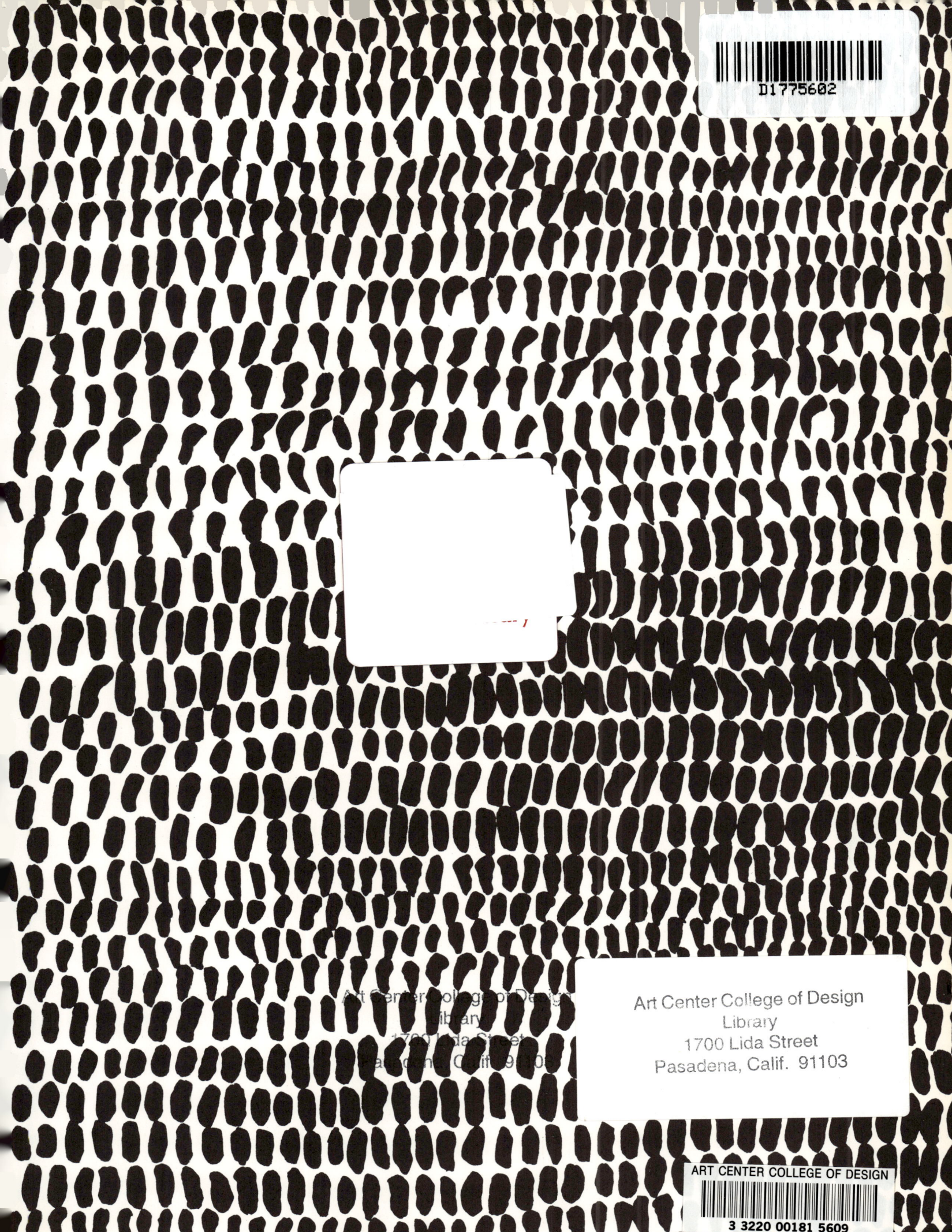

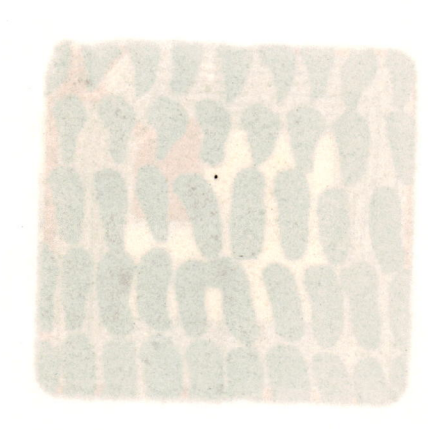

graphic beat: the soft mix vol.1

a collaboration of music and graphics

london tokyo

P·I·E BOOKS

Copyright

GRAPHIC BEAT THE SOFT MIX : LONDON / TOKYO, VOLUME 1

Copyright © 1997 P·I·E BOOKS

All rights reserved.
No part of this publication may be reproduced or used in any form or by any means graphic, electronic, or mechanical, including photocopying, recording, taping or information storage and retieval systems without written permission of the publisher.

ISBN4-89444-071-7-C3070

First Edition December 1997

P·I·E BOOKS: #301, 4-14-6 Komagome, Toshima-ku, Tokyo 170, Japan
Phone 03-3940-8302 Fax 03-3576-7361

本書は好評につき完売した「グラフィックビート ロンドン／トウキョウ Vol.1」の改訂版です。
This book was previously published in a popular hardcover edition as
"THE GRAPHIC BEAT : London / Tokyo Volume 1."

Contents

004 Foreword by Helen Rees
006 Foreword by Ryuichi Sakamoto
010 Malcolm Garrett
026 Contemporary Production
044 The Designers Republic
062 Russell Mills
078 Tadanori Yokoo
096 Peter Saville
114 Kenji Ishikawa
126 David Crow
138 Hajime Tachibana
148 David James
158 Two
168 Nobuaki Takahashi
178 Ian Swift
190 Ken Sakaguchi
200 Terry Jones
217 Acknowledgements
220 Designers' Address

ART CENTER COLLEGE OF DESIGN

Foreword by Helen Rees

Design for music is the touchstone of the work of a new generation of British and Japanese designers and artists. Although this collection shows a range of design, it is the combination of sound and image which captures a transient moment in popular culture which runs throughout the book. Ever since the first glossy, full-colour illustrated sleeves for 45rpm records burst on the scene in the 1960s, graphic designers have visualised the sounds playing across the airwaves or the dance floor. More than book jackets, record sleeves are packages to keep. More than a packet of soap powder, they endow a (visually) anonymous product with an image full of resonance.

For many young designers, working in the music business is a dream come true. Hajime Tachibana is a musician, who has played with Plastics, as well being an award winning designer. Often this work is an extremely personal responce to the music, creating an image for, as well as of a bend. Jamie Reid's collaboration with the Sex Pistols introduced a new smash-and-grab aesthetic into the music industry: the perfect graphic image for the Great Rock'n'Roll Swindle. Punk was also the supreme moment of defiance against commercialism in the music business, sparking the creation of hundreds of small, independent labels, making up in creativity what they lacked in finance.

At the same time, the impact of the Yellow Magic Orchestra (YMO) in Japan was equally dramatic: the first original Japanese rock'n'roll. Yukimasa Okumura's designs for YMO were as feted as the music, creating a style which was copied by young people all over the country. In contrast to British punk whose rejection of conventional production values was accompanied by characteristically anarchic graphics, the technological sophistication of YMO's music was reflected in Okumura's high-tech computer graphics.

That spirit has survived in the continuing commitment of musicians and designers to reject convention in favour of experimentation. They work in the knowledge that every nuance of style will be noted by the fans who make up a triangle of mutual understanding with the musicians and designers. The use of type, photography and printing on record sleeves and promotional material will be appreciated by the knowledgeable fans who are as familiar with the graphics as they are with the music. Some designers develop a particularly close relationship with one record label, such as Neville Brody for Fetish, Peter Saville for Factory and Vaughan Oliver for 4AD. Although this trend is largely confined to relatively small labels in Britain, in Japan major companies work with young designers. Yasutaka Kato, Kenji Ishikawa and Nobuaki Takahashi have all worked for Epic / Sony, and have been retained by Sony Records.

Some designers in both Japan and Britain have created identities for individual bands, for example: Ken Sakaguchi for Buck-Tick and The Street Beats; Mick Itaya for Gontiti; Katsu Nagaishi for Complex; Contemporary Production for the Flipper's Guitar and Pizzicato Five; Malcolm Garrett for Buzzcocks and Duran Duran; Peter Saville for New Order.

Style magazines which were once produced on the margins, now occupy the mainstream of youth culture. Terry Jones started i-D as a kind of fashion fanzine, filled with black and white photographs of starting and inventive people snapped going about their daily business-which was usually posing in the street. Today, the i-D style of multi-layered words and pictures, is as familiar in Tokyo as in London.

Jones' happy eclecticism contrasts with the more disciplined use of new typography in the two magazines best known for having been designed by Neville Brody, The Face and Arena. Brody has also contributed to 03-Tokyo Calling, the most influential style magazine to have come out of Tokyo in the last ten years. Hiroshi Sunto is responsible for the appearance of 03 which, like The Face, covers politics and religion, as well as music, fasion and art.

Some museums may look as though they are at the opposite end of the cultural spectrum from nightclubs, yet the Hacienda club in Manchester shares the same designers as the Boymans Museum in Rotterdam: 8vo. Similarly, both Peter Saville and Malcolm Garrett have designed logos for museums and galleries, as well as for pop groups.

The facility to move from one cultural form to another is typical of the designers from Japan and Britain represented in this collection. Though their work is very different, they each reflect and shape the patterns of contemporary culture. The designers in this book represent a range of approaches, rather than a single style. The contributors have made their own selections, giving the reader a private view of their very public art.

Helen Rees / Design Museum, London

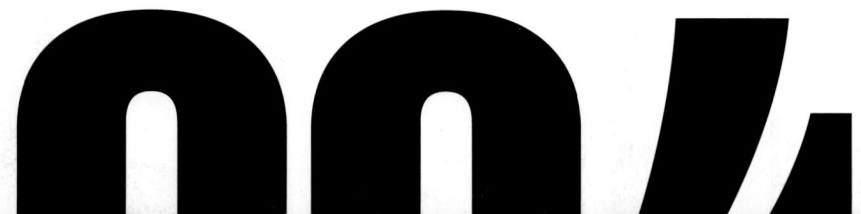

"音楽のためのデザイン"というものが、イギリスと日本の新しい世代のデザイナーやアーティストたちの間で、活動の試金石となっています。このコレクションでもデザインと名のつくものを幅広く扱っていますが、ここで言う"デザイン"は、ページの最初から最後まで流れているポップ・カルチャーの、一時的な瞬間を捉えた音とイメージの組み合せなのです。1960年代に45回転レコードのテカリのある天然色のジャケットが世に登場して以来、グラフィック・デザイナーたちはラジオやダンスフロアで流れる音楽を視覚化してきました。レコード・ジャケットというものは、本の装丁以上に保存したくなる包装であり、洗濯洗剤のあき箱以上に（視覚的に）個性を持たない商品に対して、広がりのあるイメージを多大に与えてくれるものなのです。

多くの若いデザイナーにとって、音楽産業で働くということはまさに夢の実現といえます。立花ハジメは、プラスチックスというバンドに在籍していたミュージシャンであり、同時にデザイナーとしても賞を受けています。多くの場合、彼の仕事はその音楽に対しての非常にパーソナルな反応であり、そこに創り出されるものはバンドのためのイメージであり、またバンド自身のイメージでもあります。ジェイミー・リードとセックス・ピストルズとのコラボレーションは、音楽産業に「スマッシュ・アンド・グラッブ（叩き壊してつかみ取る）」という新たな美学を吹き込みました。それは"偉大なるロックンロールの食わせ者"を正しく、完璧に表現したグラフィック・イメージだったのです。また、パンク・ムーヴメントは、音楽産業における商業主義に対する抵抗のピーク時にあり、何百というインディペンデント・レーベルの発足の刺激となりました。これらのレーベルは、財政的に弱い部分をクリエイティヴィティーでカヴァーしたのです。

同時に、日本におけるイエロー・マジック・オーケストラ（YMO）のインパクトは、同じようにドラマティックなものでした。彼らは、日本のロックンロールのオリジナリティーを初めて感じさせてくれるバンドだったのです。YMOのために奥村靫正が手がけたデザインは、その音楽と同じくらいに称賛され、日本中の若者がそのスタイルをコピーしました。伝統的な形づくりの形式を拒絶していたパンクが、それを象徴するようにアナーキーなグラフィックを採用していたのに対して、奥村のハイテックなコンピュータ・グラフィックスには、技術的に洗練されたYMOの音楽が反映されていました。

このような精神は、伝統よりは実験的なやり方を選ぶミュージシャンやデザイナーの決意のなかに生き続けています。彼らは、ファンがスタイル的にどんな微妙なニュアンスにも気づいていて、ミュージシャンやデザイナーとともに共通の理解を持った三角形を創り出していることを知った上で仕事をしています。レコードや宣伝材料にロゴ・タイプや写真を使用することは、音楽と同じくらいにグラフィックスについても知識を持っているファンには受け入れられるのです。また、この本に登場して来るデザイナーのなかには、特定のレコード・レーベルと親密な関係を持つ人もいます。例えば、フェティッシュのネヴィル・ブロディー、ファクトリーのピーター・サヴィル、そして4ADのヴォーン・オリヴァーらのように。この傾向は、ほとんどイギリスの小さなレーベルに限られていますが、日本ではメジャーな会社が若いデザイナーを起用しています。加藤靖隆、石川絢士、高橋伸明らは、同じようにみなソニーレコード、エピック・ソニー レコードでデザイナーとして活躍し、今でもその関係を続けているのです。

日本やイギリスのデザイナーのなかには、ある特定のバンドのアイデンティティーを創り出そうとした人もいます。例えば、バクチクやストリート・ビーツの坂口賢、ゴンチチのミック板谷、コンプレックスの永石勝、フリッパーズ・ギター、ピチカート・ファイヴのコンテンポラリー・プロダクション、バズコックスとデュラン・デュランのマルコム・ギャレット、ニュー・オーダーのピーター・サヴィルなどがその例です。

また、その昔採算ギリギリの線で出版されていたスタイル雑誌が、今では若者たちの文化の主流になっています。『i-D』は、テリー・ジョーンズが一種のファッション・ファン向けに始めた雑誌でした。街角でポーズを取ることを日課にしている、独創的な人々のモノクロのスナップ写真をタイトルに使用したり、文章や写真を何重にも重ねる"i-Dスタイル"は、ロンドンと同じくらいに東京でも一般的になりました。

ジョーンズのいかにも楽しい折衷主義は、ネヴィル・ブロディーがデザインした『フェイス』や『アリーナ』におけるより規律正しいタイポグラフィーの用法とは対象的です。ブロディーはまた、過去10年間で東京から発したスタイル誌のなかで、最も影響力のあった『03〜Tokyo Calling』にも寄与しています。『フェイス』のように音楽やファッション、そしてアートと同じレヴェルで政治や宗教をも扱っていた『03』については、駿東宏がアート・ディレクションを担当しています。

博物館のなかには、ナイトクラブとは文化的に正反対の位置にあるように見えながら、マンチェスターのハチエンダ・クラブのようにロッテルダム・ボイマンス博物館と同じデザイナーがデザインを手掛けているという例もあります。同様に、ピーター・サヴィルもマルコム・ギャレットも、ポップ・グループの仕事をするのと同じように、博物館のロゴをデザインしています。

あるひとつの文化的な形態から、別の形態へと移行することができる器用さは、このコレクションで代表される、日本及びイギリスのデザイナーたちに見られる典型的な資質です。彼らのそれぞれの仕事は非常に異なっていますが、いずれも現代文化のパターンを反映し、形作っているものなのです。この本で取り上げる人々は、ひとつのスタイルにとどまらず、幅広くデザインのあらゆる取り組み方をしているデザイナーの代表選手です。自らもページ作りに加わったデザイナーたちは、広く一般に知られるようになった彼らの作品について、とてもプライヴェートな見方を読者に提供してくれています。

ロンドン・デザイン美術館 ／ ヘレン・リース

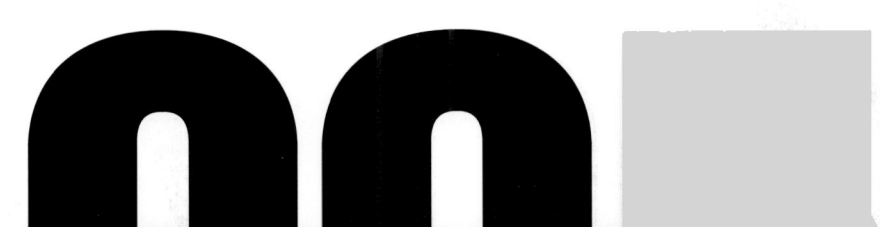

Foreword by Ryuichi Sakamoto

I believe that if the music is without some sort of universal validity, the graphic design for the packaging of that music cannot claim any real authenticity of its own. If the music has no voice, if it does not speak to people all over the world, the end product will be a specialty item tucked away in the imported record section at Tower Records. No matter how fabulous an album jacket might be, only the handful of music aficionados interested in that particular niche will ever see it. So I think it is fair to say that it is the music which gives life to the graphic design on the jacket.

I try to maintain an awareness of the universal appeal of music, and to remember that there are a lot of people out there who do not know anything about me. If I want them to know Ryuichi Sakamoto, I feel they have to know the face that goes with the Sakamoto sound, so I always make it a point to feature my face on the jacket. That is my personal visual conceit and I impose it as a required visual element for each cover. This kind of self assertion is not common in Japan, however. More often than not, Japanese musicians have nothing to say about the design of their album covers.

Probably that is why it is quite rare to see designs for music in which there is a dynamic equilibrium between the music and the visual entity that comes with it. There is an unfortunate tendency for the designer to go off on his own tangent and pursue some personal artistic objective that has nothing to do with the music. He is so busy trying to impress other artists and designers that he forgets that the music is the raison d'etre for the artwork in the first place.

When I am putting together an album, I start with an overall concept for the project and then look for an artist who is able to understand the musical intent. Only with this understanding, is there any hope of arriving at a graphic that will compliment the sound in any meaningful way.

Robert Bergman-Ungar, who was the art director on my two most recent original albums "Beauty" and "Heartbeat", took a very positive approach to the whole process and was involved long before we went to final mastering. He responded to the sound as it developed and, in a sense, the feedback from his visual imagination became incorporated into the music itself. His ideas actually helped inspire the music that would carry the banner of his graphic work out into the public marketplace. This sort of passion in a designer, that drives him to get involved in the actual making of the music, is vital if you are going to produce something that has integrity.

There are precious few designers, however, who can really relate to the sounds musicians create, especially in Japan. Perhaps the ideal example of collaboration between musician and designer would be David Sylvian and Russell Mills in London.

Like many musicians, I am not a designer. I do not so much as dabble in painting or drawing and consider myself quite hopeless at that sort of thing. Nevertheless, like most musicians, I feel that the jacket on my album is my jacket. It is, after all, what presents the music and the musician to the browsing public, and ultimately, it is the musician who gets the feedback, not the artist. If someone comes up and says that the jacket stinks, how are we to respond if we are artistically illiterate? Worse, if the musician does not have any bona fide musical aims, if he is without an authentic voice of his own, then he may not even feel he has the grounds to reject a submitted design that he does not like. He will not be able to articulate any coherent criticism.

Look at TV commercials in America; there is an odd sort of parallel here I think. If you compare them with Japanese commercials, you will find the Japanese ones much more fun, more interesting visually and created with higher production values. But one thing can be said about the American commercials; there is a logical consistency in them which recognizes that commercials exist to sell products. It is present in the cheapest, late night, junk commercials and in the most prestigious, prime-time, national brand commercials. This logical consistency would be impossible if people simply used whatever ideas that happened to pop into their heads or chance impressions borrowed randomly from elsewhere. To hold this sort of consistency, it may even be necessary to choose a concept which is not very exciting or interesting, seen purely from an artistic point of view, because it suits the rationale or the character of the product.

When you set out to create the visual aspect of a music product, you should never start with the notion that hiring the hottest designer or using state of the art equipment will solve the problem. You should start by selecting the right designer for the feel of your music. Of course, you may sometimes choose to use a high-tech graphic generator such as a Macintosh computer if it can be made to fit the theme you are working on. When putting together a team of people for the creation of an album, all those people must suit the feel of the total product. Naturally, if you want a universal quality to the product, your team should be rich in international color; it cannot consist of Japanese only. We are living in a borderless era in many ways. My band is a good example of this borderless, cross-cultural milieux, consisting of people of various nationalities from around the world. Whether you are talking about music or design, technology has brought us to the point where you can produce something superficially impressive by simply making selections from the menus on your Mac. American recording engineers, who grew up in an environment saturated with rock'n' roll on the radio had a natural feel for good sound instilled in them right from the beginning. Their Japanese counterparts have no such familiarity with good sound at this bone deep level, so they cannot really take advantage of all this state of the art equipment which is available to recording engineers everywhere. They just cannot produce, because they do not have this elementary sense of direction in either music or design. First you must have a sense of purpose — if you have that, then the direction of your creative drive is determined and everything falls into place.

Today, with CDs as the mainstream medium for music, it seems to me that, at least in the design and materials used in packaging, they are reaching the limits of what can be done. From here on in, new directions will be required and it will be exciting to see how design for music responds.

Ryuichi Sakamoto / Musician

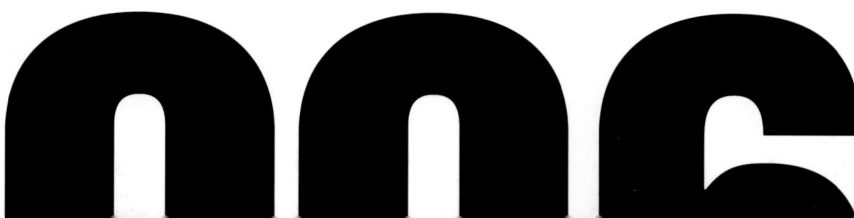

音楽じたいに国際性がなければ、それに関わるグラフィック・デザインも成り立たないと思う。例えばいくらアルバム・ジャケットが良くても、聴こえて来る音楽に世界に流通するパワーや質がなかったら、タワー・レコードの輸入盤コーナーでマニアックな人たちが買って終わり、なんてシロモノになってしまう。音楽が、ジャケットを、グラフィック・デザインを世界に引きずって行くのだ。
　"世界に流通する"という意識を、僕はつねに持つようにしている。まだ僕の事を知らない人が世界にはたくさんいるわけで、その人たちに"サカモトの顔"をインプットさせるために、ジャケット全面に自分の顔を出すように心がけている。
　そんなヴィジュアル・コンセプトを自ら持ち、発言することじたい、日本のミュージシャンはやらないケースが多い。だからかも知れないが、昨今のミュージック・デザインは、音楽性とヴィジュアルがイコールで結ばれているとはなかなか言い難い。音楽のためのジャケットのはずが、デザイナーの意向のみでアートにおぼれ、デザイナーたちのただの才能の競い合いだけになってしまう傾向がある。
　僕がアルバムを作る際には、まずこちら側で具体的なコンセプトを決め、僕たちの意志を理解した上で、それを具現化してくれるクリエイターを探すようにしている。最近発表したオリジナル・アルバム『ビューティ』と『ハートビート』でアート・ディレクションを担当してくれたロバート・バーグマン－アンガーは、レコーディング前のデモ・テープの段階から積極的にアプローチを見せ、音を聴いてはアイディアをどんどん投げかけてきた。むしろ音楽を作っている僕自身が、彼にインスパイアされた部分もあるくらいに。そんなふうにデザイナーも、音楽作りに参加するくらいの気持ちが必要なんじゃないだろうか。ロンドンで言えば、デヴィッド・シルヴィアンとラッセル・ミルズのコラボレーションのように、ミュージシャンの作る音をよくわかってくれるデザイナーは、日本ではまだまだ少ないように思える。僕はデザイナーじゃないし、絵も書けないから自分でデザインはできないけれど、ジャケットはその音楽とミュージシャンの顔だから、最終的に第三者の意見が帰って来るのはデザイナーではなく、こちら側なのだ。カッコ悪いといわれても、ミュージシャンは何も手を下せない。だが、ミュージシャン自身の主張や明確なヴィジョンを持っていないと、納得いかないデザインを前にして反論することもできない。
　音楽だけではなくて、企業のTVCMに話を置き換えても同様のことが言える。例えば、アメリカと日本のTVCMを比べてみると、おもしろさでは日本のほうが勝っているが、アメリカは"商品を売るための宣伝"という論理が首尾一貫している。それはチープな作りのものから、ベスト・クオリティのものまでに通じて。"売るための論理性"を表現するには、思い付きや、どこかから借りてきたようなアイディアで済まない。極端なことを言えば、デザイン的におもしろくないものであっても、時には商品に合わせてそれを選ぶ必要もあるのだ。
　ヴィジュアル作りは、立派な機材や旬のデザイナーを使いたい、ということから始めるものではなく、音楽のテーマ性に合ったデザイナーを選ぶことから始めるべきだと思う。そのテーマを表現する際に効率的であるために、マッキントッシュ・コンピュータなどのテクノロジーを選ぶこともある。そんな風にテーマにあったクリエイターの人選をしていると、日本人だけでなく、他国の人が混じったチームができるかもしれない。現に僕の今のバンドも様々な国籍の人たちでなりたっている。今は、そういうことが全く可能な時代なのだから。
　音楽にしろデザインにしろ、マッキントッシュのメニューをいくつかチョイスすれば、それらしいものが出来てしまうところまで来ている。幼少の頃からラジオでガンガンロックを聴きまくったために、"いい音"が自然とインプットされているアメリカのレコーディング・エンジニアに比べ、日本のエンジニアは"いい音"を聴いたことがないから、世界共通の機材を前にしてもその音がわからず、作れないでいる。音楽もデザインも、"こうしたい"という目的意識を持つことから始まって、方向性が定まって来るものなのに。
　CDが音楽ソフトのメインとなった今、早くもプラスティックやメタリックな素材で、デザインは出来る限りのことをしてしまった。ここから未来にかけてデザインがどう変わって行くのか、楽しみでもある。

ミュージシャン／坂本龍一

Editorial Notes

1. Title of Work
Intended Use and Year of Completion
PR:Product Brand Name
CD:Creative Director AD:Art Director
D:Designer P:Photographer
I:Illustrator CW:Copy Writer
S:Stylist H:Hair & Make-up
DF:Design Firm CL:Client

The words 'Company Limited' and 'Incorporated' have been omitted from the credits in this book.

1.作品タイトル
作品の使用目的 制作年度
PR:ブランド
CD:クリエイティヴ ディレクター AD:アート ディレクター
D:デザイナー P:フォトグラファー
I:イラストレーター CW:コピー ライター
S:スタイリスト H:ヘア メイク
DF:デザイン ファーム CL:クライアント

本文クレジット中、会社名については、株式(有限)会社
Company Limited、Incorporated等の表記を省略しました。

graphic beat: the soft mix vol.1

a collaboration of music and graphics

london tokyo

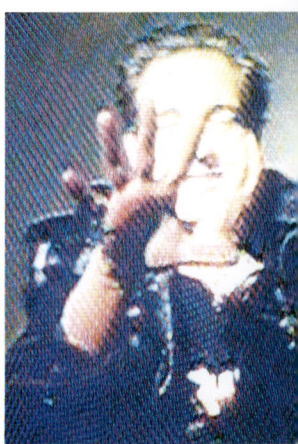
Photography / Peter Anderson

010

Malcolm Garrett

I was never one for standing still. I have always been excited by the future, what may be possible, what could be done. Media visions of the future have stimulated my imagination for as long as I can remember. The paradox is that many such visions are now part of our cultural history. This causes me no problems, for it is a particular attitude that I respect. It is part of my questioning nature (some would say my distinctly contrary nature) that has given me an appreciation of those people who challenge convention or refuse to believe that there can only be one way of addressing the world. With this in mind it is no surprise that the likes of Duchamp, Marinetti, Warhol, Zappa, Kubrick and Rotten have all helped define and channel my creative energies. I do not, however, identify with those who simply tell you what's wrong, but rather the ones who question what is right. Dogma whether positive or negative I find unpalatable.

One of my failings is the tendency to believe that merely conceiving an idea automatically makes it exist and it is therefore time to move on. Given the option, I can readily avoid applying myself the task of putting ideas into action. Mentally resolving how something should work can easily satisfy my cerebral desires. I display a tenacity of ideals but not necessarily a tenacity of performance. That said, a connecting thread of ideas link many pieces of work over the years, which allows me to return to and pick up themes discarded at an earlier time without any difficulty. This, coupled with an ability to simultaneously entertain several seemingly conflicting notions, imbues my work with a particular kind of inconsistency, and I expect makes analysis of the logic at work a puzzling task. Cynics would say I just can't make up my mind.

私はじっとしていられない質だ。いつも未来に興味を持って、物に対する可能性についエキサイトしてしまう。未来のメディアのヴィジョンは、私が物心ついた時から刺激を与えてくれていた。そのヴィジョンは、私たちが育ってきた文化の歴史とは矛盾したものになるが、別にそこにはこだわらず、私が尊敬しているのは"態度"なのた。自然に対して疑問を持つ人（自然とは対照的な人だと言われるときもある）や、臨機応変に物事を考えられる人、世界に対してもいろいろなアプローチを持っている人、普通であることに対して、反抗心を持っている人が好きだ。私にクリエイティヴなエネルギーを注ぎ込んでくれたのは、デュウシャンやマリネッティ、ウォーホル、ザッパ、キューブリック、ロッテンだ。彼らは物事に対してすぐに間違っていると決めつけず、むしろ正しいものに対して疑問を持つタイプなのだ。ポジティヴでもネガティヴでも、ドグマは好きじゃない。

　私の悪いところは、考えついたアイディアがそのまま生きるとすぐ思ってしまうところだ。そして、次の瞬間にはもう後の進行を考えていること。最高のアイディアを持っていても、アイディアを頭の中に巡らすだけで充分満足してしまうので、実際に形にしないで終わってしまう。ただし、アイディアのリンクは細い線でつながっているので、何年前のアイディアや作品であっても今そこに戻って見直したり、ピックアップして作業を続けることは簡単にできる。ふたつをいっぺんに考えられないような両極端のアイディアも、同時に頭に置くことができるのだ。そんな時の私を、シニカルな人が見たら「決断力のない奴だ」と言うかもしれないけれど。

Malcolm Garrett was born in the town of Northwich in the north of England in 1956. He studied typography and psychology at Reading University and graphic design at Manchester Polytechnic. Leaving college in 1978 he formed the design group, Assorted Images, and was joined in 1983 by partner Kasper de Graaf. He is now a self-confessed computer obsessive, doing daily digital damage to his eyesight with his beloved Macintosh.

1956年、イギリス北部のノースウィッチで誕生。 リーディング大学でタイポグラフィーと心理学を学び、マンチェスター工芸学校でグラフィック・デザインを専攻した。1978年に卒業後、デザイン・グループ「Assorted Images」を設立、1983年にキャスパ・デ・グラフとパートナー・シップを持つ。現在はコンピュータにご執心で、愛するマッキントッシュに目を痛ませる毎日。

1.

1. BUZZCOCKS / A DIFFERENT KIND OF TENSION LP 1979
CD,D: Malcolm Garrett P: Jill Furmanovsky, Kevin Cummins, Peter Monks, Gervaise Soeurouge, Judith Wrighton
DF: Assorted Images CL: United Artists
バズコックス / ア ディファレント カインド オヴ テンション LP 1979
CD,D: マルコム ギャレット P: ジル ファーマノヴスキー、ケヴィン コミンズ、ピーター モンクス、ジュディス ライトン
DF: アソーテッド イメージズ CL: ユナイテッド アーティスツ

2. BUZZCOCKS / PRODUCT LP (Box Package) 1978,1989
CD,D: Malcolm Garrett DF: Assorted Images CL: EMI
バズコックス / プロダクト LP（ボックス パッケージ） 1978,1989
CD,D: マルコム ギャレット DF: アソーテッド イメージズ CL: EMI

3. BUZZCOCKS / THE DIFFERENT KITCHEN Exhibition Brochure 1986
CD,D: Malcolm Garrett DF: Assorted Images CL: Festival of the Tenth Summer
バズコックス / ザ ディファレント キッチン 展覧会パンフレット 1986
CD,D: マルコム ギャレット DF: アソーテッド イメージズ CL: フェスティヴァル オヴ ザ テンス サマー

1.Inner Sleeve / Back

1.Inner Sleeve / Front

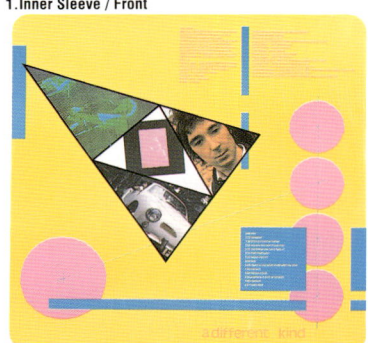

1.Back

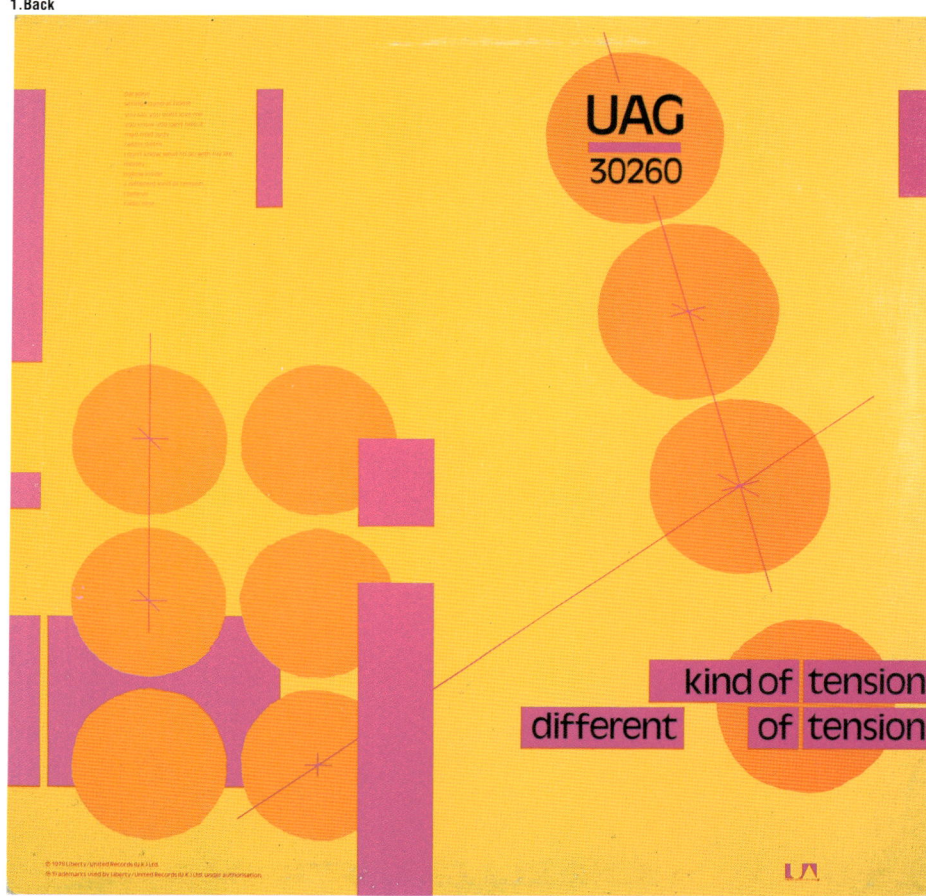

2.

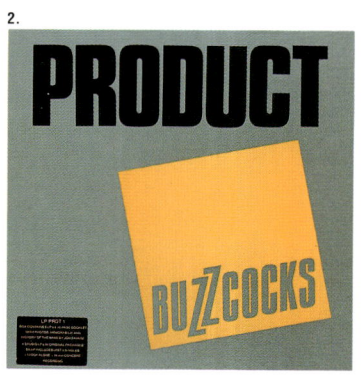

3.

4. BUZZCOCKS / THE FAB FOUR LP 1989
CD,D: Malcolm Garrett DF: Assorted Images CL: EMI
バズコックス / ザ ファブ フォー LP 1989
CD,D: マルコム ギャレット DF: アソーテッド イメージズ CL: EMI

5. BUZZCOCKS / AUF WIEDERSEHEN Video 1989
CD,D: Malcolm Garrett DF: Assorted Images CL: IKON
バズコックス / アウフ ヴィダーゼン ビデオ 1989
CD,D: マルコム ギャレット DF: アソーテッド イメージズ CL: IKON

6. BUZZCOCKS / OPERATORS MANUAL CD 1991
CD,D: Malcolm Garrett DF: Assorted Images CL: EMI
バズコックス / オペレーターズ マニュアル CD 1991
CD,D: マルコム ギャレット DF: アソーテッド イメージズ CL: EMI

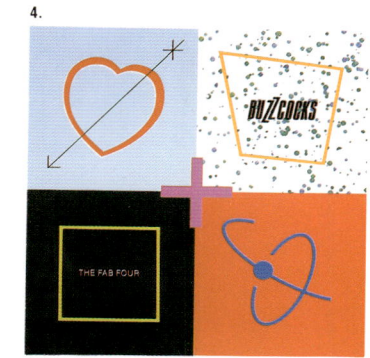

1.Front

7. Back

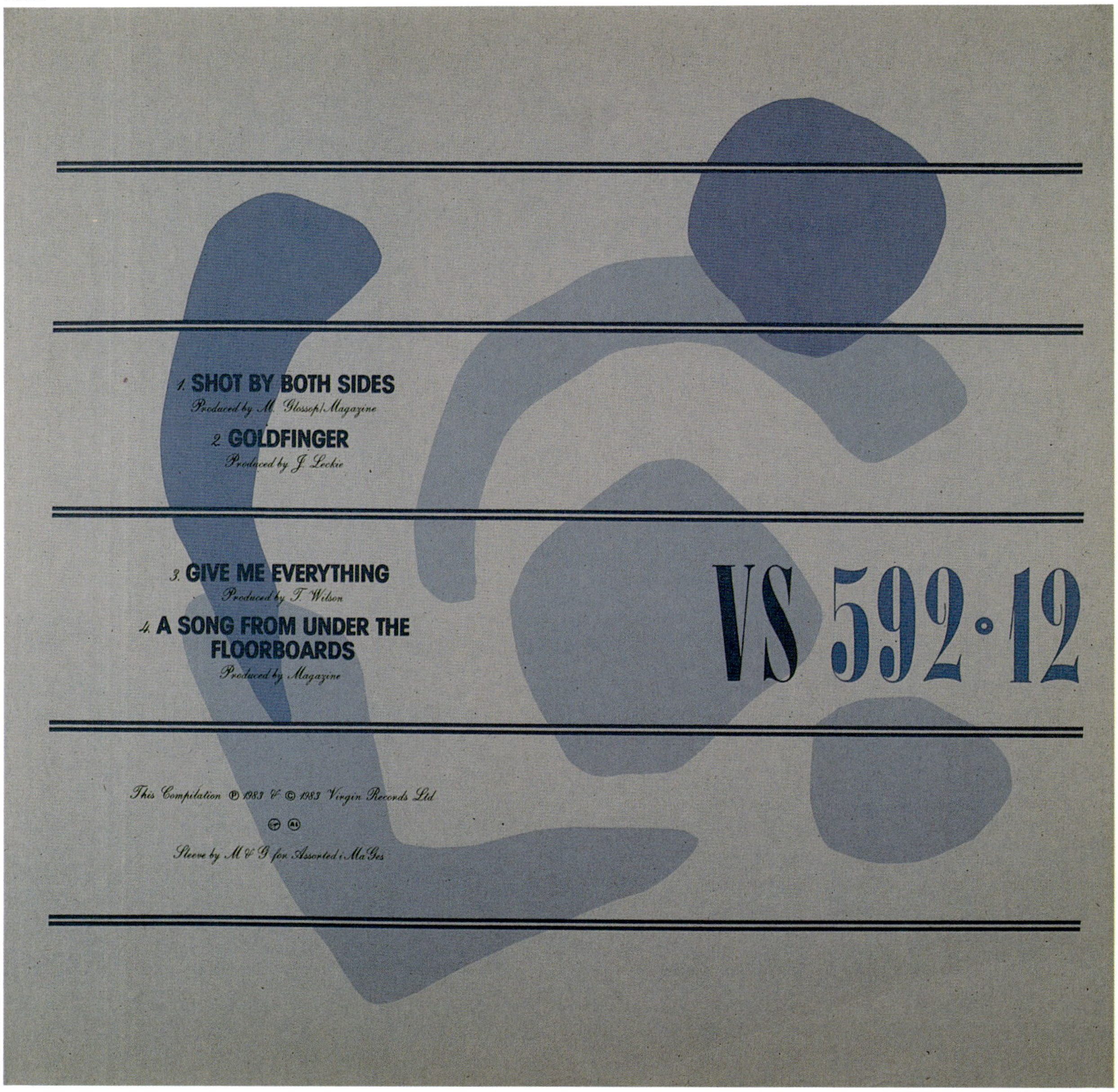

1. SHOT BY BOTH SIDES
Produced by M. Glossop/Magazine
2. GOLDFINGER
Produced by J. Leckie
3. GIVE ME EVERYTHING
Produced by T. Wilson
4. A SONG FROM UNDER THE FLOORBOARDS
Produced by Magazine

VS 592·12

This Compilation ℗ 1983 & © 1983 Virgin Records Ltd

Sleeve by M & G for Assorted iMaGes

8.

9.

7.Front

SHOT BY BOTH SIDES
GOLDFINGER
MAGAZINE
GIVE ME EVERYTHING
A SONG FROM UNDER
THE FLOORBOARDS

10.

7. MAGAZINE / FOUR TRACK EP 12-inch Single 1983
CD,D: Malcolm Garrett D: Garry Mouat DF: Assorted Images CL: Virgin Records
マガジン / フォートラックEP 12インチ シングル 1983
CD,D: マルコム ギャレット D: ゲイリー ムーアット DF: アソーテッド イメージズ CL: ヴァージン レコード

8. MAGAZINE / A SONG FROM UNDER THE FLOORBOARDS 7-inch Single 1980
CD,D: Malcolm Garrett DF: Assorted Images CL: Virgin Records
マガジン / ア ソング フロム アンダー ザ フロアボーズ 7インチ シングル 1980
CD,D: マルコム ギャレット DF: アソーテッド イメージズ CL: ヴァージン レコード

9. MAGAZINE / THE CORRECT USE OF SOAP LP 1980
CD,D: Malcolm Garrett DF: Assorted Images CL: Virgin Records
マガジン / ザ コレクト ユーズ オヴ ソープ LP 1980
CD,D: マルコム ギャレット DF: アソーテッド イメージズ CL: ヴァージン レコード

10. MAGAZINE / TOUCH AND GO 7-inch Single 1978
CD,D: Malcolm Garrett DF: Assorted Images CL: Virgin Records
マガジン / タッチ アンド ゴー 7インチ シングル 1978
CD,D: マルコム ギャレット DF: アソーテッド イメージズ CL: ヴァージン レコード

11.Back 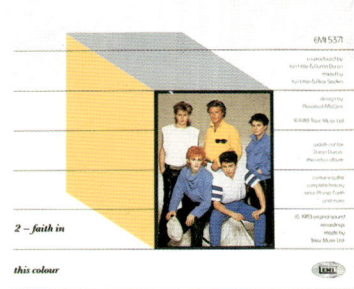 11.Front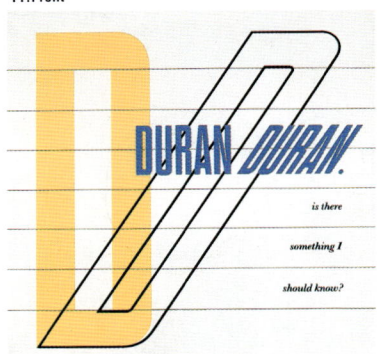

12.Front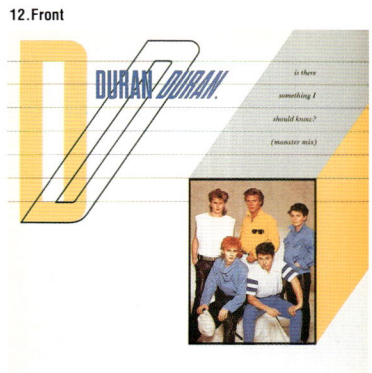

12.Back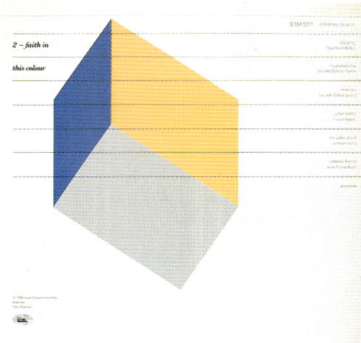

13.Back

11. DURAN DURAN / IS THERE SOMETHING I SHOULD KNOW？ 7-inch Single 1983
CD,D: Malcolm Garrett P: Brian Aris DF: Assorted Images CL: EMI
デュラン デュラン / イズ ゼア サムシング アイ シュド ノウ？ 7インチ シングル 1983
CD,D: マルコム ギャレット P: ブライアン アリス DF: アソーテッド イメージズ CL: EMI

12. DURAN DURAN / IS THERE SOMETHING I SHOULD KNOW？ 12-inch Single 1983
CD,D: Malcolm Garrett P: Brian Aris DF: Assorted Images CL: EMI
デュラン デュラン / イズ ゼア サムシング アイ シュド ノウ？ 12インチ シングル 1983
CD,D: マルコム ギャレット P: ブライアン アリス DF: アソーテッド イメージズ CL: EMI

13. DEVO / FOUR TRACK EP 12-inch Single 1983
CD,D: Malcolm Garrett P: Chalkie Davies DF: Assorted Images CL: Virgin Records
ディーヴォ / フォートラック EP 12インチ シングル 1983
CD,D: マルコム ギャレット P: チョルキー デイヴィス DF: アソーテッド イメージズ CL: ヴァージン レコード

13.Front

14.,15. NOW77
NOW77 LP 1991
CD,D: Malcolm Garrett
DF: Assorted Images
CL: EMI
ナウ77
ナウ77 LP 1991
CD,D: マルコム ギャレット
DF: アソーテッド イメージズ
CL: EMI

14.

15.

16. Back & Front A

16. DURAN DURAN
WILD BOYS
7-inch Single 1984
CD,D: Malcolm Garrett
P: Mike Owen
DF: Assorted Images
CL: EMI
デュランデュラン
ワイルド ボーイズ
7インチ シングル 1984
CD,D: マルコム ギャレット
P: マイク オーウェン
DF: アソーテッド イメージズ
CL: EMI

16. Back B

16. Back & Front C

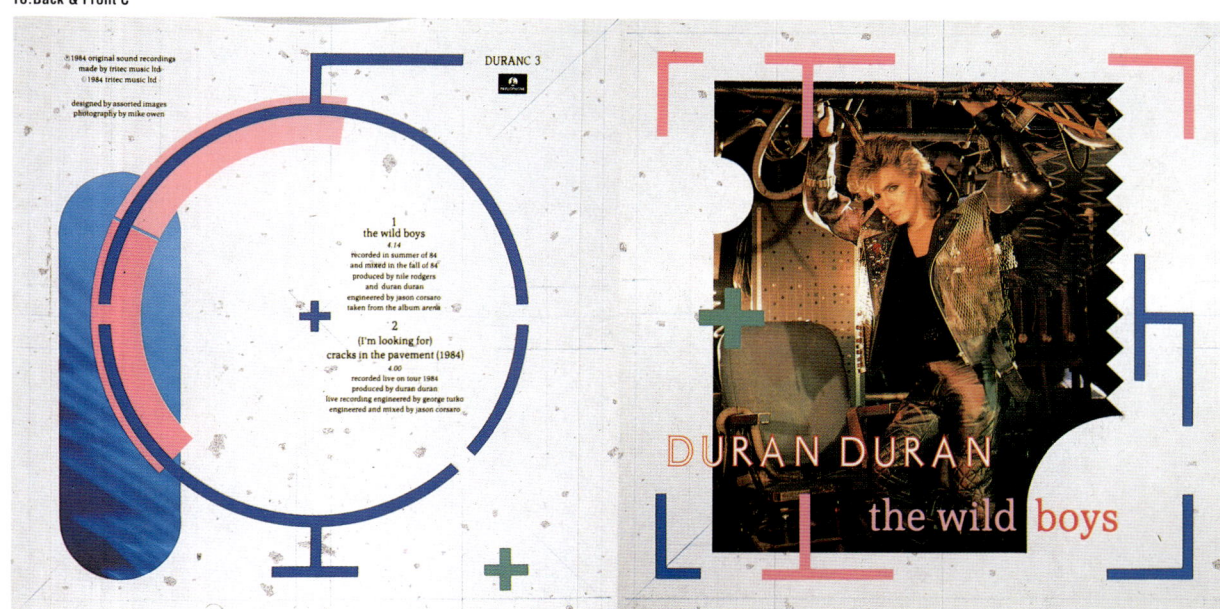

16. Back & Front D

16. Front B

16. Back & Front E

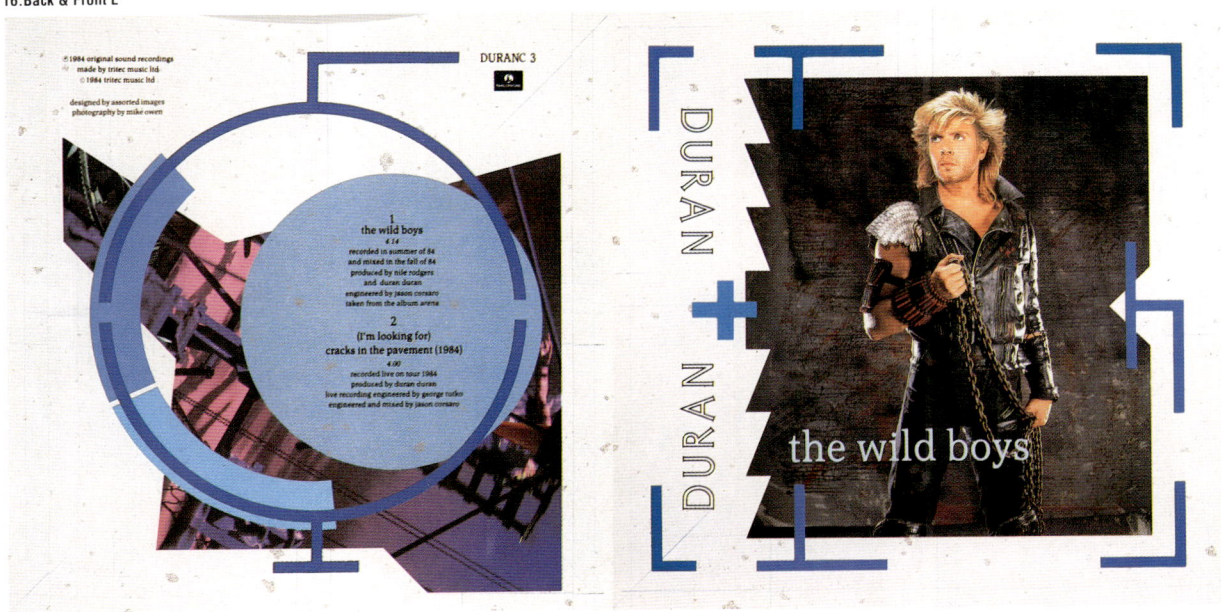

17.Front

17. SIMPLE MINDS / I TRAVEL 12-inch Single 1983
CD,D: Malcolm Garrett P: Garry Mouat DF: Assorted Images CL: Virgin Records
シンプル マインズ / ワン トラヴェル 12インチ シングル 1983
CD,D: マルコム ギャレット P: ゲイリー ムーアット DF: アソーテッド イメージズ CL: ヴァージン レコード

18. ENO / MORE BLANK THAN FRANK 12-inch Single 1986
CD,D: Malcolm Garrett CD,I: Russell Mills DF: Assorted Images CL: EG
イーノ / モア ブランク ザン フランク 12インチ シングル 1986
CD,D: マルコム ギャレット CD,I: ラッセル ミルズ DF: アソーテッド イメージズ CL: EG

19. SIMPLE MINDS / NEW GOLD DREAM LP 1982
CD,D: Malcolm Garrett DF: Assorted Images CL: Virgin Records
シンプル マインズ / ニュー ゴールド ドリーム LP 1982
CD,D: マルコム ギャレット DF: アソーテッド イメージズ CL: ヴァージン レコード

17.Back

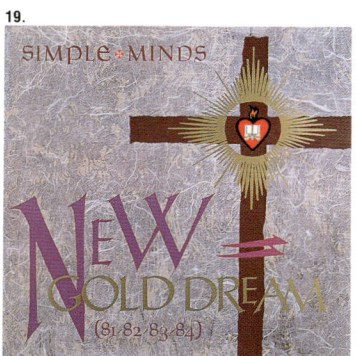

18.Back

19.

20.

**20. SIMPLE MINDS
THIS IS YOUR LAND
7-inch Single 1989**
CD,D: Malcolm Garrett
P: Guido Harari, Lawrence Watson, NASA
DF: Assorted Images CL: Virgin Records
シンプル マインズ
ディス イズ ユア ランド
7インチ シングル 1989
CD,D: マルコム ギャレット
P: ギド ハラリ, ローレンス ワトソン, NASA
DF: アソーテッド イメージズ CL: ヴァージン レコード

18.Front

21.

21. GIORGIO MORODER AND PHILIP OAKEY
TOGETHER IN ELECTRIC DREAMS
7-inch Single 1984
CD,D: Malcolm Garrett
P: Malcolm Garrett (TV screen images from film)
DF: Assorted Images **CL:** Virgin Records
ジョルジオ モロダー アンド フィリップ オーキー
トゥゲザー イン エレクトリック ドリームズ
7インチ シングル 1984
CD,D: マルコム ギャレット
P: マルコム ギャレット
DF: アソーテッド イメージズ **CL:** ヴァージン レコード

22. Back & Front

22. Inner Sleeve / Front

22. Inner Sleeve / Back

23.

22. BOY GEORGE / SOLD LP 1987
CD,D: Malcolm Garrett P: Paul Gobel, Johnny Rosza, Bill Ling DF: Assorted Images CL: Virgin Records
ボーイ ジョージ / ソールド LP 1987
CD,D: マルコム ギャレット D: ポール ゴベル、ジョニー ロザ、ビル リング DF: アソーテッド イメージズ CL: ヴァージン レコード

23. BOY GEORGE / LIVE MY LIFE 12-inch Single 1987
CD,D: Malcolm Garrett P: Mark Lebon DF: Assorted Images CL: Virgin Records
ボーイ ジョージ / ライヴ マイ ライフ 12インチ シングル 1987
CD,D: マルコム ギャレット D: マーク ルボン DF: アソーテッド イメージズ CL: ヴァージン レコード

23.Package / Front

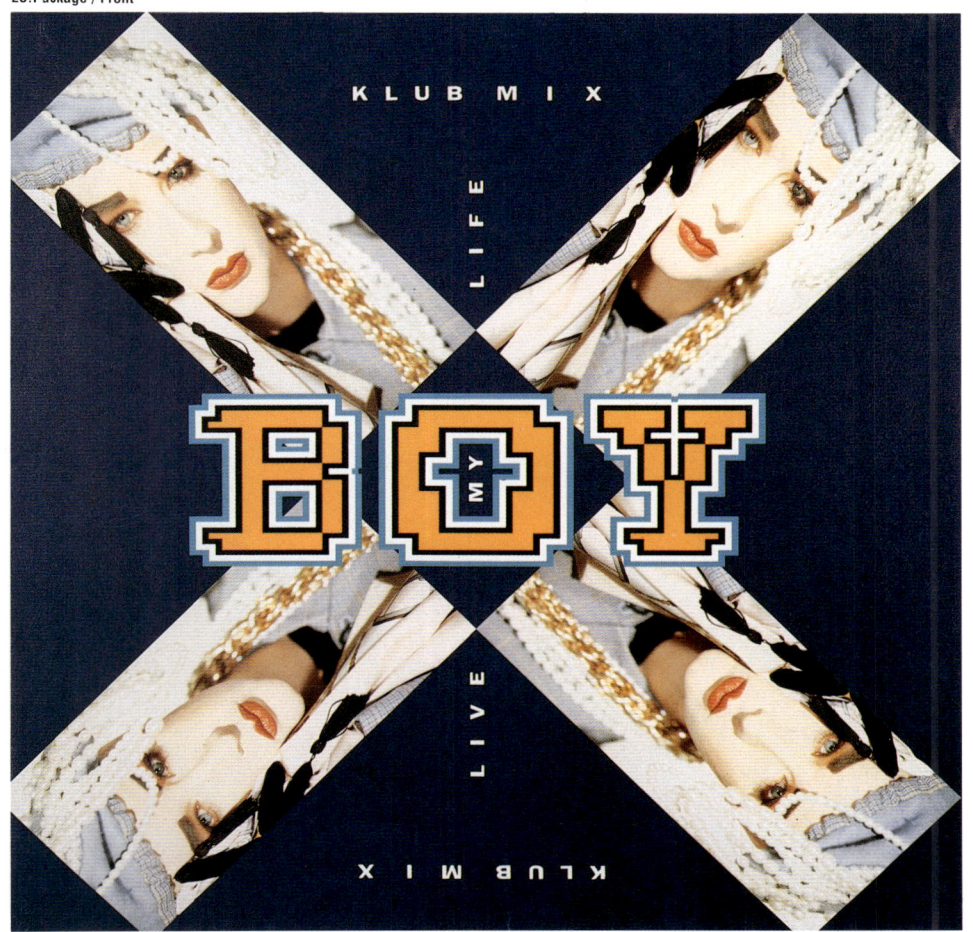

24. BOY GEORGE / TO BE REBORN 7-inch Single 1987 AD,D: Malcolm Garrett P: Andre Csillag
DF: Assorted Images CL: Virgin Records
ボーイ ジョージ / トゥー ビー リボーン 7インチ シングル 1987 AD,D: マルコム ギャレット
P: アンドレ シラー DF: アソーテッド イメージズ CL: ヴァージン レコード

24.Back & Front

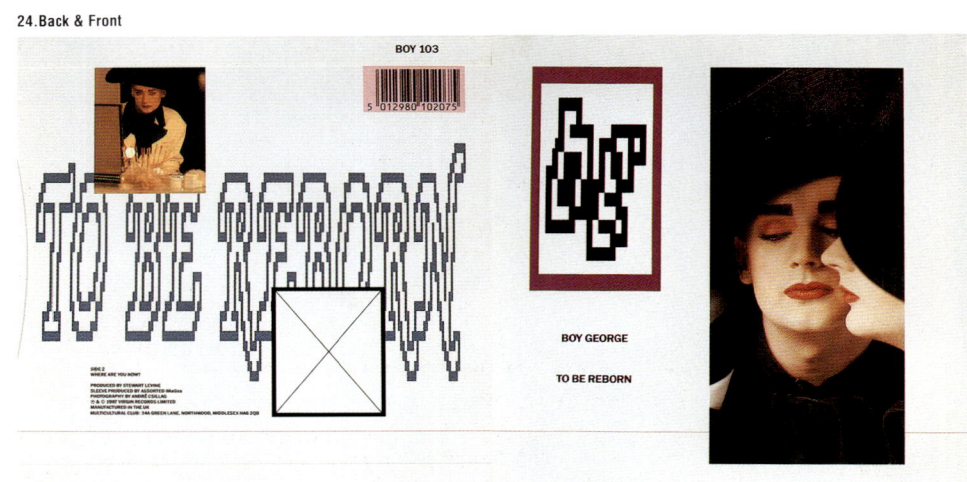

25.

25.Back

25. BEF / FEATURING BEF
CD 1991
CD,D: Malcolm Garrett
P: Kevin Westenberg
CYBEROPTICS: ZAP Factor
DF: Assorted Images CL: TEN
BEF / フィーチャリング BEF
CD 1991
CD,D: マルコム ギャレット
P: ケヴィン ウェスタンバーグ
CYBEROPTICS: ZAP ファクター
DF: アソーテッド イメージズ CL: TEN

25.Front

26.Back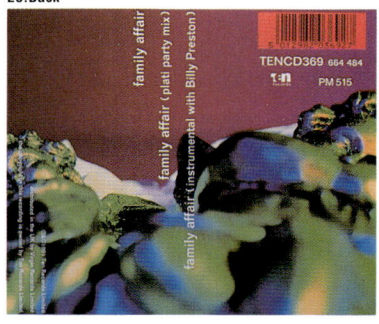

26.Front

27.

26. BEF FEATURING LALAH HATHAWAY / FAMILY AFFAIR CD 1991 CD,D: Malcolm Garrett P: Kevin Westenberg CYBEROPTICS: ZAP Factor DF: Assorted Images CL: TEN
BEF〜フィーチャリング ララ ハサウェイ / ファミリー アフェア CD 1991 CD,D: マルコム ギャレット P: ケヴィン ウェスタンバーグ CYBEROPTICS: ZAP ファクター
DF: アソーテッド イメージズ CL: TEN

27. BEF FEATURING GREEN GAURSIDE / I DON'T KNOW WHY I LOVE YOU 7-inch Single 1991 CD,D: Malcolm Garrett P: Kevin Westenberg
CYBEROPTICS: ZAP Factor DF: Assorted Images CL: TEN
BEF〜フィーチャリング グリーン ガーサイド / アイ ドント ノウ ホワイ アイ ラヴ ユー 7インチ シングル 1991 CD,D: マルコム ギャレット P: ケヴィン ウェスタンバーグ
CYBEROPTICS: ZAP ファクター DF: アソーテッド イメージズ CL: TEN

28.

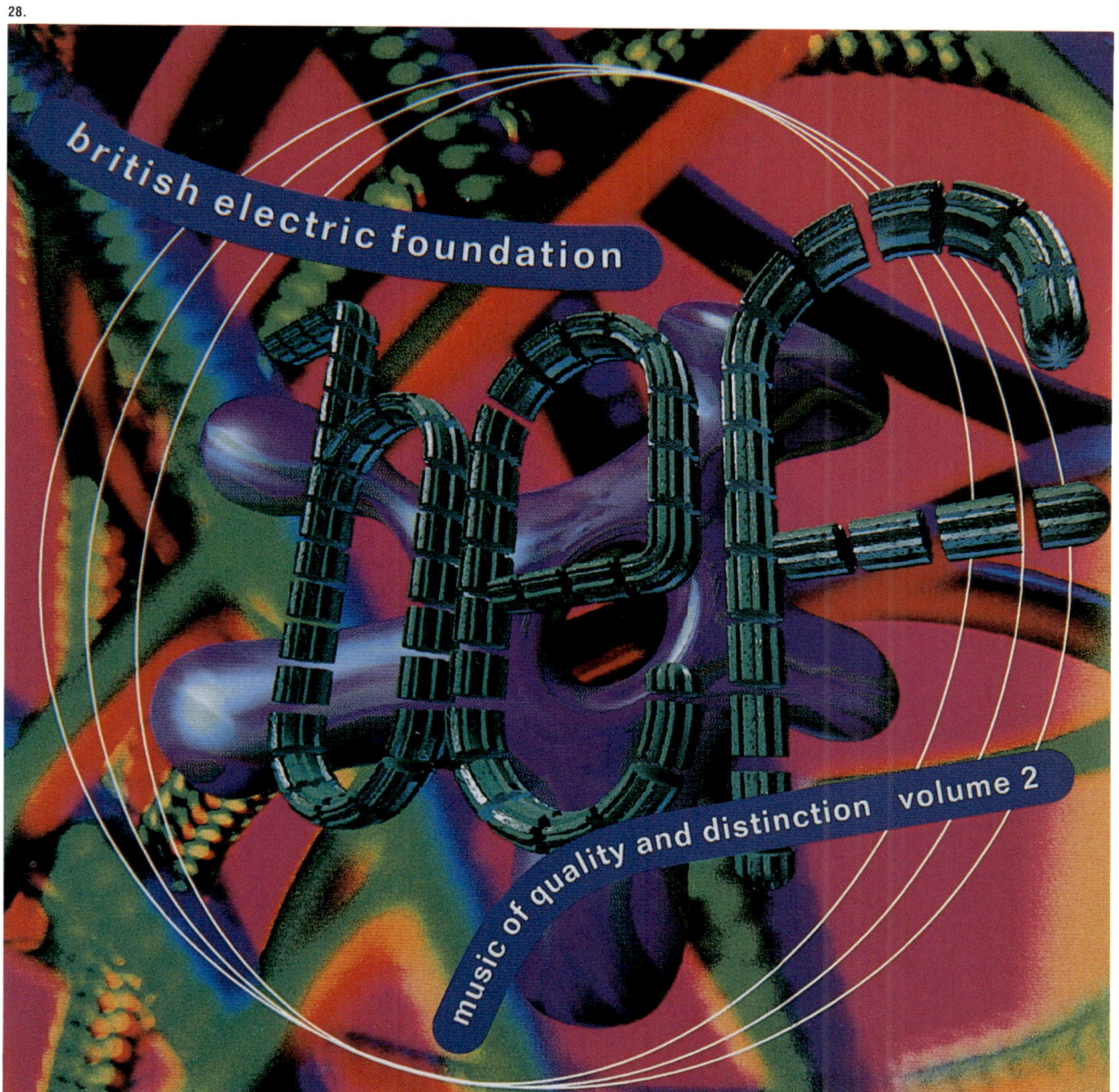

28. BEF / MUSIC OF QUALITY AND DISTINCTION VOL.2 CD 1991 CD,D: Malcolm Garrett P: Kevin Westenberg CYBEROPTICS: ZAP Factor DF: Assorted Images CL: TEN
BEF / ミュージック オヴ クウォリティ アンド ディスティンクション VOL.2 CD 1991 CD,D: マルコム ギャレット P: ケヴィン ウェスタンバーグ CYBEROPTICS: ZAP ファクター
DF: アソーテッド イメージズ CL: TEN

Photography / O.K. Young

Contemporary Production　コンテムポラリー プロダクション

Like a schizophrenic, I am able to embrace several value systems at once, and not hold one set to be absolute. At one time, I fell in love with rock'n'roll and set up a college folk band. There was a time when I went from shop to shop looking for second-hand Japanese records, and from coffee bar to coffee bar. I was drawn to hyper realism and at the same time thought *Matisse* was the greatest. There is no coherence here. If anything, it might be described as an attitude that refuses to accept that there are any absolutes— you might call it the ideology of non-ideology. The same goes for design. I approach the essence of things—with the easy-going attitude: "As long as it's cool, it's okay." Or maybe it's something that isn't too beautiful so it doesn't become decadent. I guess I'm working on the edge, where things lose their style when they have too much style, and lose their cool when they are too sophisticated. For a while I thought that my ideology, which cannot be called an ideology, might be rooted in the Buddhist sense of impermanence.

/ Mitsuo Shindo (Art Director)

僕は、分裂症的にいろんな価値観を同じレベルで好きになれるし、またこれしかないと自信を持って言える価値観もない。

ある時期には、ロックにしびれる一方、軟弱なカレッジ・フォークでバンドを組んだり、またある時期には、歌謡ポップスの中古盤探しに精を出す一方、カフェ・バー巡りをしたり、またハイパー・リアリズムにひかれる一方、やっぱりマチスが最高だと思ってみたりと……。そこには一貫したものはない。あるとすれば、絶対的なるものを認めないということかもしれないし、無思想と呼ぶ思想とも言えるかもしれない。

デザインにおいても同様に、極めて軽いノリの「カッコよけりゃいいんじゃない」的な、物事の本質に迫りそうで、迫らないもの。あるいは美を追求しすぎて耽美主義に陥らないもの、とでも言うのだろうか。もっと言えば、カッコよすぎるとカッコわるくなるし、洗練されすぎるとダサくなるし、そんな二律背反的なボーダーライン上で、僕は仕事をしているような気がする。でも、僕の持つ思想とも呼べない思想は、もしかしたら仏教的な無常感に根ざしたものかもしれない、とフッと想った。

／信藤三雄（コンテムポラリー プロダクション代表）

Established in 1985. Eighty percent of the business is music-releated, ten is general advertizing, and the remaining ten, editorial. When we design a record cover, the project includes posters, magazine ads, pamphlets, and sometimes video clips. The current members are: Mitsuo Shindo(Art director), Sawako Nakajima, Kuniko Tezuka, Satoshi Nakamura, Koichi Fujikawa, Masako Saito (Designers), Yoko Mizukoshi (Manager).

1985年に設立。業務内容は現在、音楽関係が約8割、一般企業の広告が1割、エディトリアルが1割程度という比率で行なっている。音楽の仕事に関しては、ひとつのアルバム・ジャケットをデザインした際には、それに伴うポスター、雑誌広告、パンフレット、またビデオ・クリップにいたるまで、出来る限り制作に携わるようにしている。メンバーは、信藤三雄（アート・ディレクター）、中嶋佐和子、手塚久美子、中村智、藤川浩一、斉藤雅子（デザイナー）、水越庸子（マネージャー）。

1. ORIGINAL LOVE
LOVE! LOVE! & LOVE!
CD 1991
AD: Mitsuo Shindo
D: Masako Saito, Koichi Fujikawa
P: Kenji Miura
S: Hiroko Umeyama
H: Akemi Nakano, Mika Kanzaki
DF: Contemporary Production
CL: Toshiba EMI

オリジナル ラヴ
ラヴ！ラヴ！＆ラヴ！
CD 1991
AD: 信藤三雄
D: 斉藤雅子、藤川浩一
P: 三浦憲治
S: 梅山弘子
H: 中野明美、神崎ミカ
DF: コンテンポラリー プロダクション
CL: 東芝EMI

1. Front A

1.

1.

1. Front B

1.

2. JITTERIN'JINN
HAPPY COME COME
CD 1991
AD: Mitsuo Shindo
D: Satoshi Nakamura, Koichi Fujikawa, Kumiko Tezuka
P: Mihoko Ishiguro
S: Hiroko Umeyama
H: Miho Matsuura
DF: Contemporary Production
CL: Nippon Columbia

ジッタリン ジン
ハッピーカムカム
CD 1991
AD: 信藤三雄
D: 中村 智、藤川浩一、手塚 久美子
P: 石黒 美穂子
S: 梅山弘子
H: 松浦美穂
DF: コンテムポラリー プロダクション
CL: 日本コロムビア

2. Lyrics / Outside

2. Lyrics / Inside

2.

CONTEMPORARY PRODUCTION

3. FLIPPER'S GUITAR / THREE CHEERS FOR OUR SIDE CD 1989
AD: Mitsuo Shindo D: Sawako Nakajima P: Kenji Miura S: Tamako Sato H: Masato Izumi DF: Contemporary Production CL: Polystar
フリッパーズ ギター / 海へ行くつもりじゃなかった CD 1989
AD: 信藤三雄 D: 中嶋佐和子 P: 三浦憲治 S: サトウ タマコ H: イズミ マサト DF: コンテムポラリー プロダクション CL: ポリスター

4. Lyrics

4. FLIPPER'S GUITAR / CAMERA TALK CD 1990
AD,P: Mitsuo Shindo D,H: Sawako Nakajima DF: Contemporary Production CL: Polystar
フリッパーズ ギター / カメラトーク CD 1990
AD,P: 信藤三雄 D,H: 中嶋佐和子 DF: コンテムポラリー プロダクション CL: ポリスター

5.

5. FLIPPER'S GUITAR / CAMERA! CAMERA! CAMERA! CD 1990
AD: Mitsuo Shindo D: Sawako Nakajima P: Kenji Miura H: Akemi Nakano S: Ayumi Shino DF: Contemporary Production CL: Polystar
フリッパーズ ギター / カメラ！カメラ！カメラ！ CD 1990
AD: 信藤三雄 D: 中嶋 佐和子 P: 三浦憲治 H: 中野明美 S: 篠 あゆみ DF: コンテムポラリー プロダクション CL: ポリスター

6. FLIPPER'S GUITAR / DOCTOR HEAD'S WORLD TOWER CD 1991
AD: Mitsuo Shindo D: Sawako Nakajima P: Kenji Miura S: Ayumi Shino H: Akemi Nakano SET: Satoshi Nakamura, Koichi Fujikawa
DF: Contemporary Production CL: Polystar
フリッパーズ ギター / ヘッド博士の世界塔 CD 1991
AD: 信藤三雄 D: 中嶋 佐和子 P: 三浦憲治 S: 篠 あゆみ H: 中野明美 SET: 中村 智、藤川浩一 DF: コンテムポラリー プロダクション CL: ポリスター

6.

6.

6. Lyrics

6.

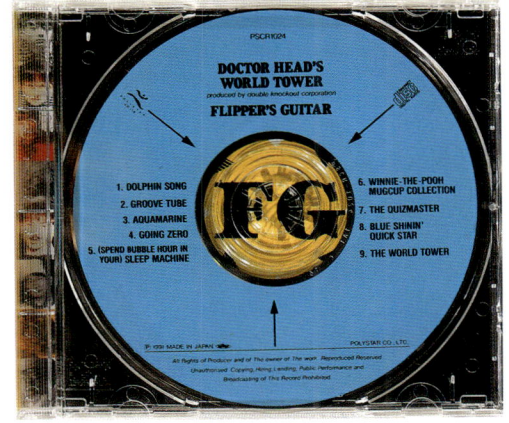

7. PIZZICATO FIVE / ON HER MAJESTY'S REQUEST CD 1989
AD,BODY PAINTING: Mitsuo Shindo D,BODY PAINTING: Naoyuki Suzuki
D: Kumiko Tezuka P: Takahisa Ide H: Eito Furukubo
DF: Contemporary Production CL: Sony Records
ピチカート ファイヴ / 女王陛下のピチカート ファイヴ CD 1989
AD,BODY PAINTING: 信藤三雄 D,BODY PAINTING: 鈴木直之
D: 手塚 久美子 P: 井出貴久 H: 古久保 英人
DF: コンテムポラリー プロダクション CL: ソニー レコード

8. Lyrics / Outside

8. Lyrics / Inside

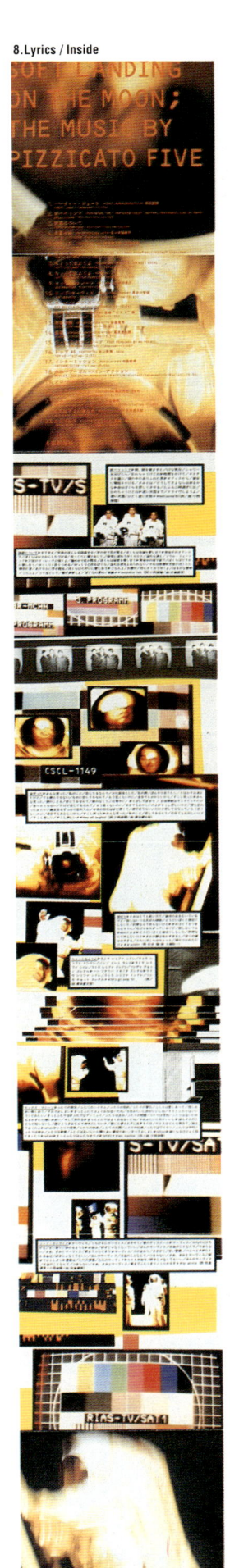

8.

8.

8. PIZZICATO FIVE / SOFT LANDING ON THE MOON CD 1990
AD: Mitsuo Shindo D: Kumiko Tezuka
P: Kozo Fukuoka S: Pizzicato Five H: Tomoichiro Satake
DF: Contemporary Production CL: Sony Records
ピチカート ファイヴ / 月面軟着陸 CD 1990
AD: 信藤三雄 D: 手塚久美子 P: 福岡耕造 S: ピチカート ファイヴ H: 佐竹 智一郎
DF: コンテムポラリー プロダクション CL: ソニー レコード

9.

9.Cover / Front & Outside Spreads

9.Cover / Inside Spread

9.PIZZICATO FIVE / LONDON-PARIS-TOKYO CD 1991
AD: Mitsuo Shindo D: Koichi Fujikawa P: Naoki Tsuruta, Manabu Matsunaga S: Mina Takayama H: Ryuji DF: Contemporary Production CL: Nippon Columbia
ピチカート ファイヴ／超音速のピチカート ファイヴ CD 1991
AD: 信藤三雄 D: 藤川浩一 P: 鶴田直樹、松永 学 S: 高山みな H: りゅうじ DF: コンテムポラリー プロダクション CL: 日本コロムビア

10. Front

10. PIZZICATO FIVE
THIS YEAR'S GIRL
CD 1991
AD: Mitsuo Shindo
D: Masako Saito,
Koichi Fujikawa
P: Naoki Tsuruta,
Manabu Matsunaga
S: Mina Takayama
H: Ryuji
DF: Contemporary Production
CL: Nippon Columbia
ピチカート ファイヴ
女性上位時代
CD 1991
AD: 信藤三雄
D: 斉藤雅子、
藤川浩一
P: 鶴田直樹、
松永 学
S: 高山みな
H: りゅうじ
DF: コンテムポラリー プロダクション
CL: 日本コロムビア

10. Lyrics

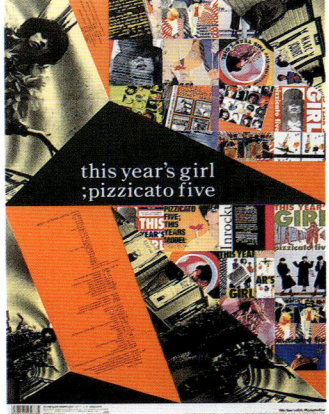

10. Back

10.

11.Lyrics / Inside Spread

11.Lyrics / Outside Spread

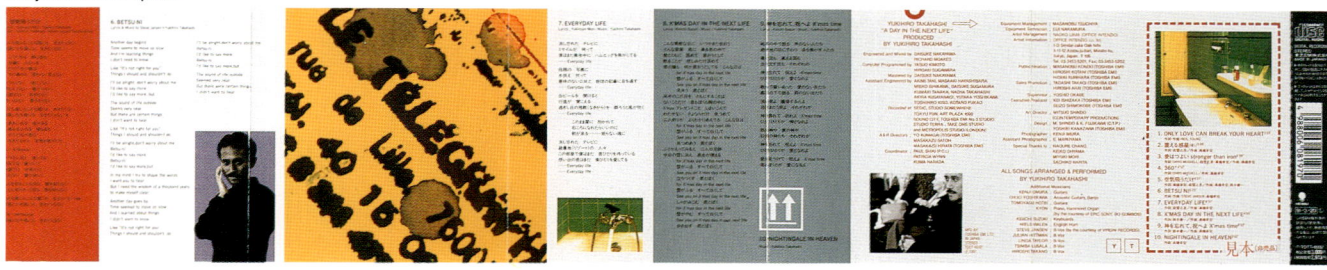

11. YUKIHIRO TAKAHASHI
A DAY IN THE NEXT LIFE
CD 1991
AD,D: Mitsuo Shindo
D: Koichi Fujikawa
P: Kenji Miura
DF: Contemporary Production
CL: Toshiba EMI
高橋幸宏
ア デイ イン ザ ネクスト ライフ
CD 1991
AD,D: 信藤三雄
D: 藤川浩一
P: 三浦憲治
DF: コンテムポラリー プロダクション
CL: 東芝EMI

12. Lyrics / Outside Spread

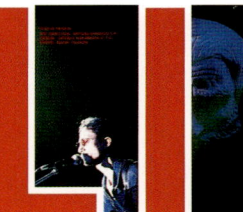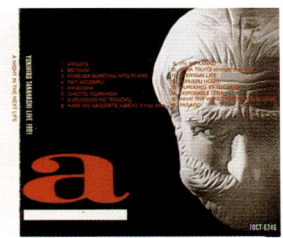

12. Lyrics / Inside Spread

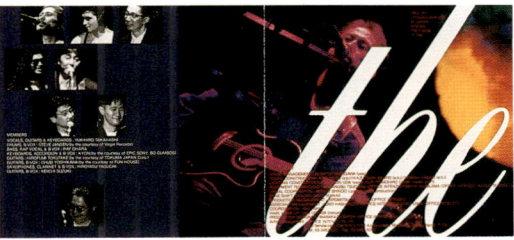

12.

12.

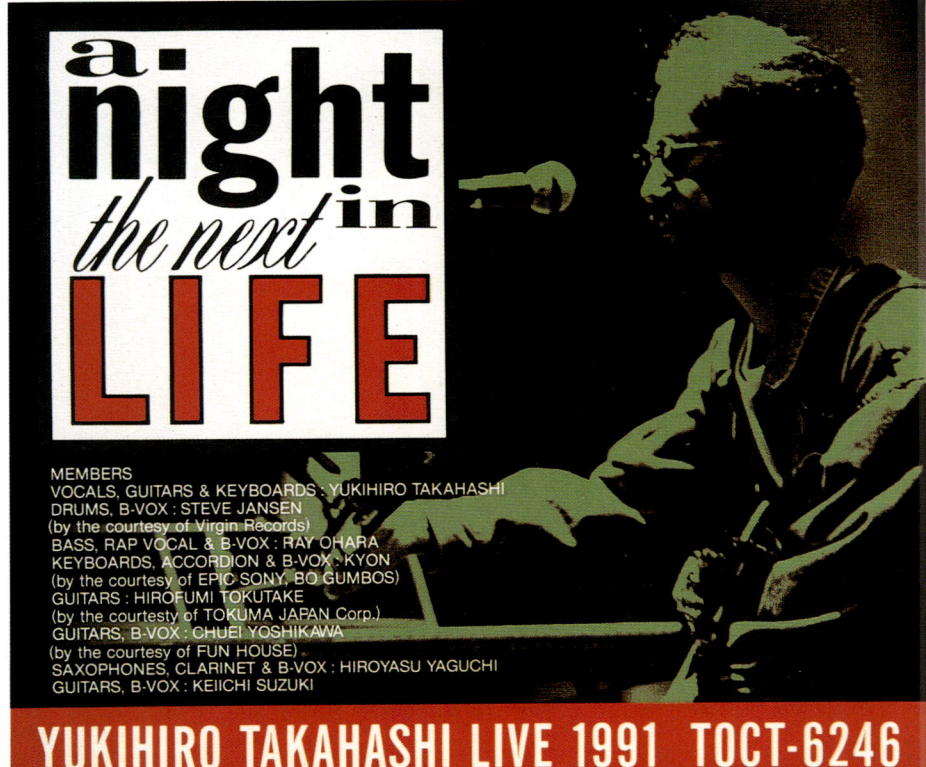

12. YUKIHIRO TAKAHASHI
A NIGHT IN THE NEXT LIFE
CD 1991
AD: Mitsuo Shindo
D: Satoshi Nakamura, Koichi Fujikawa, Masako Saito
P: Naoki Tsuruta
H: Mikio Honda (Bijin)
DF: Contemporary Production
CL: Toshiba EMI

高橋幸宏
アナイト インザ ネクスト ライフ
CD 1991
AD: 信藤三雄
D: 中村　智、藤川浩一、斉藤雅子
P: 鶴田直樹
H: ホンダ ミキオ
DF: コンテムポラリー プロダクション
CL: 東芝EMI

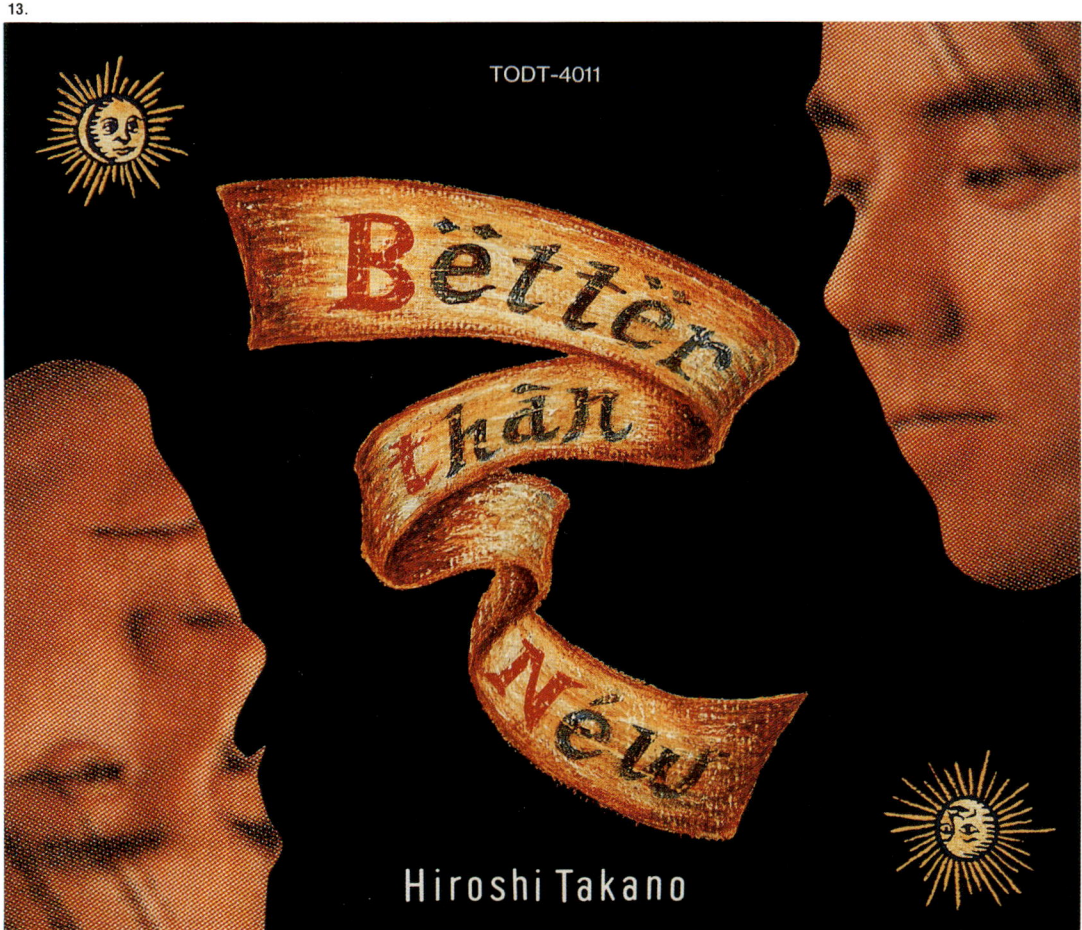

13. HIROSHI TAKANO / BETTER THAN NEW CD Single 1990 AD: Mitsuo Shindo D: Kumiko Tezuka I: Keiji Ito DF: Contemporary Production CL: Toshiba EMI
高野 寛 / ベター ザン ニュー CDシングル 1990 AD: 信藤三雄 D: 手塚久美子 I: 伊藤桂司 DF: コンテムポラリー プロダクション CL: 東芝EMI

14. Booklet / Page Spread

14. Booklet / Page Spread

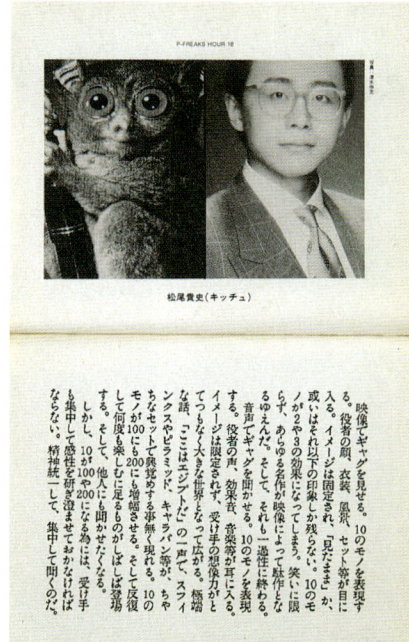

14. Booklet / Page Spread

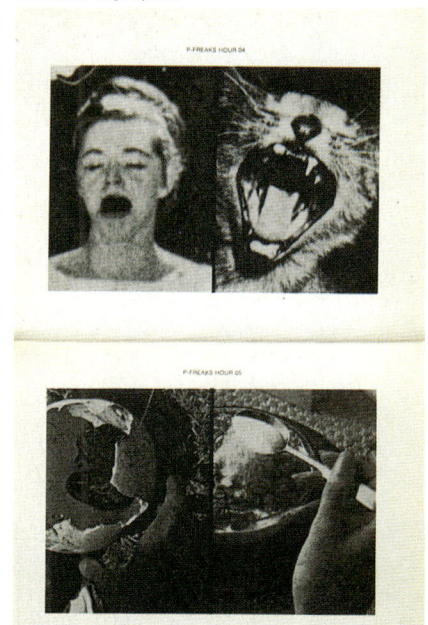

14.

14. Front

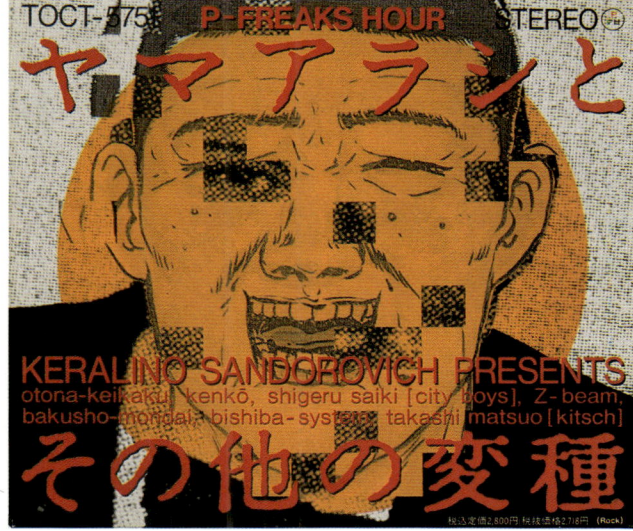

14. Back

14. P-FREAKS HOUR
PORCUPINES AND OTHER TRAVESTIES
CD 1990
AD: Mitsuo Shindo
D: Sawako Nakajima, Shinsuke Suda (Toshiba EMI)
I: Sensha Yoshida CL: Toshiba EMI
Pフリークス アワー
ヤマアラシとその他の変種
CD 1990
AD: 信藤三雄
D: 中嶋佐和子、須田真介
I: 吉田戦車 CL: 東芝EMI

15. Cover / Inside Spread

15. HIROKO YAKUSHIMARU / PRIMAVERA CD 1991 AD: Mitsuo Shindo **D:** Satoshi Nakamura **P:** Naoki Tsuruta **S:** Kazuo Hiyama **H:** Akihiko Asai
DF: Contemporary Production **CL:** Toshiba EMI
薬師丸 ひろ子 / プリマヴェーラ **CD 1991 AD:** 信藤三雄 **D:** 中村 智 **P:** 鶴田直樹 **S:** 檜山カズオ **H:** 浅井昭彦
DF: コンテムポラリー プロダクション **CL:** 東芝EMI

16.

16.

16. YUMI MATSUTOYA / THE GATES OF HEAVEN CD 1990
AD: Mitsuo Shindo D: Kumiko Tezuka, Koichi Fujikawa P: Kenji Miura
H: Akihiko Asai COSTUME DESIGN: Sachiko Ito(Sugar)
DF: Contemporary Production CL: Toshiba EMI
松任谷 由実 / 天国のドア CD 1990
AD: 信藤三雄 D: 手塚 久美子、藤川浩一 P: 三浦憲治
H: 浅井昭彦 COSTUME DESIGN: 伊藤 佐智子
DF: コンテンポラリー プロダクション CL: 東芝EMI

16. Lyrics / Outside Spread

16. Lyrics / Inside Spread

The Designers Republic

"**The Designers Republic! Yeah…What is it?** A celebration of plunder: computer age piracy on the hi-tech, where nothing's new under the sun. Big Fun! It's not theft: it's the desire to speak the language of logos a-go-go, mutated multi-national heiroglyphics speaking a global slang for the common man. It's the glory of graphic ready mades, corporations reduced to plexus: the chaos of the computer malfunction and the ghosts in the machine. The ages of chance versus change. The chips that free us from the need to be free. A blade running newspeak of slogans from "fast history rewinding into the future" to "Design or Die!" It's the religion of Popped Art American Expressionism, of consumerism and department store cathedrals; the mantras of the repeated image and the philosophy of more is more!

And some of this may be true…

「デザイナーズ・リパブリック？……なんだい、そりゃ？」
〈略奪したアイディアを祝う会〉ハイテクを駆使したコンピュータ時代の海賊行為。この世の中に全く新しいものはひとつとしてない。
〈なんと、これは盗みではない〉これは、最新のロゴマークで言語を話そうとする試みである。この「最新のロゴマーク言語」は、一般の人間には膨大なスラングにしか聞こえない言語を話す、多国籍の壁画によって変化されている。
〈これはグラフィックのレディメードの宝庫。たくさんの企業が神経のようにネットワークされている〉コンピュータの機能不全や機械内のゴーストの出現による混乱。チャンスの時代は、変化の時代でもある。我々を必要性から解放するチップは、自由でなくてはならない。「未来に向かって素早く巻戻される歴史」や「デザインか、さもなくば死か」は、ニュース・ピークなスローガンだ。
〈これは、Popped Art American Expression、コンシューマリズムとデパートメントストア・カテドラルの宗教である〉繰り返されるイメージのマントラと多くの哲学が、すべてだ。」

そして、このいくつかは事実かもしれない。

The Designers Republic was declared in July 1986 in Sheffield, England by Ian Anderson. Original team included ex-partner Nick Phillips, and Helen Betnay. The Designers Republic is currently Anderson, David Smith, Nick Bax, Michael Place & Vanessa Swetman. Exhibitions: *The Britishness of British Design* (Museum Boymans-van Beuningen Rotterdam) Spring 1989, *The Art of Selling Songs* (The Victoria & Albert Museum London) Spring 1991, Ian Anderson was a member of the D&AD Graphics Jury 1990.

デザイナーズ・リパブリックは、1986年7月に、イアン・アンダーソンによってイギリスのシェルフィールドに設立された。当初のメンバーは、ニック・フィリップスとヘレン・ベトネイ。現在は、アンダーソンとデヴィッド・スミス、ニック・バックス、マイケル・プレイス、ヴァネッサ・スウェットマンでチームを組んでいる。エキジビションとして、1989年春に「The Britishness of British Design」をロッテルダムのBoymans-van Beuningen博物館にて、1991年春に「The Art of Selling Songs」をロンドンのヴィクトリア＆アルバート美術館にて行なっている。また、イアン・アンダーソンは、1990年7月のD&ADグラフィックスの審査員だった。

1.Back

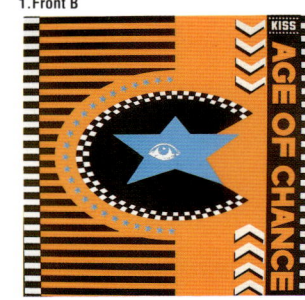
1.Front A

1.Front B

1.Front C

1.Front D

1. AGE OF CHANCE / KISS 12-inch Single 1986 AD,D: The Designers Republic DF: The Designers Republic CL: Fon Records
エイジ オヴ チャンス / キッス 12インチシングル 1986 AD,D: デザイナーズ リパブリック DF: デザイナーズ リパブリック CL: フォン レコード

2. AGE OF CHANCE / CRUSH COLLISION LP 1986 AD,D: The Designers Republic DF: The Designers Republic CL: Fon Records
エイジ オヴ チャンス / クラッシュ コリジョン LP 1986 AD,D: デザイナーズ リパブリック DF: デザイナーズ リパブリック CL: フォン レコード

3. AGE OF CHANCE / WHO'S AFRAID OF THE BIG BAD NOISE 12-inch Single 1987 AD,D: The Designers Republic DF: The Designers Republic CL: Virgin Records
エイジ オヴ チャンス / フーズ アフレイド オヴ ザ ビッグ バッド ノイズ 12インチ シングル 1987 AD,D: デザイナーズ リパブリック DF: デザイナーズ リパブリック CL: ヴァージン レコード

4. AGE OF CHANCE / TAKE IT! 12-inch Single 1988 AD,D,P: The Designers Republic DF: The Designers Republic CL: Virgin Records
エイジ オヴ チャンス / テイク イット！ 12インチ シングル 1988 AD,D,P: デザイナーズ リパブリック DF: デザイナーズ リパブリック CL: ヴァージン レコード

2.

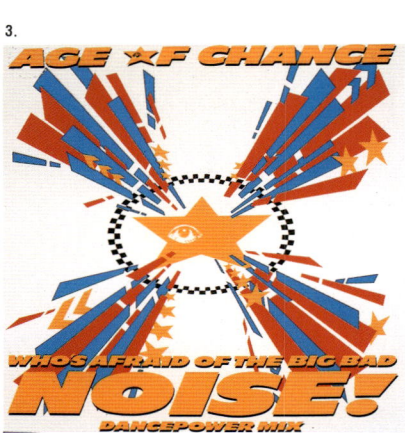
3.

4.

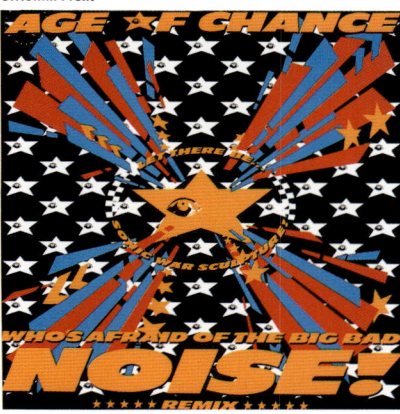
3.Remix Front

5. Front

5. AGE OF CHANCE / ONE THOUSAND YEARS OF TROUBLE LP 1987 AD,D: The Designers Republic DF: The Designers Republic CL: Virgin Records
エイジ オヴ チャンス / ワン サウザンド イヤーズ オヴ トラブル LP 1987 AD,D: デザイナーズ リパブリック DF: デザイナーズ リパブリック CL: ヴァージン レコード

5. Back

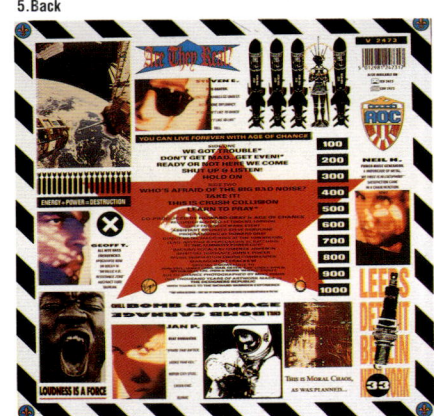

5. Inner Sleeve / Back

5. Inner Sleeve / Front

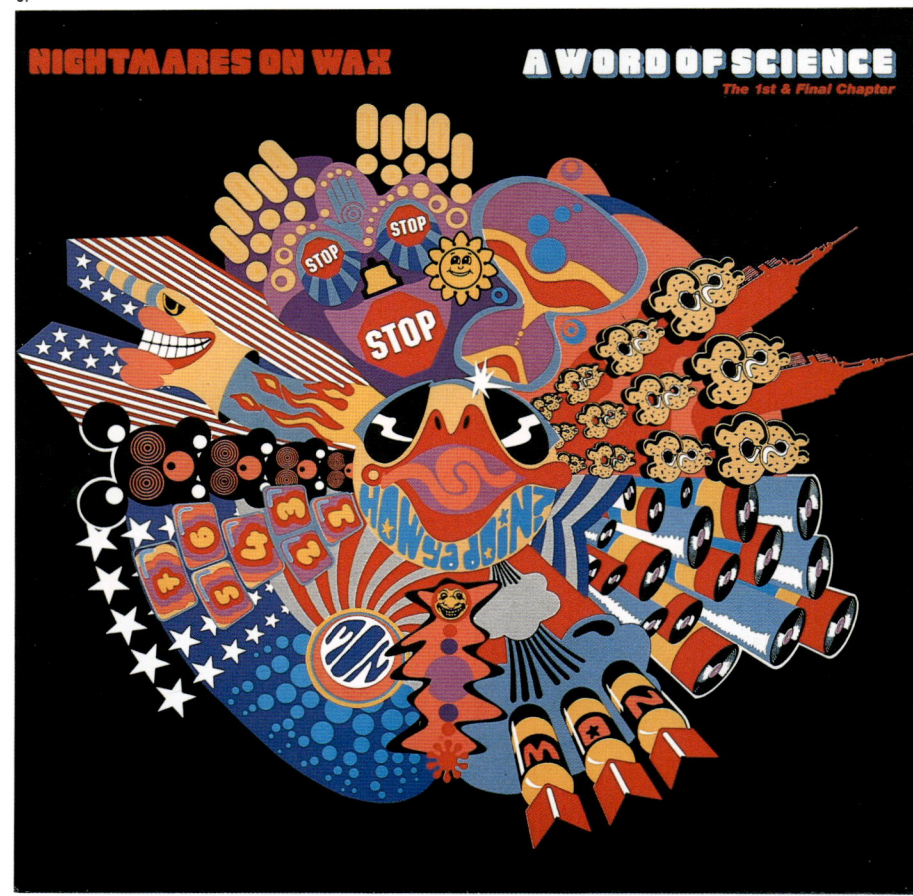

6. NIGHTMARES ON WAX / A WORD OF SCIENCE LP 1991
AD,D,I: The Designers Republic P: Luke DF: The Designers Republic CL: Warp Records
ナイトメアーズ オン ワックス / ア ワード オヴ サイエンス LP 1991
AD,D,I: デザイナーズ リパブリック P: ルーク DF: デザイナーズ リパブリック CL: ワープ レコード

7. KOROVA MILK BAR / TWISTED 12-inch Single 1990
AD,D: The Designers Republic DF: The Designers Republic CL: Chapter 22 Records
コロヴァ ミルク バー / ツイステッド 12インチ シングル 1990
AD,D: デザイナーズ リパブリック DF: デザイナーズ リパブリック CL: チャプター22レコード

8. FANGORIA / SALTO MORTAL LP 1990
AD,D: The Designers Republic DF: The Designers Republic CL: EMI, HISPAVOX
ファンゴリア / サルト モルタル LP 1990
AD,D: デザイナーズ リパブリック DF: デザイナーズ リパブリック CL: EMI, ヒスパヴォックス

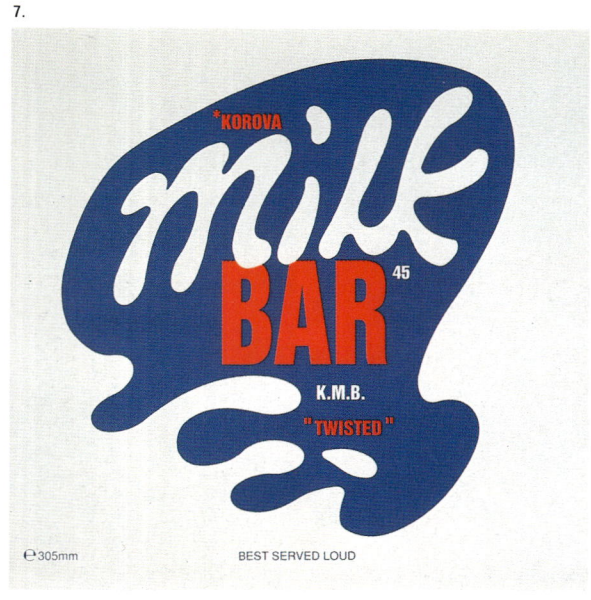

9. NATION 12 / REMEMBER 12-inch Single 1990 AD,D: The Designers Republic DF: The Designers Republic CL: Rhythm King
ネイション 12 / リメンバー 12インチ シングル 1990
AD,D: デザイナーズ リパブリック DF: デザイナーズ リパブリック CL: リズム キング

10. MARATHON / MOVIN' 12-inch Single 1990 AD,D: The Designers Republic DF: The Designers Republic CL: EG Records
マラソン / ムーヴィング 12インチ シングル 1990
AD,D: デザイナーズ リパブリック DF: デザイナーズ リパブリック CL: EG レコード

11. ASHLEY AND JACKSON / SWEET TIME 12-inch Single 1991 AD,D: The Designers Republic DF: The Designers Republic CL: Big Life
アシュレイ アンド ジャクソン / スウィート タイム 12インチ シングル 1991
AD,D: デザイナーズ リパブリック DF: デザイナーズ リパブリック CL: ビッグ ライフ

12. NIXON / SUBMISSION 12-inch Single 1991 AD,D,I: The Designers Republic DF: The Designers Republic CL: MCA
ニクソン / サブミッション 12インチ シングル 1991
AD,D,I: デザイナーズ リパブリック DF: デザイナーズ リパブリック CL: MCA

13. NIXON / SWEET TEMPTATION 12-inch Single 1990 AD,D: The Designers Republic DF: The Designers Republic CL: MCA
ニクソン / スウィート テンプテーション 12インチ シングル 1990
AD,D: デザイナーズ リパブリック DF: デザイナーズ リパブリック CL: MCA

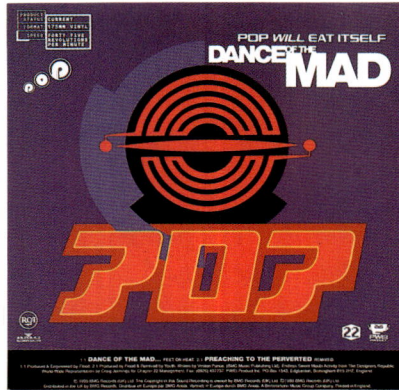
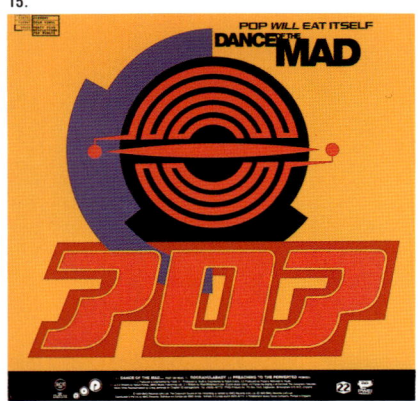
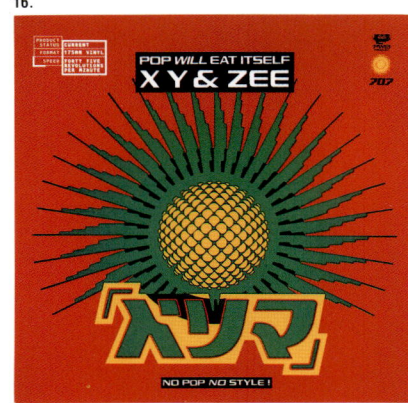

14. POP WILL EAT ITSELF / DANCE OF THE MAD 7-inch Single 1990
AD,D: The Designers Republic DF: The Designers Republic CL: RCA
ポップ ウィル イート イットセルフ / ダンス オヴ ザ マッド 7インチ シングル 1990
AD,D: デザイナーズ リパブリック DF: デザイナーズ リパブリック CL: RCA

15. POP WILL EAT ITSELF / DANCE OF THE MAD 12-inch Single 1990
AD,D: The Designers Republic P: Science Photo Library DF: The Designers Republic CL: RCA
ポップ ウィル イート イットセルフ / ダンス オヴ ザ マッド 12インチ シングル 1990
AD,D: デザイナーズ リパブリック P: サイエンス フォト ライブラリー DF: デザイナーズ リパブリック CL: RCA

16. POP WILL EAT ITSELF / X Y & ZEE 7-inch Single 1991
AD,D: The Designers Republic DF: The Designers Republic CL: RCA
ポップ ウィル イート イットセルフ / X Y & ZEE 7インチ シングル 1991
AD,D: デザイナーズ リパブリック DF: デザイナーズ リパブリック CL: RCA

17. POP WILL EAT ITSELF / WISE UP! SUCKER 12-inch Single 1989
AD,D: The Designers Republic DF: The Designers Republic CL: RCA
ポップ ウィル イート イットセルフ / ワイズ アップ! サッカー 12インチ シングル 1989
AD,D: デザイナーズ リパブリック DF: デザイナーズ リパブリック CL: RCA

18. POP WILL EAT ITSELF / TOUCHED BY THE HAND OF CICCIOLINA 12-inch Single 1990
AD,D: The Designers Republic DF: The Designers Republic CL: RCA
ポップ ウィル イート イットセルフ / タッチド バイ ザ ハンド オヴ チチョリーナ 12インチ シングル 1990
AD,D: デザイナーズ リパブリック DF: デザイナーズ リパブリック CL: RCA

19. POP WILL EAT ITSELF / 92°F 12-inch Single 1991
AD,D: The Designers Republic DF: The Designers Republic CL: RCA
ポップ ウィル イート イットセルフ / 92°F 12インチ シングル 1991
AD,D: デザイナーズ リパブリック DF: デザイナーズ リパブリック CL: RCA

20. POP WILL EAT ITSELF / 92°F (REMIX) 10-inch Single 1991
AD,D: The Designers Republic DF: The Designers Republic CL: RCA
ポップ ウィル イート イットセルフ / 92°F (リミックス) 10インチ シングル 1991
AD,D: デザイナーズ リパブリック DF: デザイナーズ リパブリック CL: RCA

17.Front
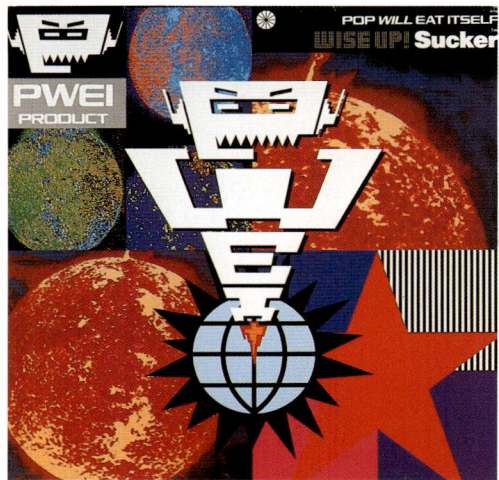

17.Back

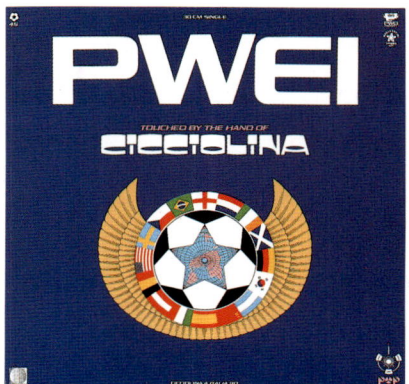

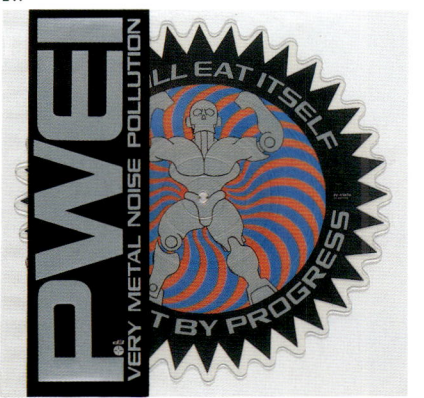

21. **POP WILL EAT ITSELF / VERY METAL NOISE POLLUTION** 10-inch Single 1989
AD,D: The Designers Republic DF: The Designers Republic CL: RCA
ポップ ウィル イート イットセルフ / ヴェリー メタルノイズ ポリューション 10インチ シングル 1989
AD,D: デザイナーズ リパブリック DF: デザイナーズ リパブリック CL: RCA

22. **POP WILL EAT ITSELF / VERY METAL NOISE POLLUTION** Cassette 1989
AD,D: The Designers Republic DF: The Designers Republic CL: RCA
ポップ ウィル イート イットセルフ / ヴェリー メタルノイズ ポリューション カセット 1989
AD,D: デザイナーズ リパブリック DF: デザイナーズ リパブリック CL: RCA

23. **POP WILL EAT ITSELF / CURE FOR SANITY** LP 1991
AD,D: The Designers Republic DF: The Designers Republic CL: RCA
ポップ ウィル イート イットセルフ / キュア フォー サニティ LP 1991
AD,D: デザイナーズ リパブリック DF: デザイナーズ リパブリック CL: RCA

24. **POP WILL EAT ITSELF / WISE UP! SUCKER** 7-inch Single 1989
AD,D: The Designers Republic DF: The Designers Republic
CL: RCA
ポップ ウィル イート イットセルフ / ワイズ アップ！ サッカー 7インチ シングル 1989
AD,D: デザイナーズ リパブリック DF: デザイナーズ リパブリック CL: RCA

25. **POP WILL EAT ITSELF / VERY METAL NOISE POLLUTION** 7-inch Single 1989
AD,D: The Designers Republic DF: The Designers Republic CL: RCA
ポップ ウィル イート イットセルフ / ヴェリー メタルノイズ ポリューション 7インチ シングル 1989
AD,D: デザイナーズ リパブリック DF: デザイナーズ リパブリック CL: RCA

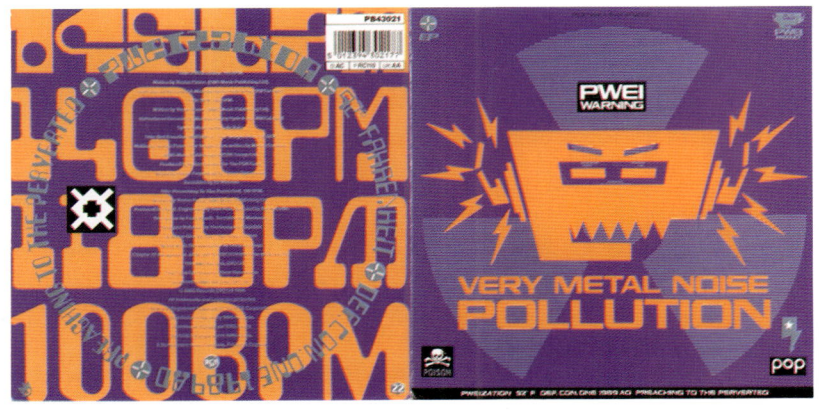

26.

27.Back

28.

27.Front

26. THE FUNKY WORM / HUSTLE 12-inch Single 1988 **AD,D,I:** The Designers Republic **DF:** The Designers Republic **CL:** Fon Records, WEA
ザ ファンキー ウォーム / ハッスル 12インチ シングル 1988 **AD,D,I:** デザイナーズ リパブリック **DF:** デザイナーズ リパブリック **CL:** フォン レコード、WEA

27. THE FUNKY WORM / THE SPELL! 12-inch Single 1988 **AD,D,I:** The Designers Republic **DF:** The Designers Republic **CL:** Fon Records, WEA
ザ ファンキー ウォーム / ザ スペル！ 12インチ シングル 1988 **AD,D,I:** デザイナーズ リパブリック **DF:** デザイナーズ リパブリック **CL:** フォン レコード、WEA

28. FUZZBOX / BIG BANG! LP 1989 **AD:** Rob Dickens **D:** The Designers Republic **P:** Bob Carlos Clarke **DF:** The Designers Republic **CL:** WEA
ファズボックス / ビッグ バン！ LP 1989 **AD:** ロブ ディケンズ **D:** デザイナーズ リパブリック **P:** ボブ カルロス クラーク **DF:** デザイナーズ リパブリック **CL:** WEA

29. JOY-FEATURING GLADNESS RUSSELL / HALF PAST MIDNIGHT 12-inch Single 1988 **AD,D:** The Designers Republic **DF:** The Designers Republic **CL:** Submission Records
ジョイ〜フィーチャリング グラッドネス ラッセル / ハーフ パスト ミッドナイト 12インチ シングル 1988 **AD,D:** デザイナーズ リパブリック **DF:** デザイナーズ リパブリック **CL:** サブミッション レコード

30. KRUSH / HOUSE ARREST 12-inch Single 1987 **AD,D:** The Designers Republic **DF:** The Designers Republic **CL:** Fon Records, Phonogram
クラッシュ / ハウス アレスト 12インチ シングル 1987 **AD,D:** デザイナーズ リパブリック **DF:** デザイナーズ リパブリック **CL:** フォン レコード、フォノグラム

31. KRUSH / HOUSE ARREST (REMIX) 12-inch Single 1987 **AD,D:** The Designers Republic **DF:** The Designers Republic **CL:** Fon Records, Phonogram
クラッシュ / ハウス アレスト（リミックス） 12インチ シングル 1987 **AD,D:** デザイナーズ リパブリック **DF:** デザイナーズ リパブリック **CL:** フォン レコード、フォノグラム

29.

30.

31.

32. LFO / WE ARE BACK (REMIX) 12-inch Single 1991 AD,D: The Designers Republic DF: The Designers Republic CL: Warp Records
LFO / ウィ アー バック（リミックス） 12インチ シングル 1991 AD,D: デザイナーズ リパブリック DF: デザイナーズ リパブリック CL: ワープ レコード

33. VARIOUS ARTISTS-OZONE COMPILATION / HARDBEAT & BASS LINE LP 1991 AD,D: The Designers Republic DF: The Designers Republic CL: A Native Release
ヴァリアス アーティスト〜オゾン コンピレーション / ハードビート & ベース ライン LP 1991 AD,D: デザイナーズ リパブリック DF: デザイナーズ リパブリック CL: ア ネイティヴ リリース

34. THE ORB / ADVENTURES BEYOND THE ULTRA WORLD LP 1991 AD,D: The Designers Republic P: Richard Cheadle, Paul Evans, N.A.S.A.
DF: The Designers Republic CL: Wau! Mr Modo, Big Life
THE ORB / アドヴェンチャーズ ビヨンド ジ ウルトラワールド LP 1991 AD,D: デザイナーズ リパブリック P: リチャード チードル、ポール エバンス、N.A.S.A.
DF: デザイナーズ リパブリック CL: ワウ！ミスター モード、ビッグ ライフ

35. THE ORB / LITTLE FLUFFY CLOUDS (REMIX) 12-inch Single 1990 AD,D: The Designers Republic P: N.A.S.A. DF: The Designers Republic CL: Wau! Mr Modo, Big Life
THE ORB / リトル フラフィ クラウズ（リミックス） 12インチ シングル 1990 AD,D: デザイナーズ リパブリック P: N.A.S.A. DF: デザイナーズ リパブリック
CL: ワウ！ミスター モード、ビッグ ライフ

36.

37. Front & Outside Spreads

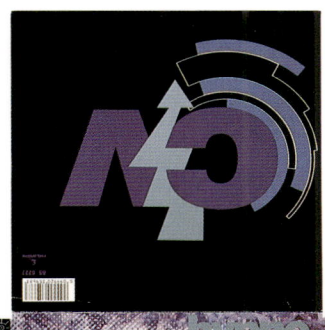

38.

36. BLEEP AND BOOSTER / GENKI-ELECTRO CITY 12-inch Single 1990
AD,D: The Designers Republic P: Christopher Reid
DF: The Designers Republic CL: Tove Corporation
ブリープ アンド ブースター / ゲンキ-エレクトロ シティ 12インチ シングル 1990
AD,D: デザイナーズ リパブリック P: クリストファー リード
DF: デザイナーズ リパブリック CL: トヴ コーポレーション

37. CABARET VOLTAIRE / HYPNOTISED 7-inch Single 1989
AD,D: The Designers Republic DF: The Designers Republic CL: EMI Records
キャバレー ヴォルテール / ヒプノタイズ 7インチ シングル 1989
AD,D: デザイナーズ リパブリック DF: デザイナーズ リパブリック CL: EMIレコード

38. THE ORB / PERPETUAL DAWN 12-inch Single 1991
AD,D: The Designers Republic I: Rainbow Paterson
DF: The Designers Republic CL: Wau! Mr Modo, Big Life
THE ORB / パーペチュアル ダウン 12インチ シングル 1991
AD,D: デザイナーズ リパブリック I: レインボー パターソン
DF: デザイナーズ リパブリック CL: ワウ！ ミスター モード、ビッグ ライフ

39.Inner Sleeve / Front

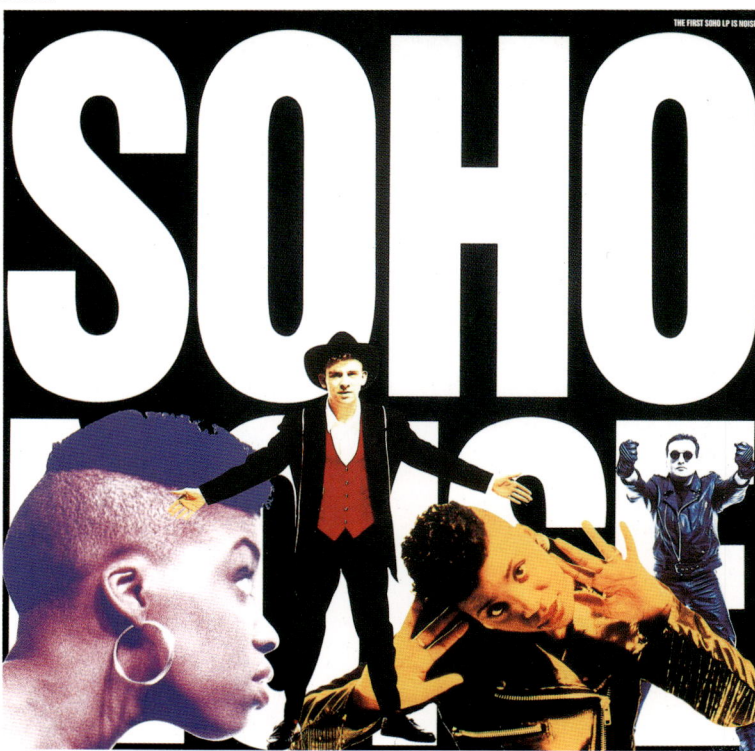

39.Front

39. SOHO / NOISE LP 1989 AD,D: The Designers Republic P: Peter Ashworth Ultraphotography DF: The Designers Republic CL: Virgin Records
ソーホー / ノイズ LP 1989 AD,D: デザイナーズ リパブリック P: ピーター アシュワース ウルトラフォトグラフィー DF: デザイナーズ リパブリック CL: ヴァージン レコード

40. THE DARLING BUDS / SHAME ON YOU 12-inch Single 1987 AD,D,P: The Designers Republic DF: The Designers Republic CL: Native Records
ザ ダーリン バッズ / シェーム オン ユー 12インチ シングル 1987 AD,D,P: デザイナーズ リパブリック DF: デザイナーズ リパブリック CL: ネイティヴ レコード

41. THE DARLING BUDS / HIT THE GROUND 12-inch Single 1989 AD,D: The Designers Republic P: Andy Gray DF: The Designers Republic CL: Native Records, Epic
ザ ダーリン バッズ / ヒット ザ グラウンド 12インチ シングル 1989 AD,D: デザイナーズ リパブリック P: アンディ グレイ DF: デザイナーズ リパブリック CL: ネイティヴ レコード、エピック

40.

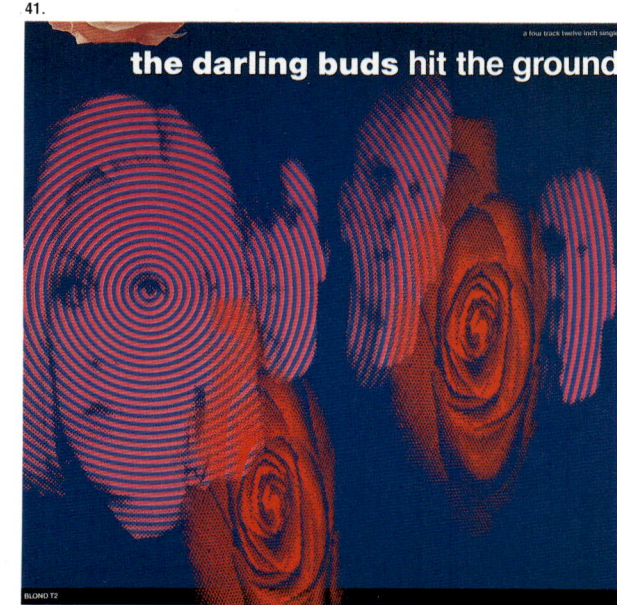

41.

39.Back

39.Inner Sleeve / Back

42. SOHO / LOVE GENERATION 12-inch Single 1991 AD,D: The Designers Republic DF: The Designers Republic CL: Savage Records
ソーホー / ラヴ ジェネレーション 12インチ シングル 1991 AD,D: デザイナーズ リパブリック DF: デザイナーズ リパブリック CL: サヴィジ レコード

42.Back

42.Front

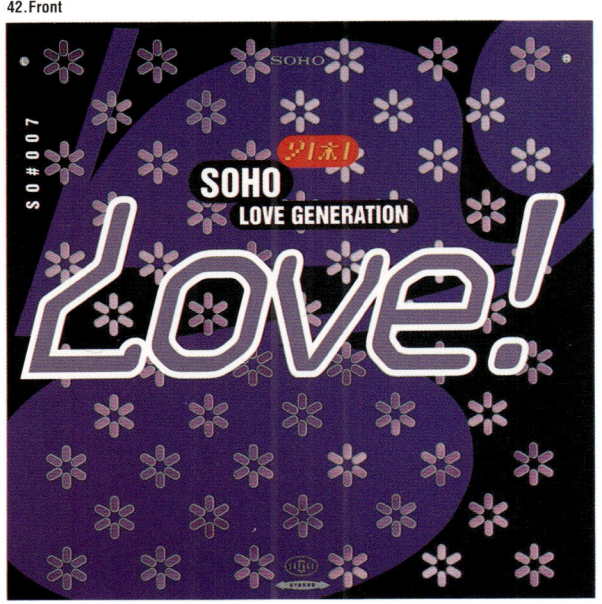

43.Back

43.Front

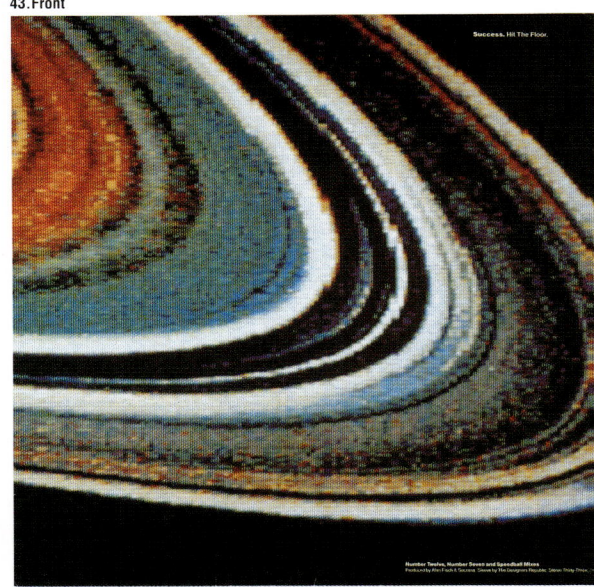

43. SUCCESS / HIT THE FLOOR 12-inch Single 1989
AD,D: The Designers Republic DF: The Designers Republic CL: Native Records
サクセス / ヒット ザ フロア 12インチ シングル 1989
AD,D: デザイナーズ リパブリック DF: デザイナーズ リパブリック
CL: ネイティヴ レコード

44. SUCCESS / WORLD CRASH LP 1989 AD,D: The Designers Republic P: N.A.S.A.
DF: The Designers Republic CL: Native Records
サクセス / ワールド クラッシュ LP 1989
AD,D: デザイナーズ リパブリック P: N.A.S.A.
DF: デザイナーズ リパブリック CL: ネイティヴ レコード

45. SUCCESS / TRIP WIRE 12-inch Single 1989
AD,D: The Designers Republic DF: The Designers Republic CL: Ozone Records
サクセス / トリップ ワイアー 12インチ シングル 1989
AD,D: デザイナーズ リパブリック DF: デザイナーズ リパブリック CL: オゾン レコード

44.

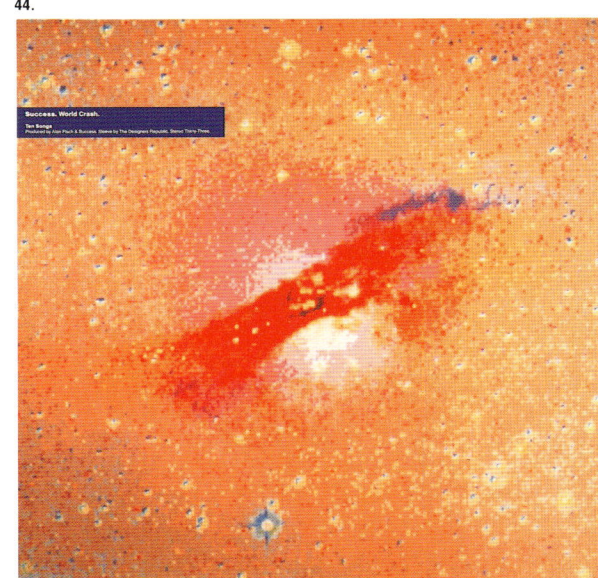

45.Back

45.Front

46. Back

47.

46. Front

46. NINE INCH NAILS / SIN 12-inch Single 1990
AD,D: The Designers Republic   DF: The Designers Republic   CL: TVT Records
ナイン インチ ネイルズ / SIN 12インチ シングル 1990
AD,D: デザイナーズ リパブリック   DF: デザイナーズ リパブリック   CL: TVTレコード

47. SMASHING ORANGE / SMASHING ORANGE LP 1991
AD,D: The Designers Republic   DF: The Designers Republic   CL: A Native Release
スマッシング オレンジ / スマッシング オレンジ LP 1991
AD,D: デザイナーズ リパブリック   DF: デザイナーズ リパブリック
CL: ア ネイティヴ リリース

48. WHYCLIFFE / ROUGH SIDE LP 1991
AD,D: The Designers Republic
P: Peter Ashworth Ultraphotography, Jeurgen Teller, Shaun Bloodworth, Alex Bailey
DF: The Designers Republic   CL: Submission Records, MCA
ホワイクリフ / ラフ サイド LP 1991
AD,D: デザイナーズ リパブリック
P: ピーター アシュワース ウルトラフォトグラフィー、ジョーガン テラー、
シャウン ブラッドワース、アレックス ベイリー
DF: デザイナーズ リパブリック   CL: サブミッション レコード、MCA

48. Inner Sleeve / Back

48. Inner Sleeve / Front

49. **THE DESIGNERS REPUBLIC - STATIONERY** Business Stationery 1990 **AD,D:** The Designers Republic **DF:** The Designers Republic
デザイナーズ リパブリック ステーショナリー ビジネス ステーショナリー 1990
AD,D: デザイナーズ リパブリック **DF:** デザイナーズ リパブリック

50. **VOUT OROONIE** Promotional Kit 1990 **AD,D:** The Designers Republic **DF:** The Designers Republic **CL:** The Leadmill
ヴー オローニー 販促用キット 1990 **AD,D:** デザイナーズ リパブリック **DF:** デザイナーズ リパブリック **CL:** ザ レッドミル

51. **SHAUN BLOODWORTH - STATIONERY** Business Stationery 1990
AD,D: The Designers Republic **DF:** The Designers Republic **CL:** Shaun Bloodworth
シャウン ブラッドワース ステーショナリー ビジネス ステーショナリー 1990
AD,D: デザイナーズ リパブリック **DF:** デザイナーズ リパブリック **CL:** シャウン ブラッドワース

52. **CHAPTER 22 MANAGEMENT - STATIONERY** Business Stationery 1990
AD,D: The Designers Republic **DF:** The Designers Republic **CL:** Chapter 22 Management
チプター22 マネージメント ステーショナリー ビジネス ステーショナリー 1990
AD,D: デザイナーズ リパブリック **DF:** デザイナーズ リパブリック **CL:** チプター22 マネージメント

53. **OZONE RECORDINGS - STATIONERY** Business Stationery 1990
AD,D: The Designers Republic **DF:** The Designers Republic **CL:** Ozone Recordings
オゾン レコーディング ステーショナリー ビジネス ステーショナリー 1990
AD,D: デザイナーズ リパブリック **DF:** デザイナーズ リパブリック **CL:** オゾン レコーディング

55.

56.

57.

58. Logo

54. UNITY RECORDS - STATIONERY
Business Stationery 1990
AD,D: The Designers Republic
DF: The Designers Republic CL: Unity Records
ユニティ レコード ステーショナリー
ビジネス ステーショナリー 1990
AD,D: デザイナーズ リパブリック
DF: デザイナーズ リパブリック CL: ユニティ レコード

55. THE ART OF SELLING SONGS 1690-1990
Exhibition Poster 1991
AD,D: The Designers Republic DF: The Designers Republic
CL: The Victoria & Albert Museum
ジ アート オヴ セリング ソングズ 1690-1990
展覧会ポスター 1991
AD,D: デザイナーズ リパブリック
DF: デザイナーズ リパブリック
CL: ヴィクトリア & アルバート ミュージアム

56. DEPARTMENT STORES ARE OUR NEW CATHEDRALS
Promotional Poster 1989
AD,D: The Designers Republic DF: The Designers Republic
デパートメントストア アー アワー ニュー カセドラル
宣伝用ポスター 1989
AD,D: デザイナーズ リパブリック
DF: デザイナーズ リパブリック

57. HEY THINK! IT AIN'T ILLEGAL YET
Promotional Poster 1990
AD,D: The Designers Republic DF: The Designers Republic
ヘイ シンク！ イット エイント イリーガル イエット
宣伝用ポスター 1990
AD,D: デザイナーズ リパブリック
DF: デザイナーズ リパブリック

58. SUPERSONIC 1989
Promotional T-Shirt 1989
AD,D: The Designers Republic DF: The Designers Republic
スーパーソニック 1989
販促用 T シャツ 1989
AD,D: デザイナーズ リパブリック
DF: デザイナーズ リパブリック

Photography / ©1991 The Douglas Brothers

Russell Mills

As an independent artist/designer I have avoided the limitations of both specialized areas of work and the obligations of commitment required in a design studio company. I prefer to work alone thereby having more options to experiment, change and choose commissions of a wider diversity (from publishing to set designs, record covers to installations, corporate work to unique commissions). My approach to all works is inspired and informed by nature's lessons, the wonders of random order, the regenerative cycle and the marvels of nature which humankind cannot replicate. What I do is not a 'job' but a vocation, something that is fundamental to my life. I will only accept commissions I believe in and can support morally, socially and politically. This approach leads me into essentially close relationships with 'clients'. Future hopes include continually challenging the accepted notions of applied arts, experimenting with unknown materials, to extend work into a wider diversity of projects and to work with more environmentally aware clients.

私は独立したアーティスト及びデザイナーとして、仕事の専門領域や、デザイン会社で要求される仕事の契約事項を、制約されることを嫌ってきた。様々な種類の仕事の依頼（出版からステージ・セットまで、レコードジャケットから機械装置まで、企業の仕事からユニークな仕事まで）を、変更や選択が許される、フリーの立場で関わっていきたいと考えている。

私の仕事への姿勢は、自然の教え、不規則状態の不思議、再生の循環、人類が複製することのできない自然の驚異、などによって影響を受け、また活気づく。私がやっているのは「仕事」ではなく、使命、すなわち、生活の根源をつくり出すものなのである。そのため自分が信頼できて、道徳的、社会的、政治的にも支持できる依頼しか受けないことにしている。このような取り組み方をしていると、私と「クライアント」の関係は、どうしても密接になってくるのだ。

今後の希望としては、一般に認められた実用的なアートに引き続き挑戦すること、未知の素材を実験してみること、さらに広範囲に仕事を広げて行くこと、そして、環境問題に意識の強いクライアントと仕事をしていくことである。

1977 MA Degree, Royal College of Art London. Since, has worked extensively in record covers, book covers, magazine/editorial, illustration and design, advertising, corporate work, stage sets/lighting for contemporary dance and music, video and environmental installations and has lectured at art colleges in Europe and America. His paintings have been exhibited in the UK, USA, Japan, France, Denmark and Germany.

1977年にローヤル・カレッジ・オヴ・アート・ロンドンで修士号をとる。以来、その仕事は、レコードジャケット、本の表紙、雑誌、エディトリアルのイラストやデザイン、広告、企業の仕事、ステージ・セット、最新のダンスや音楽の照明、ビデオ及び環境装置など、多種多様にわたる。またヨーロッパとアメリカの美術学校で、講師もつとめている。彼の絵は、イギリス、アメリカ、日本、フランス、デンマーク、ドイツで公開されている。

1. JANET FRAME / DAUGHTER BUFFALO Book Cover 1990 ASSEMBLAGE: Russell Mills P: David Buckland CL: Unwin,Pandora Books
ジャネット フレイム / ドーター バッファロー　単行本 1990　ASSEMBLAGE: ラッセル ミルズ　P: デヴィッド バックランド　CL: アンウィン、パンドラ ブックス

2.

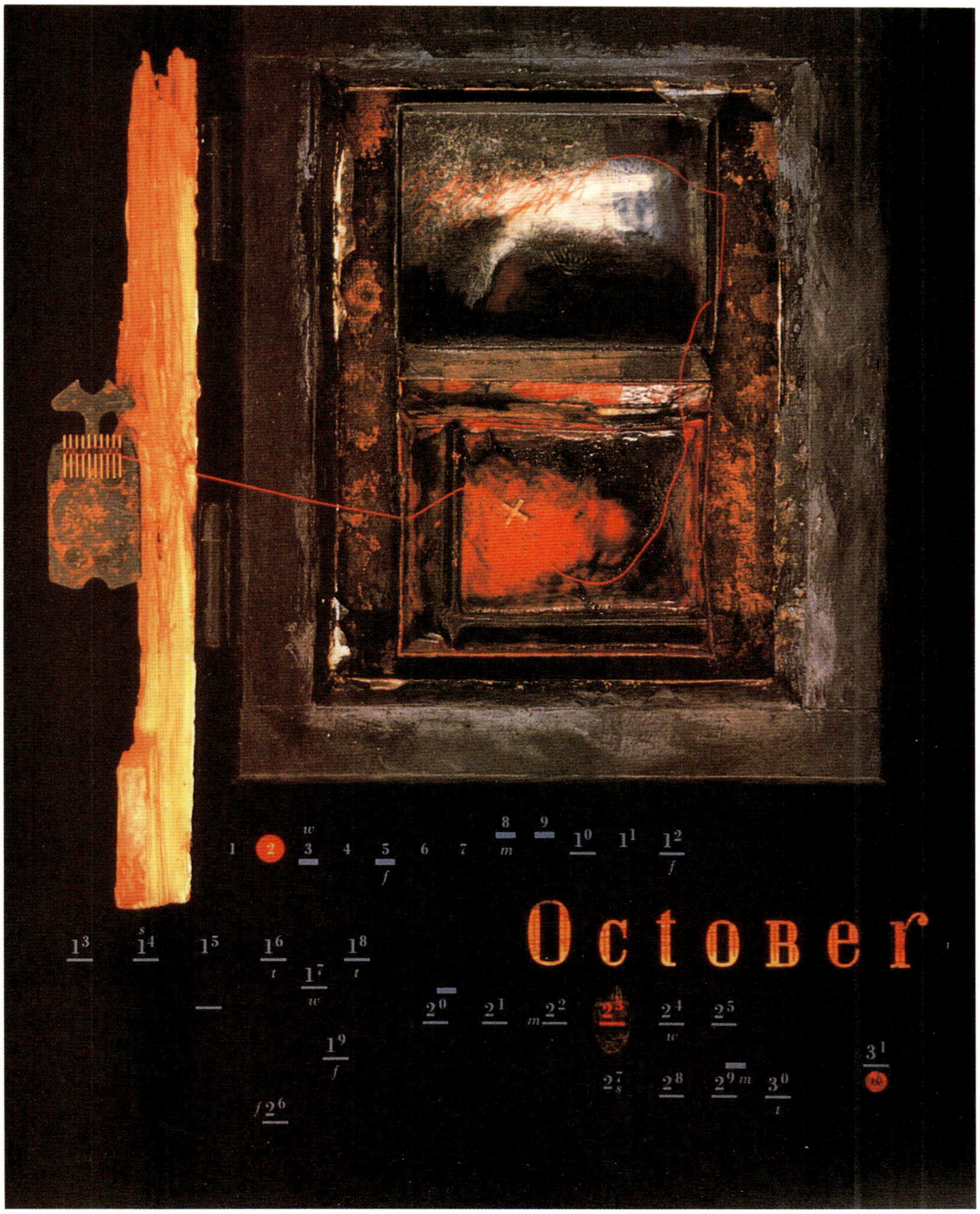

3.

2. OCTOBER 1990 Promotional Calendar 1989
AD: Vaughan Oliver P: David Buckland
I: Russell Mills CL: 4AD Records
オクトーバー 1990 販促用カレンダー 1989
AD: ヴォーン オリヴァー P: デヴィッド バックランド
I: ラッセル ミルズ CL: 4AD レコード

3. ROGER ENO / BETWEEN TIDES LP 1988
D,I: Russell Mills D: Dave Coppenhall
P: David Buckland CL: Land Warners, Brian Eno
ロジャー イーノ / ビトウィーン タイズ LP 1988
D,I: ラッセル ミルズ D: デイヴ カペンホール
P: デヴィッド バックランド
CL: ランド ワーナーズ、ブライアン イーノ

4.

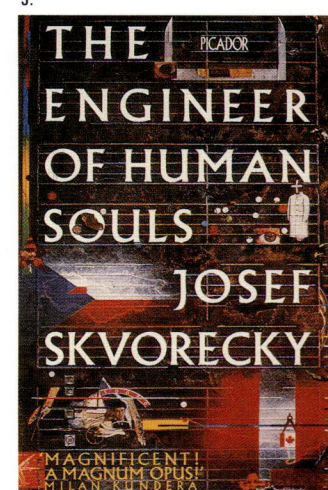

4. JOSEF SKVORECKY / THE SWELL SEASON Book Cover 1989
CD,CONSTRUCTION: Russell Mills P: David Buckland CL: Picador Books
ヨセフ スコレッキー / ザ スウェル シーズン 単行本 1989
CD,CONSTRUCTION: ラッセル ミルズ
P: デヴィッド バックランド CL: ピカドール ブックス

5. JOSEF SKVORECKY / THE ENGINEER OF HUMAN SOULS Book Cover 1986
CD,CONSTRUCTION: Russell Mills
P: David Buckland CL: Picador Books
ヨセフ スコレッキー / ジ エンジニア オヴ ヒューマン ソウルス 単行本 1986
CD,CONSTRUCTION: ラッセル ミルズ
P: デヴィッド バックランド CL: ピカドール ブックス

5.

6.

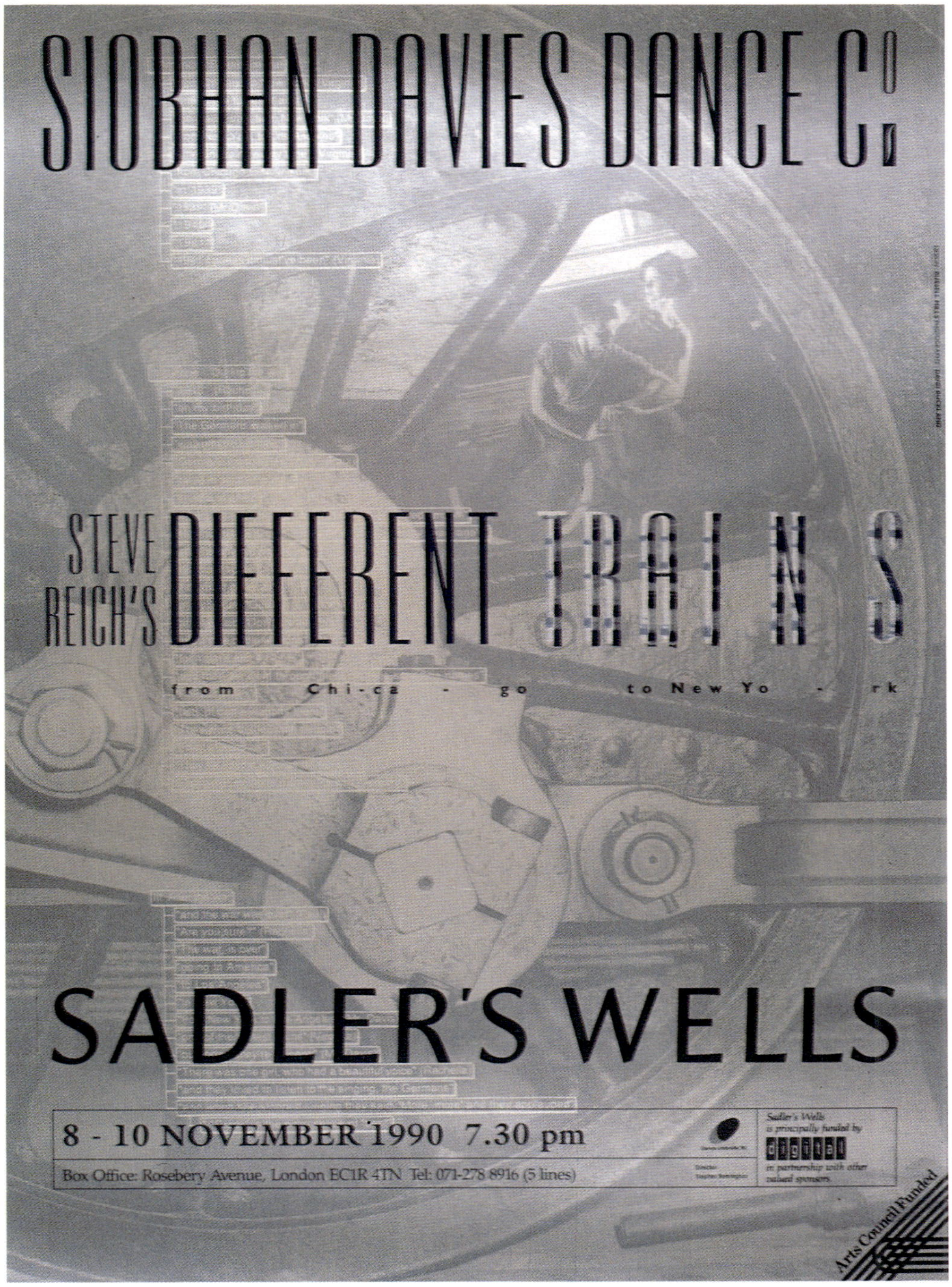

6. DIFFERENT TRAINS
Promotional Poster 1990
D: Russell Mills
P: David Buckland
CL: Siobhan Davies Dance Company
ディファレント トレインズ
宣伝用ポスター 1990
D: ラッセル ミルズ
P: デヴィッド バックランド
CL: ショーバン デイヴィーズ ダンス カンパニー

7. SAMUEL BECKETT
THE BECKETT TRILOGY
Book Cover 1982
D: Russell Mills
P: Christina Birrer
CL: Picador Books
サミュエル ベケット
ザ ベケット トリロジー
単行本 1982
D: ラッセル ミルズ
P: クリスティーナ ビラー
CL: ピカドール ブックス

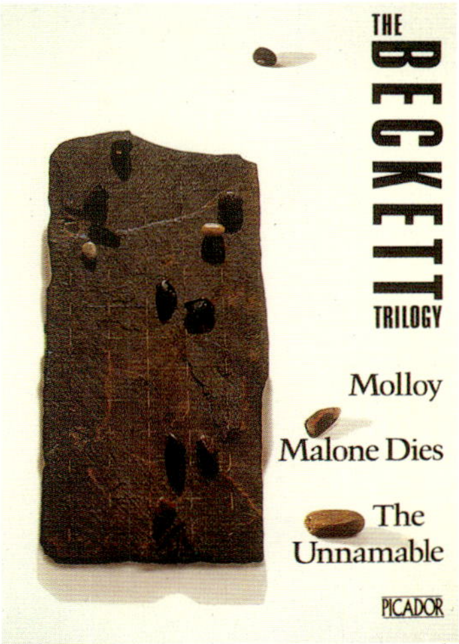

8. SAMUEL BECKETT
MORE PRICKS THAN KICKS
Book Cover 1982
D: Russell Mills
P: Christina Birrer
CL: Picador Books
サミュエル ベケット
モア プリックス ザン キックス
単行本 1982
D: ラッセル ミルズ
P: クリスティーナ ビラー
CL: ピカドール ブックス

7.   8.

9. LIVINGSTONE FISHER
Promotional Brochure 1990
PAINTING,CONSTRUCTION: Russell Mills
D: Vernon Oakley Design
P: David Buckland
CL: Livingstone Fisher
リヴィングストーン フィッシャー
販促用パンフレット 1990
PAINTING,CONSTRUCTION: ラッセル ミルズ
D: ヴァーノン オークレイ デザイン
P: デヴィッド バックランド
CL: リヴィングストーン フィッシャー

10. DOCUMENTCONCERT 'A'
Personal Work 1985
PAINTING,ASSEMBLAGE: Russell Mills
P: David Buckland
ドキュメント 'A'
コンサート
個人作品 1985
PAINTING,ASSEMBLAGE: ラッセル ミルズ
P: デヴィッド バックランド

9.

9.

9.

10.

11. EMBER GLANCE / THE PERMANENCE OF MEMORY Stage Setting 1990 CONCEIVE,CONSTRUCTION: Russell Mills, David Sylvian CL: T. S. Planning
アンバー グランス / ザ パーマネンス オヴ メモリー 舞台装置 1990 CONCEIVE,CONSTRUCTION: ラッセル ミルズ、デヴィッド シルヴィアン CL: T. S. プランニング

12. PROTEM / STILL REIGNS AND REIGNS Personal Work 1990 PAINTING,ASSEMBLAGE: Russell Mills P: David Buckland
プロテム / スティル レインズ アンド レインズ 個人作品 1990 PAINTING,ASSEMBLAGE: ラッセル ミルズ P: デヴィッド バックランド

13. CHANT / SPIN Personal Work 1990 PAINTING,ASSEMBLAGE: Russell Mills P: David Buckland
チャント / スピン 個人作品 1990 PAINTING,ASSEMBLAGE: ラッセル ミルズ P: デヴィッド バックランド

11.

11.

11. EMBER GLANCE / THE PERMANENCE OF MEMORY Stage Setting 1990 CONCEIVE,CONSTRUCTION: Russell Mills, David Sylvian CL: T. S. Planning
アンバー グランス / ザ パーマネンス オヴ メモリー　舞台装置 1990　CONCEIVE,CONSTRUCTION: ラッセル ミルズ、デヴィッド シルヴィアン　CL: T. S. プランニング

11.

11.

14. JIM CRACE
CONTINENT
Book Cover 1986
ASSEMBLAGE: Russell Mills
P: David Buckland
CL: William Heinemann,Son
ジム クレイス
コンチネント
単行本 1986
ASSEMBLAGE: ラッセル ミルズ
P: デヴィッド バックランド
CL: ウィリアム ヘインマン

15. MILAN KUNDERA
THE BOOK OF LAUGHTER AND FORGETTING
Book Cover 1982
ASSEMBLAGE: Russell Mills
CL: Faber & Faber
ミラン クンデーラ
ザ ブック オヴ ラフター アンド フォゲッティング
単行本 1982
ASSEMBLAGE: ラッセル ミルズ
CL: フェーバー & フェーバー

16. FRANÇOIS ELIE ROULIN
DISQUE ROUGE
CD 1989
D,I: Russell Mills
CL: Land Warners,
François Elie Roulin
フランソワーズ エリー ルーラン
ディスク ルージュ
CD 1989
D,I: ラッセル ミルズ
CL: ランド ワーナーズ、
フランソワーズ エリー ルーラン

17. HUGO LARGO
TURTLE SONG
12-inch Single 1989
D: Russell Mills,Dave Coppenhall
CL: Land Warners,Hugo Largo
ヒューゴ ラーゴ
タートル ソング
12インチ シングル 1989
D: ラッセル ミルズ
デイヴ カペンホール
CL: ランド ワーナーズ、
ヒューゴ ラーゴ

14.Back & Front

15.Back & Front
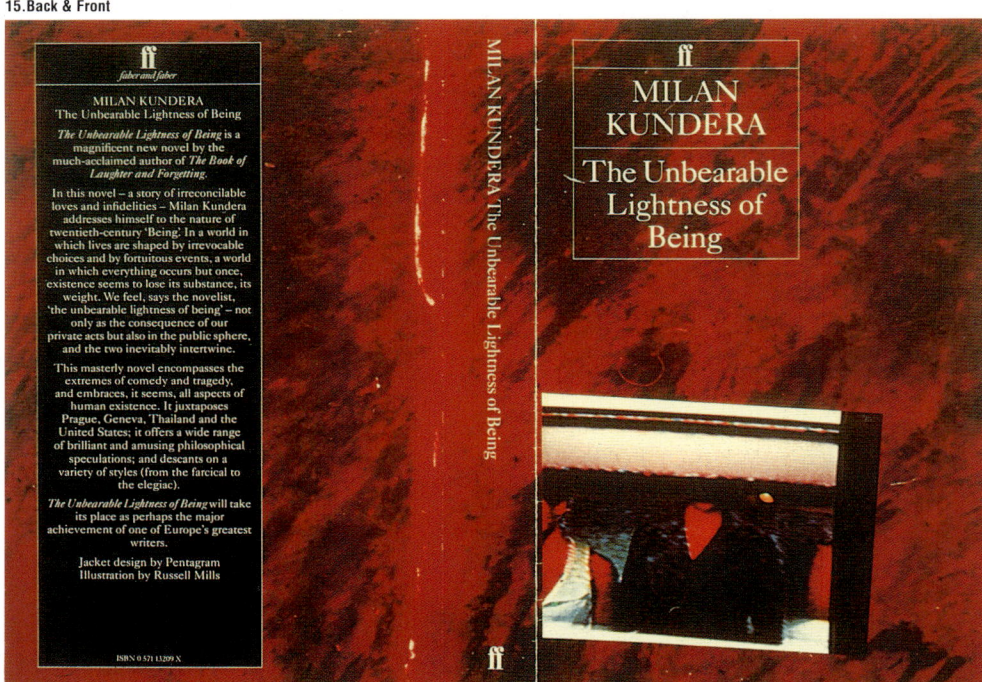

16.

17.
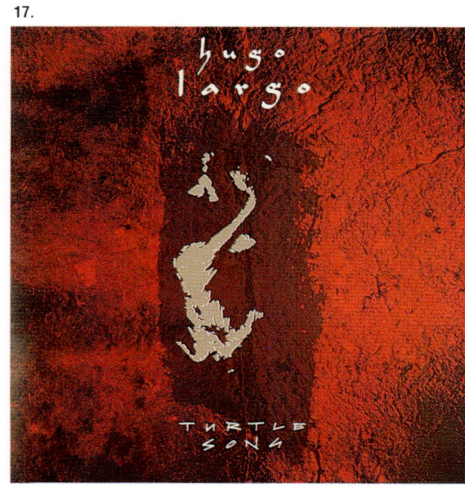

18. Back & Front

19. Back & Front

20.

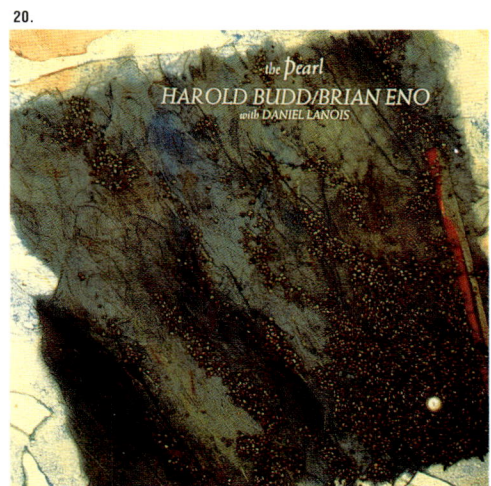

18. CHRISTOPH RANSMAYR / THE LAST WORLD Book Cover 1989
D,CONSTRUCTION: Russell Mills D: Dave Coppenhall P: David Buckland CL: Chatto & Windus
クリストフ ランズメイア / ザ ラスト ワールド 単行本 1989
D,CONSTRUCTION: ラッセル ミルズ D: デイヴ カペンホール P: デヴィッド バックランド CL: チャット & ウィンダス

19. YOUSSOU N'DOUR / SET LP 1990
D: Russell Mills, Dave Coppenhall P: David Buckland, Jack Kilby CL: Virgin Records, Youssou N'dour
ユッスー ンドゥール / SET LP 1990
D: ラッセル ミルズ、デイヴ カペンホール P: デヴィッド バックランド、ジャック キルビー
CL: ヴァージン レコード、ユッスー ンドゥール

20. HAROLD BUDD, BRIAN ENO / THE PEARL LP 1984
D,I: Russell Mills P: David Buckland CL: Editions EG, Brian Eno, Harold Budd
ハロルド バッド、ブライアン イーノ / ザ パール LP 1984
D,I: ラッセル ミルズ P: デヴィッド バックランド CL: エディションズ EG、ブライアン イーノ、ハロルド バッド

21. Back & Front

22. Cover / Front & Outside Spreads

21. TORU TAKEMITSU CD 1991 D: Russell Mills P: David Buckland CL: Virgin Classics, Toru Takemitsu
武満 徹 CD 1991 D: ラッセル ミルズ P: デヴィッド バックランド CL: ヴァージン クラシックス、武満 徹

22. DAVID SYLVIAN / IN PRAISE OF SHAMANS Concert Program 1988 D: Russell Mills, Dave Coppenhall P: David Buckland CL: Opium(Arts), David Sylvian
デヴィッド シルヴィアン / イン プレイズ オヴ シャーマンズ コンサート パンフレット 1988 D: ラッセル ミルズ、デイヴ カペンホール
P: デヴィッド バックランド CL: オピウム（アーツ）、デヴィッド シルヴィアン

23.

23. Package

23. Booklet & Covers / Front

23. DAVID SYLVIAN / WEATHER BOX Single CD Box Kit 1989 D: Russell Mills, Dave Coppenhall CL: Virgin Records, David Sylvian
デヴィッド シルヴィアン / ウェザー ボックス シングル CD ボックス キット 1989 D: ラッセル ミルズ、デイヴ カペンホール CL: ヴァージン レコード、デヴィッド シルヴィアン

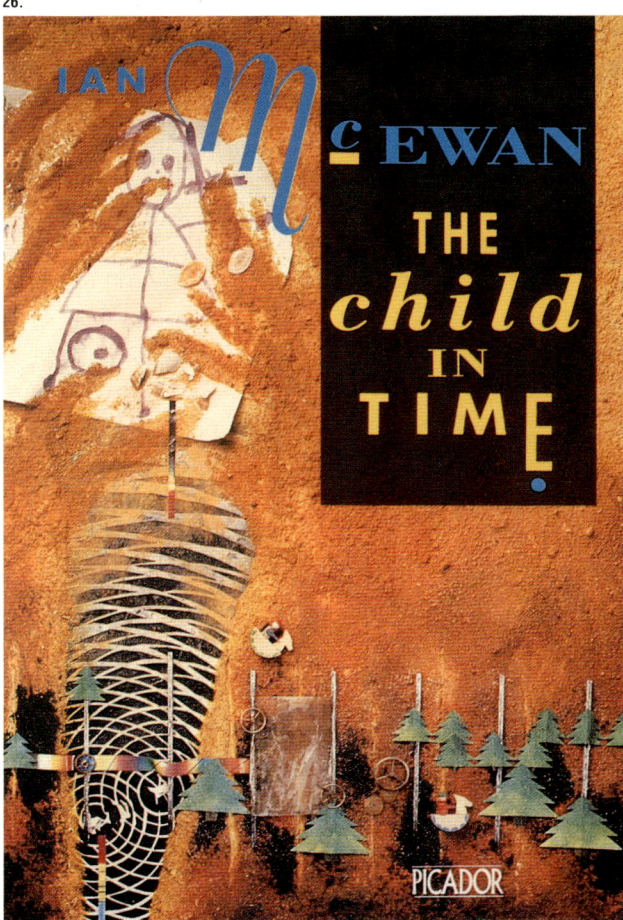

24. IAN MCEWAN
FIRST LOVES LAST RITES
Book Cover 1982
CD,CONSTRUCTION: Russell Mills
P: David Buckland
TYPOGRAPHY: Vaughan Oliver
CL: Picador Books
イアン マックイーワン
ファースト ラヴズ ラスト ライツ
単行本 1982
CD,CONSTRUCTION: ラッセル ミルズ
P: デヴィッド バックランド
TYPOGRAPHY: ヴォーン オリヴァー
CL: ピカドール ブックス

25. IAN MCEWAN
THE IMITATION GAME
Book Cover 1982
CD,CONSTRUCTION: Russell Mills
P: David Buckland
TYPOGRAPHY: Vaughan Oliver
CL: Picador Books
イアン マックイーワン
ジ イミテーション ゲーム
単行本 1982
CD,CONSTRUCTION: ラッセル ミルズ
P: デヴィッド バックランド
TYPOGRAPHY: ヴォーン オリヴァー
CL: ピカドール ブックス

26. IAN MCEWAN
THE CHILD IN TIME
Book Cover 1988
CD,CONSTRUCTION: Russell Mills
P: David Buckland
CL: Picador Books
イアン マックイーワン
ザ チャイルド イン タイム
単行本 1988
CD,CONSTRUCTION: ラッセル ミルズ
P: デヴィッド バックランド
CL: ピカドール ブックス

27.

27. RAIN TREE CROW / RAIN TREE CROW LP 1991 D: Russell Mills **P:** Shinya Fujiwara **CL:** Virgin Records
レイン トゥリー クロウ / レイン トゥリー クロウ **LP 1991 D:** ラッセル ミルズ **P:** 藤原新也 **CL:** ヴァージン レコード

Photography / Kosei Yoshida

Tadanori Yokoo 横尾忠則

Born in 1936. Painter. Yokoo won the 1969 *Paris Youth Biennale woodblock print prize*. An exhibition of his works in New York in 1972 established his international reputation. In 1981, he retired from graphic design to become a painter. He has since been exhibited at biennales in Paris, San Paolo, and Bangladesh. In addition to painting, Yokoo is active in a variety of fields, including printmaking, ceramics, and video art. Collected works: *Ryu No Utsuwa* (Parco), *Tadanori Yokoo The Complete prints* (Kodansha), *The Graphics of Tadanori Yokoo* (Kodansha). He has written several books, including *Indo E* (Bunshun Bunko), *Gaka No Nikki* (Art Digest), and *Waga Zazen Shugyo-ki* (Kodansha).

1936年生まれ。画家。1969年に受けたパリ青年ビエンナーレ版画部門大賞ほか、受賞多数。1972年ニューヨーク近代美術館で個展を開くなど、国際的に高い評価を受ける。1981年にグラフィック・デザイナーから画家に転向。以降もパリ、サンパウロ、バングラデシュの各ビエンナーレなどの国際展に招待出品。絵画のほか立体作品、版画、陶版、ビデオアートなど幅広い制作を続けている。作品集として『龍の器』（パルコ出版）、『横尾忠則の版画』（講談社）、『横尾忠則グラフィック大全』（講談社）を、著書として『インドへ』（文春文庫）、『画家の日記』（アートダイジェスト）、『わが座禅修行記』（講談社）ほかを出版。

1. AMAZON Promotional Poster 1989 AD,D: Tadanori Yokoo CL: Amazon
アマゾン 販促用ポスター 1989 AD,D: 横尾忠則 CL: アマゾン

2. **KAKURE-CHRISTIAN** LP 1973 AD,D: Tadanori Yokoo CL: Phonogram
隠れ切支丹 LP 1973 AD,D: 横尾忠則 CL: 日本フォノグラム

3. **ISAO TOMITA / THE BERMUDA TRIANGLE** LP 1978 AD,D: Tadanori Yokoo CL: RCA
富田 勲 / バミューダ トライアングル LP 1978 AD,D: 横尾忠則 CL: RCA

4. **KENJI ENDO / KENJI** Promotional Poster 1974 AD,D: Tadanori Yokoo CL: Polydor Records
遠藤賢司 / ケンジ 販促用ポスター 1974 AD,D: 横尾忠則 CL: ポリドール レコード

5.

6.

5. TADANORI YOKOO EXHIBITION Exhibition Poster 1991
AD,D,I: Tadanori Yokoo CL: Osaka German Cultural Center
横尾忠則展 展覧会ポスター 1991
AD,D,I: 横尾忠則 CL: 大阪ドイツ文化センター

6. ANNABELLA / BOW WOW WOW Promotional Poster 1982
AD,D,I: Tadanori Yokoo CL: RCA
アンナベラ / バウ ワウ ワウ 販促用ポスター 1982
AD,D,I: 横尾忠則 CL: RCA

7. LONDON PHILHARMONIC ORCHESTRA / THE PLANETS LP 1978
AD,D,I: Tadanori Yokoo CL: King Records
ロンドン フィルハーモニック オーケストラ / 惑星 LP 1978
AD,D,I: 横尾忠則 CL: キング レコード

8. KAORI MOMOI / KAORI Promotional Poster 1982
AD,D,I: Tadanori Yokoo CL: Sony Records
桃井かおり / カオリ 販促用ポスター 1982
AD,D,I: 横尾忠則 CL: ソニー レコード

9. GINJI ITO / BABY BLUE LP 1982
AD,D,I: Tadanori Yokoo CL: Polystar
伊藤銀次 / ベイビー ブルー LP 1982
AD,D,I: 横尾忠則 CL: ポリスター

7.

8.

9.

10. SANTANA
LOTUS
Promotional Poster 1974
AD,D: Tadanori Yokoo
CL: Sony Records
サンタナ
ロータス
販促用ポスター 1974
AD,D: 横尾忠則
CL: ソニー レコード

11. SANTANA
AMIGOS
LP 1974
AD,D,I: Tadanori Yokoo
CL: Sony Records
サンタナ
アミーゴ
LP 1974
AD,D,I: 横尾忠則
CL: ソニー レコード

12. SANTANA
LOTUS
LP 1973
AD,D: Tadanori Yokoo
CL: Sony Records
サンタナ
ロータス
LP 1973
AD,D: 横尾忠則
CL: ソニー レコード

12.Back & Front

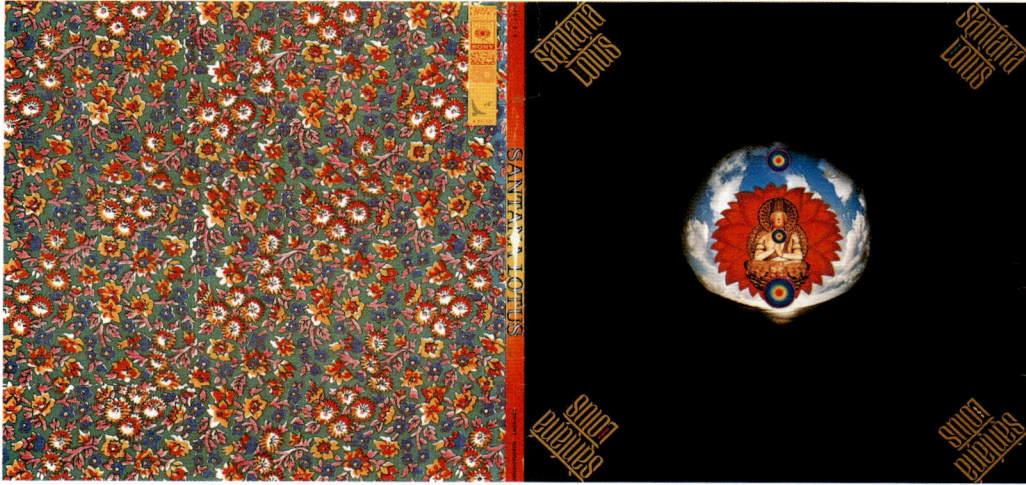

12.Cover / Inside Spread

13. BEATLES FESTIVAL Event Poster 1972
AD,D,I: Tadanori Yokoo CL: Daimaru Department Store
ビートルズ フェスティヴァル イヴェント ポスター 1972
AD,D,I: 横尾忠則 CL: 大丸

14. BEATLES STAR CLUB Promotional Poster 1977
AD,D: Tadanori Yokoo
CL: Victor Musical Industries
ビートルズ スター クラブ 販促用ポスター 1977
AD,D: 横尾忠則 CL: ビクター音楽産業

15. EARTH WIND AND FIRE
EARTH WIND AND FIRE Promotional Poster 1976
AD,D: Tadanori Yokoo CL: Sony Records
アース ウィンド アンド ファイアー
アース ウィンド アンド ファイアー 販促用ポスター 1976
AD,D: 横尾忠則 CL: ソニー レコード

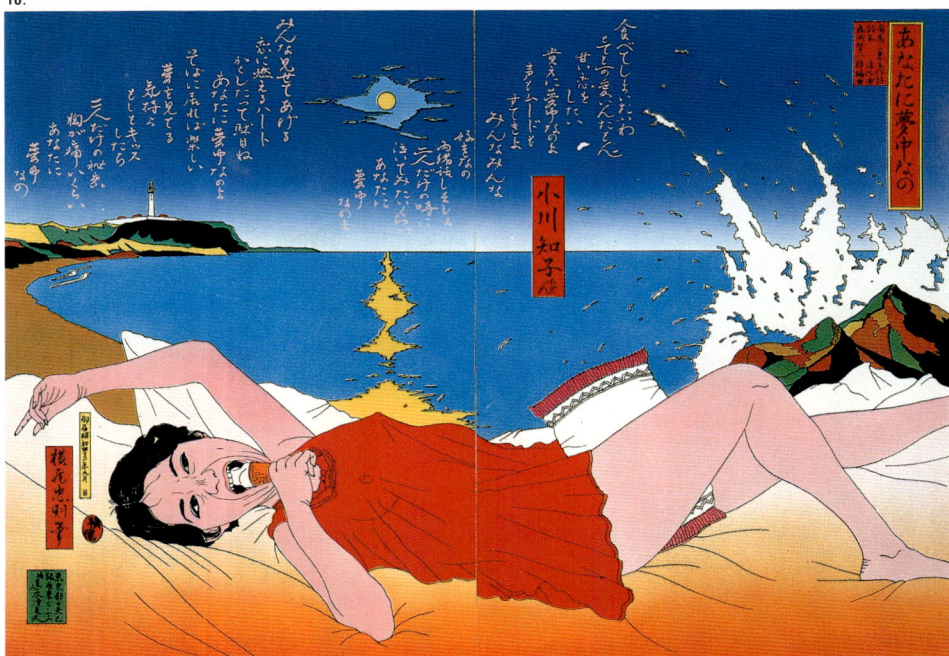
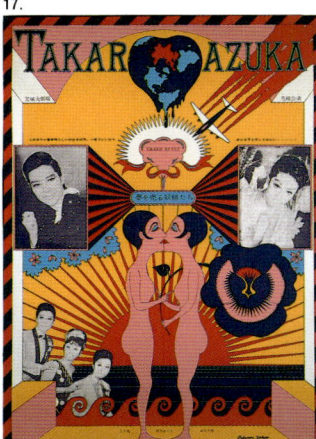

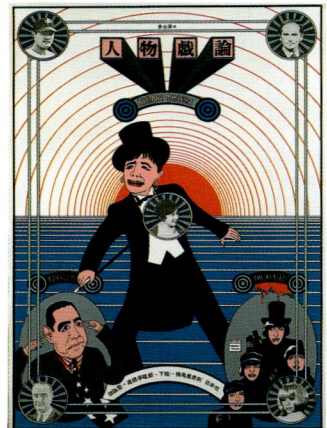

16. TOMOKO OGAWA / I AM MADLY IN LOVE WITH YOU Magazine Illustration 1968 AD,D,I: Tadanori Yokoo CL: Heibon Publishing
小川知子／あなたに夢中なの　個人作品（雑誌掲載用）　1968 AD,D,I: 横尾忠則 CL: 平凡出版

17. FAIRY DREAM VENDORS Theatrical Performance Poster 1965 AD,D,I: Tadanori Yokoo CL: Takarazuka Dance-Theatre
夢を売る妖精たち　演劇ポスター　1965 AD,D,I: 横尾忠則 CL: 宝塚歌劇団

18. HIBOTAN-BAKUTO LP 1969 AD,D,I: Tadanori Yokoo CL: Victor Musical Industries
緋牡丹博徒　LP 1969 AD,D,I: 横尾忠則 CL: ビクター音楽産業

19. HACHIRO KASUGA / SING A SONG Concert Poster 1964 D,I: Tadanori Yokoo CL: Kyoto Worker's Music Committee
春日八郎／艶歌を歌う　コンサート ポスター　1964 D,I: 横尾忠則 CL: 京都勤労者音楽協議会

20. JINBUTSU GIRON Promotional Poster 1966 AD,D,I: Tadanori Yokoo CL: Nippon-sha
人物戯論　宣伝用ポスター　1966 AD,D,I: 横尾忠則 CL: 日本社

21. STONE / AIMING SOUND Concert Poster 1974 AD,D,I: Tadanori Yokoo CL: Kazumichi Fujiwara
ストーン／音響標定　コンサートポスター　1974 AD,D,I: 横尾忠則 CL: 藤原和道

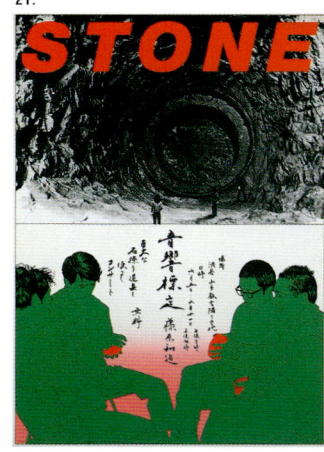

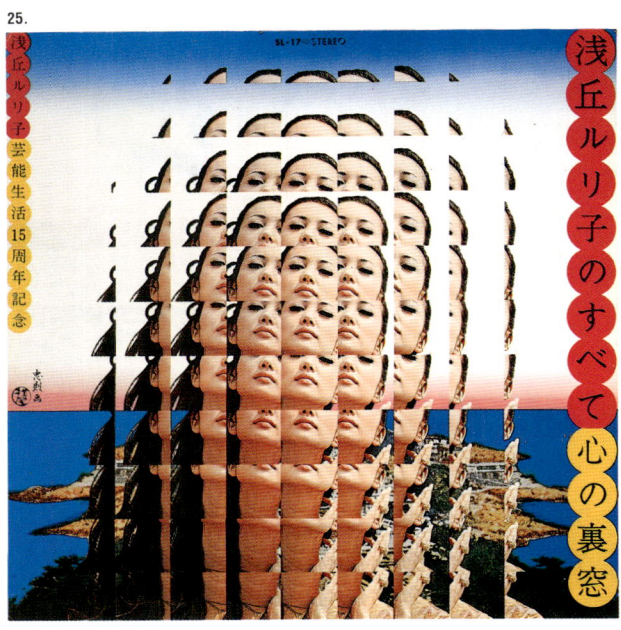

22. KUMOI-NO-HOTOTOGISU-KOKU Concert Poster 1979
AD,D: Tadanori Yokoo CL: Tokyo Philharmonic Orchestra
雲井時鳥国 コンサートポスター 1979
AD,D: 横尾忠則 CL: 東京フィルハーモニー交響楽団

23. JASRAC Promotional Poster 1988
AD,D: Tadanori Yokoo CL: Japanese Society for Right of Authors, Composers and Publishers
JASRAC 宣伝用ポスター 1988
AD,D: 横尾忠則 CL: 日本音楽著作権協会

24. GRAPHIC DESIGN 29 Magazine Cover 1967
AD,D,I: Tadanori Yokoo CL: Graphic-sha
グラフィックデザイン29 雑誌 1967
AD,D,I: 横尾忠則 CL: グラフィック社

25. RURIKO ASAOKA / ALL ABOUT RURIKO ASAOKA <REAR WINDOW OF THE MIND> LP 1969
AD,D: Tadanori Yokoo CL: Teichiku Records
浅丘ルリ子／浅丘ルリ子のすべて＜心の裏窓＞ LP 1969
AD,D: 横尾忠則 CL: テイチク レコード

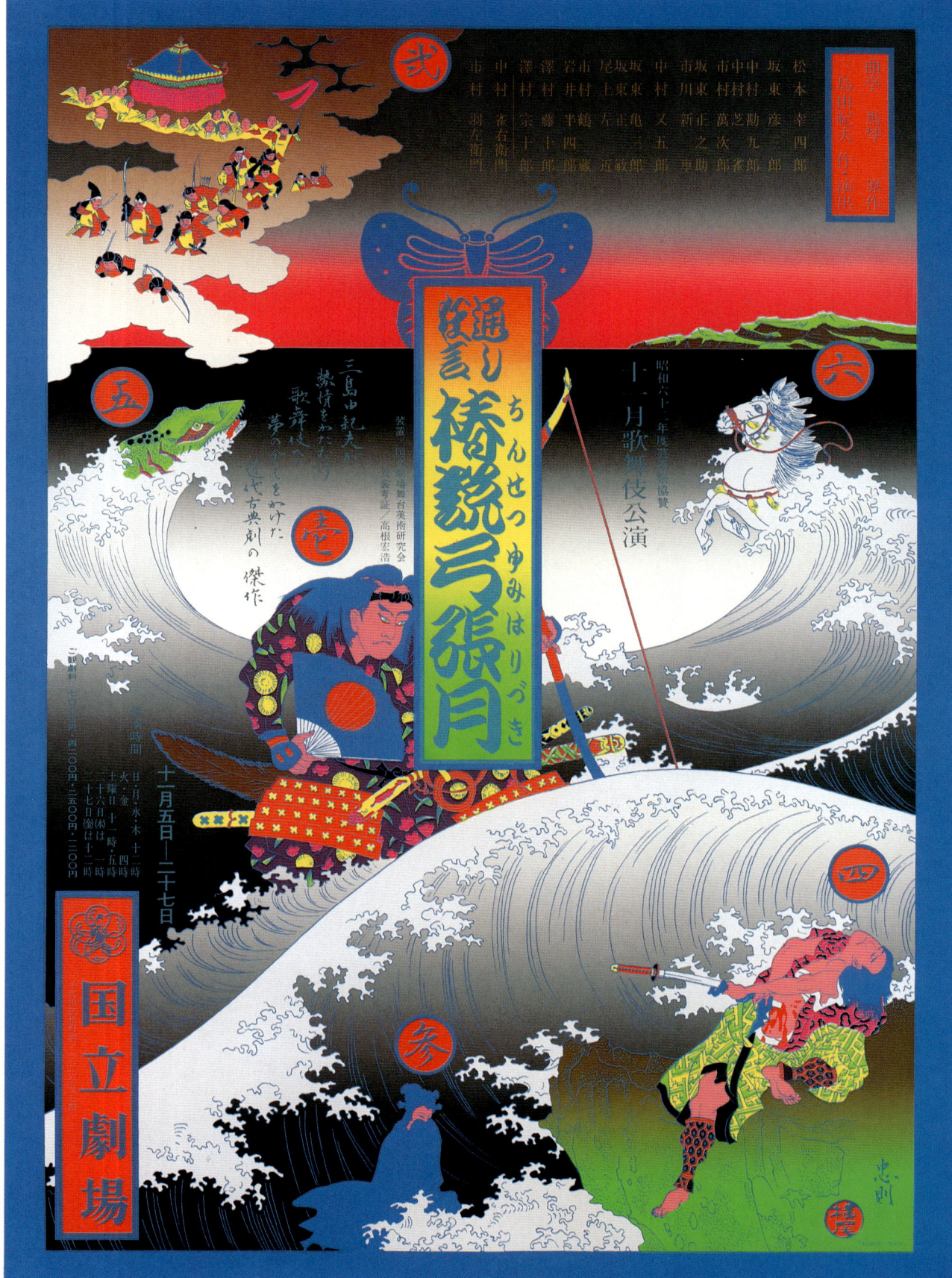

26. CHINSETSU-YUMIHARIZUKI Theatrical Performance Poster 1987 AD,D: Tadanori Yokoo CL: The National Theater
椿説弓張月 演劇（歌舞伎）ポスター 1987 AD,D: 横尾忠則 CL: 国立劇場

28.

29.

**28. YUKIHIRO TAKAHASHI
BROADCAST FROM HEAVEN**
Promotional Poster 1990
AD,D: Tadanori Yokoo   CL: Toshiba EMI
高橋幸宏
ブロードキャスト フロム ヘヴン
販促用ポスター 1990
AD,D: 横尾忠則   CL: 東芝EMI

29. VITAR
Promotional Poster
AD,D: Tadanori Yokoo   CL: Vitar
ヴィタール
販促用ポスター
AD,D: 横尾忠則   CL: ヴィタール

30.

31.

30. KOKA
Promotional Poster 1989
AD,D,I: Tadanori Yokoo CL: Koka
廣家
宣伝用ポスター 1989
AD,D,I: 横尾忠則 CL: 廣家

31. TADANORI YOKOO TOTAL GRAPH-T.Y.EXHIBITION
Exhibition Poster 1989
AD,D: Tadanori Yokoo
CL: Seiyu Department Store in Michinoo
横尾忠則TOTAL GRAPH-T.Y.展
展覧会ポスター 1989
AD,D: 横尾忠則
CL: 道の尾 西友

32. TADANORI YOKOO 1989 EXHIBITION Exhibition Poster 1989
AD,D: Tadanori Yokoo CL: Okanoyama Museum of Art in Nishiwaki City
横尾忠則1989展 展覧会ポスター 1989
AD,D: 横尾忠則 CL: 西脇市岡之山美術館

33. DAISUKE Promotional Poster 1989
AD,D,I: Tadanori Yokoo CL: Daisuke Nakatsuka Advertising Agency
ダイスケ 宣伝用ポスター 1989
AD,D,I: 横尾忠則 CL: 中塚大輔広告事務所

34. EXHIBITION OF TATSUMI HIJIKATA AND HIS SURROUNDINGS Exhibition Poster 1989
AD,D: Tadanori Yokoo CL: Yokohama Citizen's Gallery
土方巽とその周辺展 展覧会ポスター 1989
AD,D: 横尾忠則 CL: 横浜市民ギャラリー

35. TADANORI YOKOO PRINT EXHIBITION Exhibition Poster 1989
AD,D: Tadanori Yokoo CL: Nikkei Art Gallery
横尾忠則版画展 展覧会ポスター 1989
AD,D: 横尾忠則 CL: 日経アートギャラリー

36. RADO CERAMICA Promotional Poster 1989 AD,D: Tadanori Yokoo CL: Sakai Timepiece Trading
ラドー セラミカ 販促用ポスター 1989 AD,D: 横尾忠則 CL: 酒井時計貿易

37. 1ST NAGOYA THEATRICAL PERFORMANCE FESTIVAL Event Poster 1989 AD,D,I: Tadanori Yokoo CL: 1st NAGOYA Theatrical Performance Festival Organizing Committee
第1回NAGOYA演劇遊戯祭 イヴェントポスター 1989 AD,D,I: 横尾忠則 CL: 第1回NAGOYA演劇遊戯祭実行委員会

38. 3RD ASIAN ART SHOW Exhibition Poster 1989 AD,D,I: Tadanori Yokoo CL: Fukuoka Municipal Museum of Art
第3回アジア美術展 展覧会ポスター 1989 AD,D,I: 横尾忠則 CL: 福岡市美術館

39.

39. TADANORI YOKOO TOTAL GRAPH-T.Y.EXHIBITION Exhibition Poster 1989
AD,D: Tadanori Yokoo CL: Seibu Department Store in Numazu
横尾忠則TOTAL GRAPH-T.Y.展 展覧会ポスター 1989
AD,D: 横尾忠則 CL: 沼津 西武

40. FANCY DANCE Promotional Poster 1989
AD,D: Tadanori Yokoo CL: Daiei Movie Company
ファンシイ ダンス 宣伝用ポスター 1989
AD,D: 横尾忠則 CL: 大映

40.

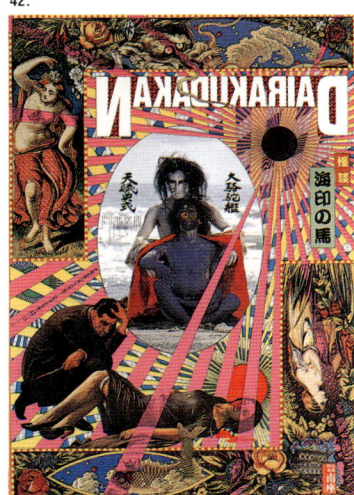

41. TADANORI YOKOO CERAMIC ART EXHIBITION Exhibition Poster 1989
AD,D,I: Tadanori Yokoo CL: Okanoyama Museum of Art in Nishiwaki City
横尾忠則セラミックアート展 展覧会ポスター 1989
AD,D,I: 横尾忠則 CL: 西脇市岡之山美術館

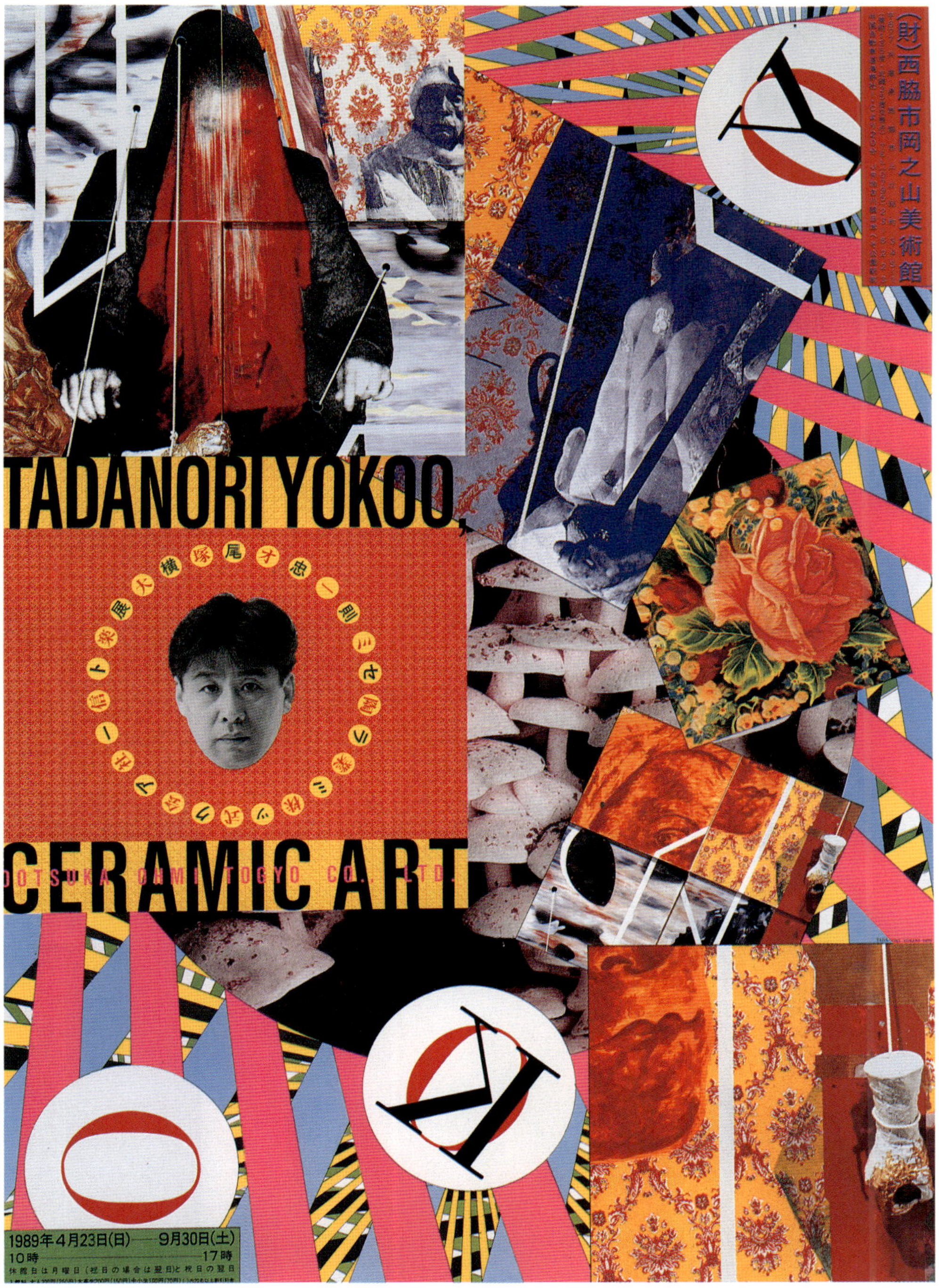

42. THE GHOST STORY A HORSE OF KANIN Theatrical Performance Poster 1989
AD,D,I: Tadanori Yokoo CL: Dairakudakan Tenputenshiki
怪談 海印の馬 演劇（舞踏）ポスター 1989
AD,D,I: 横尾忠則 CL: 大駱駝艦 天賦典式

096

Peter Saville

Under Peter's art direction, Factory's packaging came to epitomize the New Wave culture of the late 70's and early 80's. PSA's work is noted for the colour, overall minimalism and the frequent use of object rather than person centered photography. Titles and credits are often willfully omitted or carefully hidden, lending a fascination to the design. Peter's ability to predict cultural trends, then express these through graphic design and the considered deployment of photographic art direction techniques, has gained him an international reputation. PSA's work is seen by some as precious and dedicated works of fine design and as mass produced commodities at one and the same time.

ピーターがアート・ディレクターをつとめたファクトリー・レコードのパッケージングは、1970年代後半から1980年代始めのニューウェーヴ文化の縮図となった。PSAの作品は、色彩、全体的なミニマリズム、写真に人物よりも物を多用すること、などが特徴である。タイトルとクレジットは、わざと省略したり、巧妙に隠したりするパターンが多く、またそこにデザインの魅力を感じることができる。

　ピーターは、文化的トレンドを予想できるだけでなく、グラフィック・デザインや、フォト・アート・ディレクションの技術を通じてこれらをかたちにすることができるため、国際的に高い評価を得てきた。そしてPSAの作品のもうひとつの特徴は、ある人の目には貴重でひたむきな優れたデザイン作品と映るのに対し、また一方では大量生産的な作品とも見られることである。

After graduating from Manchester Polytechnic in 1978, Peter became art director for *Factory Records*. From 1979-83 he was art director for *Din Disc Records* and in 1983 he established his own practice, Peter Saville Associates (PSA) with designer Brett Wickens. He joined Pentagram as a partner in 1990.

1978年にマンチェスター工芸学校を卒業後、ファクトリー・レコードのアート・ディレクターとなる。1979年から1983年までは、ディン・ディスク・レコードのアート・ディレクターをつとめ、その後デザイナーのブレット・ウィケンズとともに、自分の会社、ピーター・サヴィル・アソシエイツ（PSA）を設立した。また1990年に、パートナーとしてペンタグラムに参加した。

1.

2.

3.

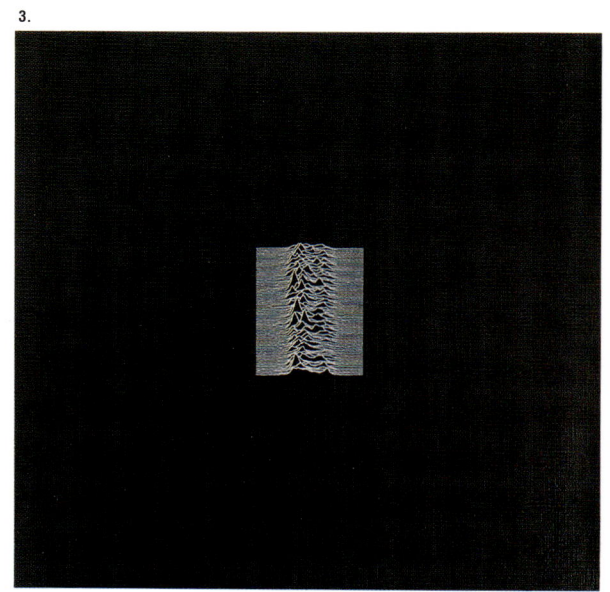

4.

1. JOY DIVISION / ATMOSPHERE 12-inch Single 1980 AD,D: Peter Saville P: Charles Meecham DF: Peter Saville Associates CL: Factory Communications
ジョイ ディヴィジョン / アトモスフィア 12インチ シングル 1980 AD,D: ピーター サヴィル P: チャールズ ミーカム
DF: ピーター サヴィル アソシエイツ CL: ファクトリー コミュニケーションズ

2. JOY DIVISION / CLOSER LP 1980 AD,D: Peter Saville D: Martyn Atkins P: Bernard Pierre Wolff DF: Peter Saville Associates CL: Factory Communications
ジョイ ディヴィジョン / クローザー LP 1980 AD,D: ピーター サヴィル D: マーティン アトキンズ P: バーナード ピエール ウルフ
DF: ピーター サヴィル アソシエイツ CL: ファクトリー コミュニケーションズ

3. JOY DIVISION / UNKNOWN PLEASURES LP 1979 AD,D: Peter Saville DF: Peter Saville Associates CL: Factory Communications
ジョイ ディヴィジョン / アンノウン プレジャーズ LP 1979 AD,D: ピーター サヴィル DF: ピーター サヴィル アソシエイツ CL: ファクトリー コミュニケーションズ

4. JOY DIVISION / LOVE WILL TEAR US APART 7-inch Single 1980 AD,D: Peter Saville P: Trevor Key DF: Peter Saville Associates CL: Factory Communications
ジョイ ディヴィジョン / ラヴ ウィル ティア アス アパート 7インチ シングル 1980 AD,D: ピーター サヴィル P: トレヴァー キィ
DF: ピーター サヴィル アソシエイツ CL: ファクトリー コミュニケーションズ

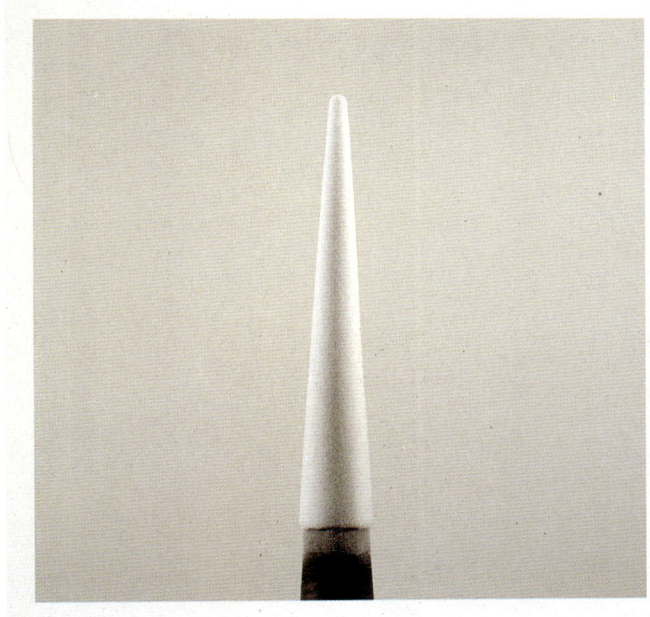

5. JOY DIVISION / SUBSTANCE Promotional Poster 1988
AD: Peter Saville D: Brett Wickens P: Trevor Key OBJECT: Jan Van Munster
DF: Peter Saville Associates CL: Factory Communications
ジョイ ディヴィジョン / サブスタンス 販促用ポスター 1988
AD: ピーター サヴィル D: ブレット ウィッケンズ
P: トレヴァー キィ OBJECT: ジャン ヴァン ムンスター
DF: ピーター サヴィル アソシエイツ CL: ファクトリー コミュニケーションズ

6. JOY DIVISION / LOVE WILL TEAR US APART 12-inch Single 1980
AD,D: Peter Saville D: Martyn Atkins P: Bernard Pierre Wolff
DF: Peter Saville Associates CL: Factory Communications
ジョイ ディヴィジョン / ラヴ ウィル ティア アス アパート 12インチ シングル 1980
AD,D: ピーター サヴィル D: マーティン アトキンス P: バーナード ピエール ウルフ
DF: ピーター サヴィル アソシエイツ CL: ファクトリー コミュニケーションズ

7. JOY DIVISION / ATMOSPHERE Promotional Poster 1988
AD: Peter Saville D: Brett Wickens P: Trevor Key OBJECT: Jan Van Munster
DF: Peter Saville Associates CL: Factory Communications
ジョイ ディヴィジョン / アトモスフィア 販促用ポスター 1988
AD: ピーター サヴィル D: ブレット ウィッケンズ P: トレヴァー キィ
OBJECT: ジャン ヴァン ムンスター
DF: ピーター サヴィル アソシエイツ CL: ファクトリー コミュニケーションズ

8. DEPECHE MODE
EVERYTHING COUNTS
12-inch Single 1988
AD: Peter Saville
AD,D: Brett Wickens
D: Paul West
P: Anton Corbijn
DF: Peter Saville Associates
CL: Mute Records
デペッシュ モード
エヴリシング カウンツ
12インチ シングル 1988
AD: ピーター サヴィル
AD,D: ブレット ウィッケンズ
D: ポール ウエスト
P: アントン コルビン
DF: ピーター サヴィル アソシエイツ
CL: ミュート レコード

9. PETER GABRIEL
RED RAIN
12-inch Single 1986
PR: Charisma Records
AD,D: Peter Saville
D: Brett Wickens
P: Trevor Key
DF: Peter Saville Associates
CL: Peter Gabriel Limited
ピーター ガブリエル
レッド レイン
12インチ シングル 1986
PR: カリスマ レコード
AD,D: ピーター サヴィル
D: ブレット ウィッケンズ
P: トレヴァー キィ
DF: ピーター サヴィル アソシエイツ
CL: ピーター ガブリエル リミテッド

10. Back 10. Front

11. Cover & Inner Sleeve

10. PETER GABRIEL / SO LP 1986
PR: Charisma Records AD,D: Peter Saville
D: Brett Wickens P: Trevor Key
DF: Peter Saville Associates CL: Peter Gabriel Limited
ピーター ガブリエル / ソー LP 1986
PR: カリスマ レコード AD,D: ピーター サヴィル
D: ブレット ウィッケンズ P: トレヴァー キィ
DF: ピーター サヴィル アソシエイツ CL: ピーター ガブリエル リミテッド

11. MIDGE URE / ANSWERS TO NOTHING LP 1987
AD,D: Peter Saville D: Brett Wickens
P: Robin Barton I: Georges Mathieu
DF: Peter Saville Associates CL: Chrysalis Records
ミッジ ウール / アンスワーズ トゥ ナッシング LP 1987
AD,D: ピーター サヴィル D: ブレット ウィッケンズ
P: ロビン バートン I: ジョージェス マシュー
DF: ピーター サヴィル アソシエイツ CL: クリサリス レコード

12. PETER GABRIEL / SLEDGEHAMMER 12-inch Single 1986
PR: Charisma Records AD,D: Peter Saville
D: Brett Wickens P: Trevor Key
DF: Peter Saville Associates CL: Peter Gabriel Limited
ピーター ガブリエル / スレッジハマー 12インチ シングル 1986
PR: カリスマ レコード AD,D: ピーター サヴィル
D: ブレット ウィッケンズ P: トレヴァー キィ
DF: ピーター サヴィル アソシエイツ CL: ピーター ガブリエル リミテッド

12.

13.

13. WHAM / I'M YOUR MAN 12-inch Single 1985 PR: CBS,Epic AD,D: Peter Saville D: Brett Wickens DF: Peter Saville Associates CL: George Michael
ワム / アイム ユア マン 12インチ シングル 1985 PR: CBS、エピック AD,D: ピーター サヴィル D: ブレット ウィッケンズ
DF: ピーター サヴィル アソシエイツ CL: ジョージ マイケル

14. MARTHA AND THE MUFFINS / METRO MUSIC LP 1980 AD,D: Peter Saville DF: Peter Saville Associates CL: Din Disc
マーサ アンド ザ マフィンズ / メトロ ミュージック LP 1980 AD,D: ピーター サヴィル DF: ピーター サヴィル アソシエイツ CL: ディン ディスク

15. JOY DIVISION / TRANSMISSION 12-inch Single 1979 AD,D: Peter Saville P: Charles Herring DF: Peter Saville Associates CL: Factory Communications
ジョイ ディヴィジョン / トランスミッション 12インチ シングル 1979 AD,D: ピーター サヴィル P: チャールズ ヘリング
DF: ピーター サヴィル アソシエイツ CL: ファクトリー コミュニケーションズ

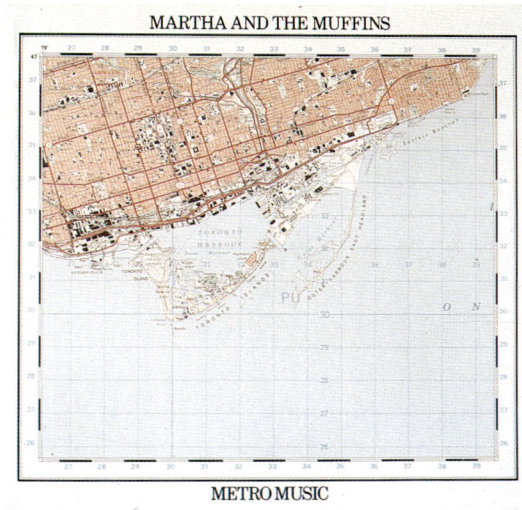

14.

15.

16. GEORGE MICHAEL / I WANT YOUR SEX 12-inch Single 1987
PR: CBS,Epic AD: Peter Saville D: Brett Wickens P: James Wedge
DF: Peter Saville Associates CL: George Michael
ジョージ マイケル / アイ ウォント ユア セックス 12インチ シングル 1987
PR: CBS、エピック AD: ピーター サヴィル D: ブレット ウィッケンズ
P: ジェイムズ ウェッジ DF: ピーター サヴィル アソシエイツ
CL: ジョージ マイケル

17. ELECTRONIC / GETTING AWAY WITH IT 12-inch Single 1990
AD,D: Peter Saville D: Julian Morey P: Image Bank
DF: Peter Saville Associates CL: Factory Communications
エレクトロニック / ゲッティング アウェイ ウィズ イット 12インチ シングル 1990
AD, D: ピーター サヴィル D: ジュリアン モーリー P: イメージ バンク
DF: ピーター サヴィル アソシエイツ CL: ファクトリー コミュニケーションズ

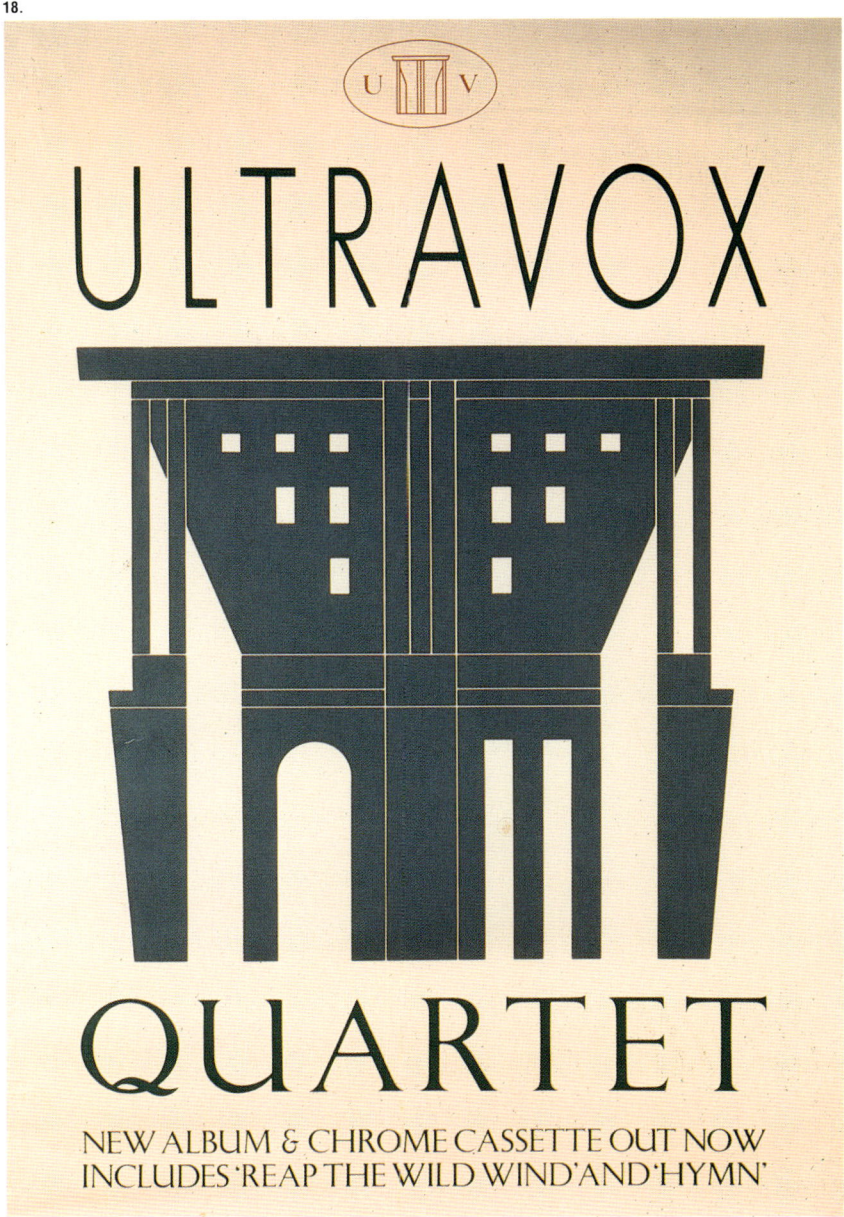

18. ULTRAVOX / QUARTET Promotional Poster 1982
AD,D: Peter Saville D: Brett Wickens D,I: Ken Kennedy DF: Peter Saville Associates CL: Chrysalis Records
ウルトラヴォックス / カルテット 販促用ポスター 1982
AD, D: ピーター サヴィル D: ブレット ウィッケンズ D,I: ケン ケネディ DF: ピーター サヴィル アソシエイツ
CL: クリサリス レコード

19.

20.

21.

22.

19. ULTRAVOX / REAP THE WILD WIND 12-inch Single 1982 AD,D: Peter Saville D: Brett Wickens D,I: Ken Kennedy DF: Peter Saville Associates CL: Chrysalis Records
ウルトラヴォックス / リープ ザ ワイルド ウィンド 12インチ シングル 1982 AD, D: ピーター サヴィル D: ブレット ウィッケンズ D,I: ケン ケネディ
DF: ピーター サヴィル アソシエイツ CL: クリサリス レコード

20. OMD / DAZZLESHIPS LP 1983 AD,D: Peter Saville D: Brett Wickens, Malcolm Garrett, Ken Kennedy, Phil Pennington DF: Peter Saville Associates CL: Virgin Records
OMD / ダズルシップス LP 1983 AD,D: ピーター サヴィル D: ブレット ウィッケンズ、マルコム ギャレット、ケン ケネディ、フィル ペニングトン
DF: ピーター サヴィル アソシエイツ CL: ヴァージン レコード

21. ULTRAVOX / HYMN 12-inch Single 1982 AD, D: Peter Saville D: Brett Wickens, Ken Kennedy DF: Peter Saville Associates CL: Chrysalis Records
ウルトラヴォックス / ヒム 12インチ シングル 1982 AD, D: ピーター サヴィル D: ブレット ウィッケンズ、ケン ケネディ DF: ピーター サヴィル アソシエイツ CL: クリサリス レコード

22. ULTRAVOX / VIENNA 12-inch Single 1981 AD,D: Peter Saville P: Time Life Books DF: Peter Saville Associates CL: Chrysalis Records
ウルトラヴォックス / ヴィエンナ 12インチ シングル 1981 AD,D: ピーター サヴィル P: タイム ライフ ブックス DF: ピーター サヴィル アソシエイツ CL: クリサリス レコード

23. BRETT WICKENS AND JAH WOBBLE / BETWEEN TWO FREQUENCIES 12-inch Single 1985 PR: General Kinetics CD,D: Brett Wickens AD,D: Peter Saville DF: Peter Saville Associates CL: Brett Wickens
ブレット ウィッケンズ アンド ジャー ウッブル / ビトウィーン トゥー フリークウァンシズ 12インチ シングル 1985 PR: ゼネラル キネティクス CD,D: ブレット ウィッケンズ AD,D: ピーター サヴィル DF: ピーター サヴィル アソシエイツ CL: ブレット ウィッケンズ

24. KINETIC IDEALS / REASON 7-inch Single 1981 AD,D: Peter Saville DF: Peter Saville Associates CL: Mannequin Records
キネティク アイディアルズ / リーズン 7インチ シングル 1981 AD,D: ピーター サヴィル DF: ピーター サヴィル アソシエイツ CL: マネキン レコード

25. SECTION 25 / ALWAYS NOW LP 1981-1982 AD,D: Peter Saville DF: Peter Saville Associates CL: Factory Communications
セクション 25 / オールウェイズ ナウ LP 1981-1982 AD,D: ピーター サヴィル DF: ピーター サヴィル アソシエイツ CL: ファクトリー コミュニケーションズ

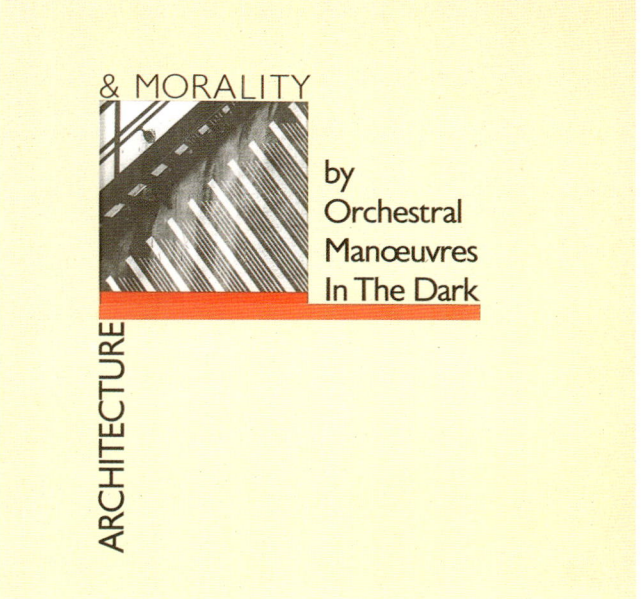
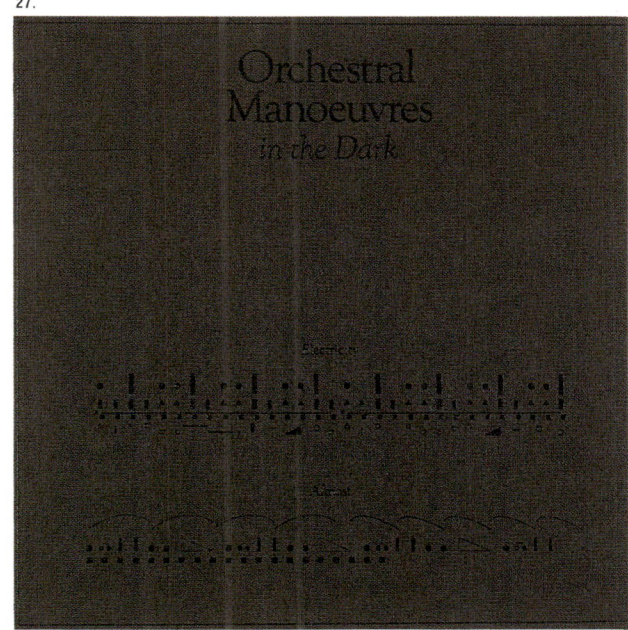

26. OMD / ARCHITECTURE & MORALITY LP 1981
AD,D: Peter Saville D: Brett Wickens P: Robin Roddey DF: Peter Saville Associates CL: Din Disc
OMD / アーキテクチャー & モラリティ LP 1981
AD,D: ピーター サヴィル D: ブレット ウィッケンズ P: ロビン ロディ DF: ピーター サヴィル アソシエイツ CL: ディン ディスク

27. OMD / ELECTRICITY 7-inch Single 1979 AD,D: Peter Saville DF: Peter Saville Associates CL: Din Disc
OMD / エレクトリシティ 7インチ シングル 1979
AD,D: ピーター サヴィル DF: ピーター サヴィル アソシエイツ CL: ディン ディスク

28. OMD / TESLA GIRLS 12-inch Single 1984
AD,D: Peter Saville P: Trevor Key DF: Peter Saville Associates CL: Virgin Records
OMD / テスラ ガールズ 12インチ シングル 1984
AD,D: ピーター サヴィル P: トレヴァー キィ DF: ピーター サヴィル アソシエイツ CL: ヴァージン レコード

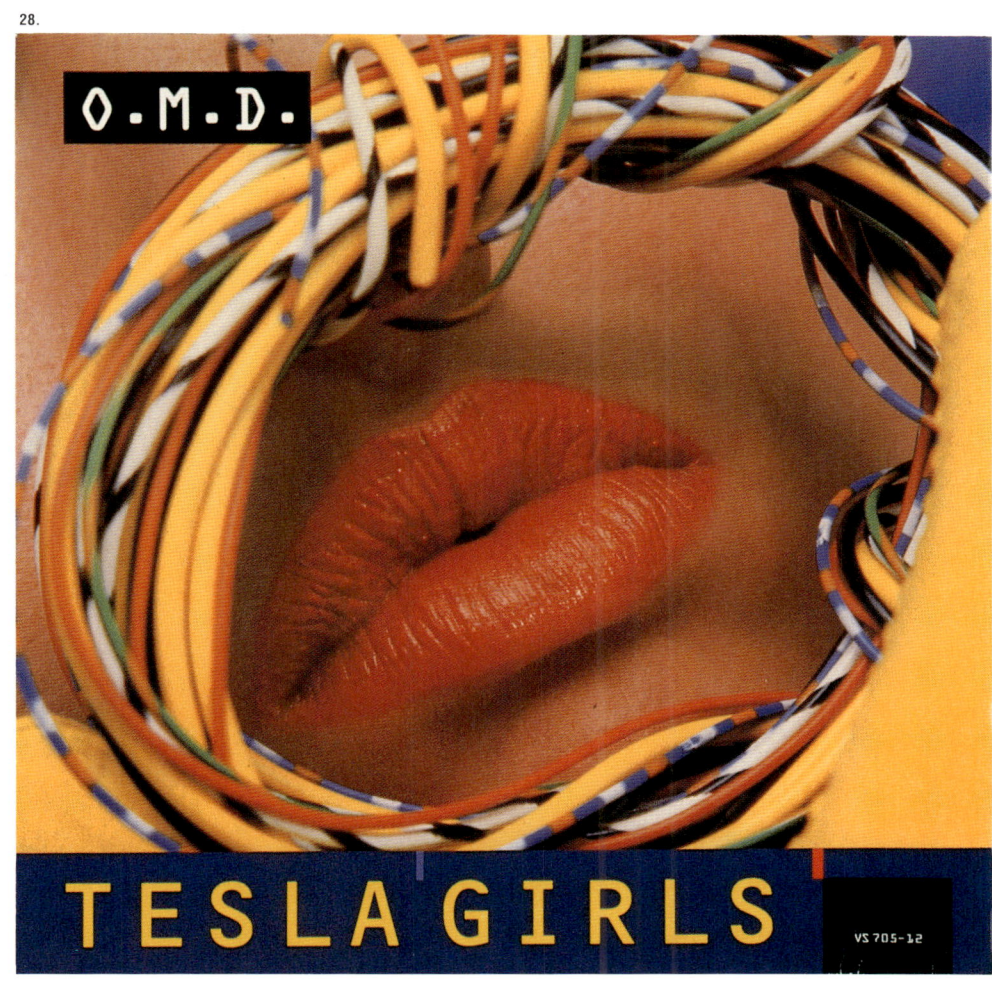

29. NEW ORDER / CONFUSION 12-inch Single 1983 AD,D: Peter Saville D: Phil Pennington DF: Peter Saville Associates CL: Factory Communications
ニュー オーダー / コンフュージョン 12インチ シングル 1983 AD,D: ピーター サヴィル D: フィル ペニングトン
DF: ピーター サヴィル アソシエイツ CL: ファクトリー コミュニケーションズ

30. NEW ORDER / CEREMONY 12-inch Single 1981 AD,D: Peter Saville DF: Peter Saville Associates CL: Factory Communications
ニュー オーダー / セレモニー 12インチ シングル 1981 AD,D: ピーター サヴィル DF: ピーター ナヴィル アソシエイツ CL: ファクトリー コミュニケーションズ

31. NEW ORDER / EVERYTHING'S GONE GREEN 7-inch Single 1981 AD,D: Peter Saville D: Brett Wickens
DF: Peter Saville Associates CL: Factory Communications
ニュー オーダー / エヴリシングズ ゴーン グリーン 7インチ シングル 1981 AD,D: ピーター サヴィル D: ブレット ウィッケンズ
DF: ピーター サヴィル アソシエイツ CL: ファクトリー コミュニケーションズ

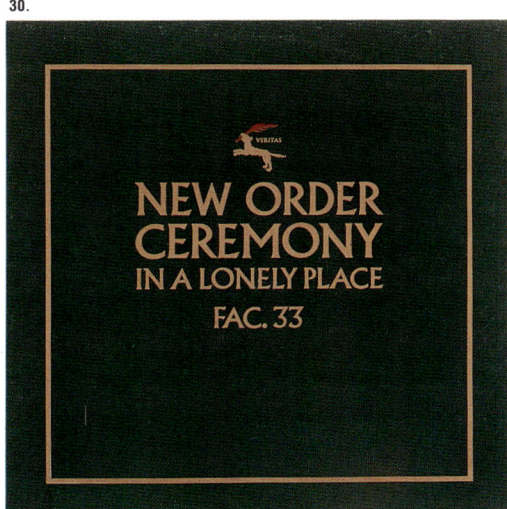

32.

33.

32. NEW ORDER
LOW LIFE
LP 1985
AD,D: Peter Saville
D: Garry Mouat
P: Trevor Key
DF: Peter Saville Associates
CL: Factory Communications
ニュー オーダー
ロウ ライフ
LP 1985
AD,D: ピーター サヴィル
D: ゲイリー ムーアット
P: トレヴァー キィ
DF: ピーター サヴィル アソシエイツ
CL: ファクトリー コミュニケーションズ

33. NEW ORDER
POWER, CORRUPTION AND LIES
LP 1983
AD,D: Peter Saville
I: Fantin-Latour
DF: Peter Saville Associates
CL: Factory Communications
ニュー オーダー
パワー、コラプション アンド ライズ
LP 1983
AD,D: ピーター サヴィル
I: ファンティン ラトゥール
DF: ピーター サヴィル アソシエイツ
CL: ファクトリー コミュニケーションズ

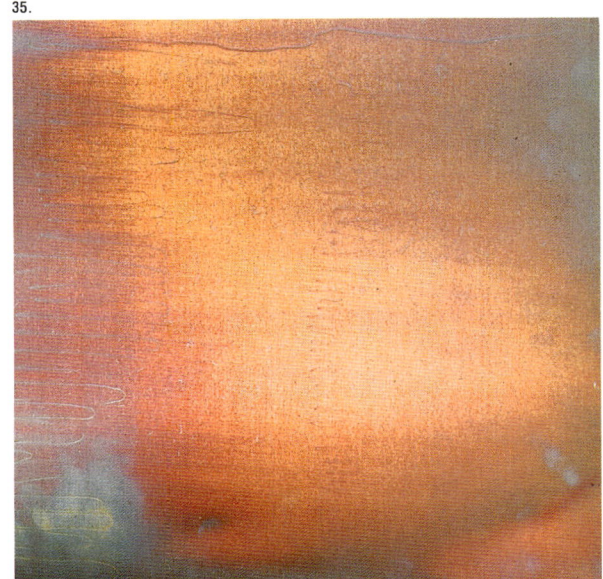

34. NEW ORDER / STATE OF THE NATION 12-inch Single 1986 AD,D: Peter Saville D: Chris Mathan P: Trevor Key DF: Peter Saville Associates CL: Factory Communications
ニュー オーダー / ステイト オヴ ザ ネイション 12インチ シングル 1986 AD,D: ピーター サヴィル D: クリス マサン P: トレヴァー キィ
DF: ピーター サヴィル アソシエイツ CL: ファクトリー コミュニケーションズ

35. NEW ORDER / BIZARRE LOVE TRIANGLE 12-inch Single 1986 AD,D: Peter Saville D: Chris Mathan P: Trevor Key DF: Peter Saville Associates CL: Factory Communications
ニュー オーダー / ビザール ラヴ トライアングル 12インチ シングル 1986 AD,D: ピーター サヴィル D: クリス マサン P: トレヴァー キィ
DF: ピーター サヴィル アソシエイツ CL: ファクトリー コミュニケーションズ

36. NEW ORDER / BROTHERHOOD LP 1988 AD,D: Peter Saville D: Chris Mathan, Brett Wickens P: Trevor Key DF: Peter Saville Associates CL: Factory Communications
ニュー オーダー / ブラザーフッド LP 1988 AD,D: ピーター サヴィル D: クリス マサン、ブレット ウィッケンズ P: トレヴァー キィ
DF: ピーター サヴィル アソシエイツ CL: ファクトリー コミュニケーションズ

37. Cover & Inner Sleeve

38. Cover & Inner Sleeve

37. NEW ORDER / SUBSTANCE LP 1987 AD: Peter Saville D: Brett Wickens P: Trevor Key DF: Peter Saville Associates CL: Factory Communications
ニュー オーダー / サブスタンス LP 1987 AD: ピーター サヴィル D: ブレット ウィッケンズ P: トレヴァー キィ DF: ピーター サヴィル アソシエイツ CL: ファクトリー コミュニケーションズ

38. NEW ORDER / TRUE FAITH 12-inch Single 1987 AD,D: Peter Saville D: Brett Wickens P: Trevor Key DF: Peter Saville Associates CL: Factory Communications
ニュー オーダー / トゥルー フェイス 12インチ シングル 1987 AD,D: ピーター サヴィル D: ブレット ウィッケンズ P: トレヴァー キィ DF: ピーター サヴィル アソシエイツ
CL: ファクトリー コミュニケーションズ

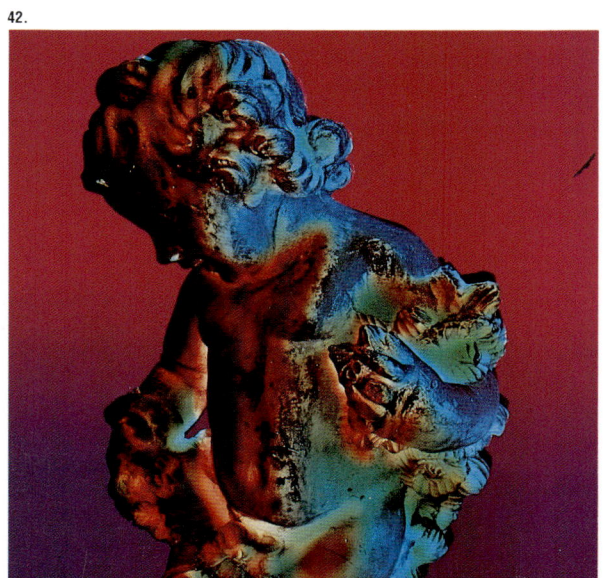

39. NEW ORDER / ROUND & ROUND 12-inch Single 1989 AD,D: Peter Saville D: Brett Wickens, Julian Morey DF: Peter Saville Associates CL: Factory Communications
ニュー オーダー / ラウンド & ラウンド 12インチ シングル 1989 AD,D: ピーター サヴィル D: ブレット ウィッケンズ、ジュリアン マレー DF: ピーター サヴィル アソシエイツ
CL: ファクトリー コミュニケーションズ

40. NEW ORDER / ROUND & REMIX 12-inch Single 1989 AD,D: Peter Saville D: Brett Wickens, Julian Morey P: Trevor Key DF: Peter Saville Associates CL: Factory Communications
ニュー オーダー / ラウンド & リミックス 12インチ シングル 1989 AD,D: ピーター サヴィル D: ブレット ウィッケンズ、ジュリアン マレー P: トレヴァー キィ
DF: ピーター サヴィル アソシエイツ CL: ファクトリー コミュニケーションズ

41. NEW ORDER / WORLD IN MOTION (REMIX) 12-inch Single 1990 AD: Peter Saville D: Brett Wickens, Marc Wood DF: Peter Saville Associates CL: Factory Communications
ニュー オーダー / ワールド イン モーション（リミックス） 12インチ シングル 1990 AD: ピーター サヴィル D: ブレット ウィッケンズ、マーク ウッド
DF: ピーター サヴィル アソシエイツ CL: ファクトリー コミュニケーションズ

42. NEW ORDER / TECHNIQUE LP 1989 AD,D: Peter Saville D: Brett Wickens P: Trevor Key DF: Peter Saville Associates CL: Factory Communications
ニュー オーダー / テクニック LP 1989 AD,D: ピーター サヴィル D: ブレット ウィッケンズ P: トレヴァー キィ DF: ピーター サヴィル アソシエイツ CL: ファクトリー コミュニケーションズ

43.

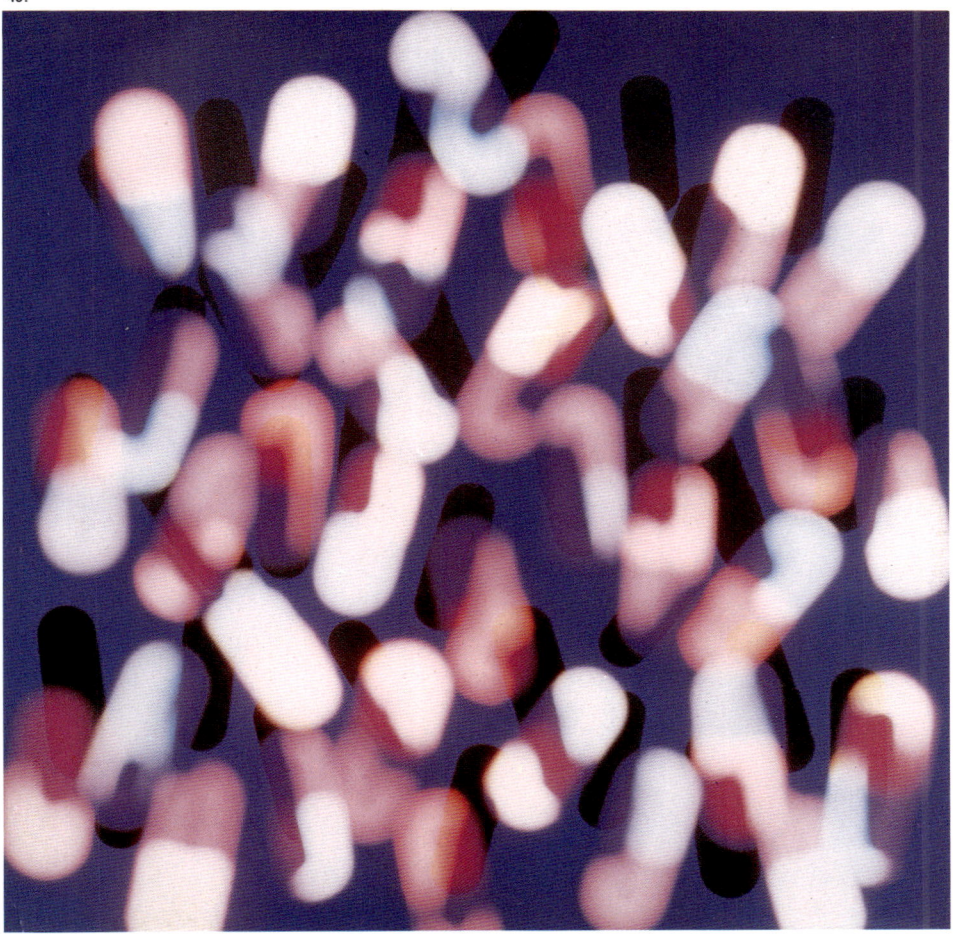

44.

43. NEW ORDER
FINE TIME (REMIX)
12-inch Single 1988
AD,D: Peter Saville
D: Brett Wickens
P: Trevor Key
DF: Peter Saville Associates
CL: Factory Communications
ニュー オーダー
ファイン タイム（リミックス）
12インチ シングル 1988
AD,D: ピーター サヴィル
D: ブレット ウィッケンズ
P: トレヴァー キィ
DF: ピーター サヴィル アソシエイツ
CL: ファクトリー コミュニケーションズ

44. NEW ORDER
RUN 2
12-inch Single 1989
AD,D: Peter Saville
D: Brett Wickens, Julian Morey
DF: Peter Saville Associates
CL: Factory Communications
ニュー オーダー
ラン2
12インチ シングル 1989
AD,D: ピーター サヴィル
D: ブレット ウィッケンズ、ジュリアン マレー
DF: ピーター サヴィル アソシエイツ
CL: ファクトリー コミュニケーションズ

Photography / Yorihito Yamauchi

Kenji Ishikawa 石川絢士

It all started in 1956 in a sweet shop in Anjo, Aichi prefecture. The boy grew up with beauty and plenty of sensibility. He spent many evenings looking out of the window drinking a bottle of soda, pretending it was a glass of wine. The adolescent ran around the athletic track in the afternoon, and ran his brush over canvas in his room. Possessed by beauty and beautiful music, the man found himself working in solitude with twilight-colored canvases in his arms. After all these years, every time Kenji the artist heaves an amber sigh, calls me up in the middle of the night, and says, "It's done." I go out to experience the moment I most look forward to: when I meet Kenji with his golden eyes.

/ Takashi Sotoma (Musician)

He works a lot. I rarely see him in the morning because he works mainly at night. When I do see him, which is not often, he looks at me with half-closed eyes, and says,"I haven't slept much." But he doesn't seem to mind. He loves being a designer.So he does a tremendous amount of work, and, of course, it's not just quantity. He's got a strong, almost stubborn character that nobody could fail to notice. But it's not an intolerant spirit that can be written off as stubbornness. He is a romantic at heart, and he stays true to his dreams and ideals. I'd call him a "fantasist", with respect; only "fantasists" can create the past the future.

/ Tomohiko Fukuoka (Director: Epic/Sony Records)

ことの起こりは1956年、愛知県安城市のとある駄菓子屋に始まる。少年は端正な顔立ちと豊かな感受性をあわせ持って育ち、やがては自室の窓辺にすわり、ワインに見立てたラムネを片手にいくつもの夕景を眺めて過ごす。青年は午後のグラウンドを短距離走者として駆け抜け、夜は部屋で絵筆を走らせた。美しいもの、美しい音楽に心をうばわれてしまった男は、黄昏色のカンヴァスを携えて孤独な仕事に就いた。
かくして芸術家・絢士は、真夜中の仕事場で琥珀色のためいきをついては、眠りについたばかりの僕に電話をよこす。「できたよ」——と。こうして僕は出かけていき、とても楽しみな瞬間を迎える。作品を手に、黄金色に染まった瞳で微笑む絢士に会えるその瞬間を。

／外間隆史（音楽家）

まったくよく働く男である。だいたい夜型なので、午前中にはめったに顔をあわせないが、たまにいるかと思うとトロンとした目で「寝てないんだよ」なんて言ってる。しかし、さしてそれを苦にするふうでもない。デザインという仕事が好きでたまらないのである。だからすごい量の仕事をこなしているが、もちろん量だけじゃない。一目で彼の作品と判る、頑固なまでの個性の強さ。しかしそれは「頑固」という言葉でくくられるような偏狭な精神ではない。彼は自分の内なる夢と理想に正直であり続けるロマンチストなのだ。
こういう人を、僕は敬意をこめて「ファンタジアン」と呼ぶ。そしてこれまでも、これからも、「ファンタジアン」のみが時代をつくる。

／福岡知彦（エピック・ソニー レコード ディレクター）

1. EBI / MUSÉE Promotional Poster 1991
AD,D,I,OBJECT DESIGN: Kenji Ishikawa
D: Yoko Kobayashi P: Yorihito Yamauchi
S: Mitsunori Aoyagi (Hamish)
OBJECT: Kengo Yoshida (Space Product)
DF: The Garden CL: Sony Records
エビ / ミュゼ 販促用ポスター 1991
AD,D,I,OBJECT DESIGN: 石川絢士
D: 小林陽子 P: 山内順仁
S: 青柳光則 OBJECT: 吉田健吾
DF: ザ ガーデン CL: ソニー レコード

2. EBI / MUSÉE CD 1991
AD,D,I,OBJECT DESIGN: Kenji Ishikawa
D: Yoko Kobayashi P: Yorihito Yamauchi
S: Mitsunori Aoyagi (Hamish)
OBJECT: Kengo Yoshida (Space Product)
DF: The Garden CL: Sony Records
エビ / ミュゼ CD 1991
AD,D,I,OBJECT DESIGN: 石川絢士
D: 小林陽子 P: 山内順仁
S: 青柳光則 OBJECT: 吉田健吾
DF: ザ ガーデン CL: ソニー レコード

3. MIMORI YUSA / HARMONIODEON CD 1989
AD,D,OBJECT DESIGN: Kenji Ishikawa
D: Shingo Minowa P: Yorihito Yamauchi
S: Haruri Sono
OBJECT: Kengo Yoshida (Space Product)
DF: The Garden CL: Epic / Sony Records
遊佐未森 / ハルモニオデオン
CD 1989
AD,D,OBJECT DESIGN: 石川絢士
D: 箕輪信吾 P: 山内順仁
S: 園 春利 OBJECT: 吉田健吾
DF: ザ ガーデン CL: エピック ソニー レコード

4. MIMORI YUSA / HITOMI SUISHO
Promotional CD Booklet 1988
AD,D: Kenji Ishikawa D: Yukio Miyazaki
P: Gen Murakoshi DF: The Garden
CL: Epic / Sony Records
遊佐未森 / 瞳水晶
販促用CD ブックレット 1988
AD,D: 石川絢士 D: 宮崎幸生
P: 村越 元 DF: ザ ガーデン
CL: エピック ソニー レコード

5. MIMORI YUSA / SORAMIMI ON THE HILL CD 1988
AD,D: Kenji Ishikawa D: Yukio Miyazaki
P: Gen Murakoshi DF: The Garden
CL: Epic / Sony Records
遊佐未森 / 空耳の丘 CD 1988
AD,D: 石川絢士 D: 宮崎幸生 P: 村越 元
DF: ザ ガーデン CL: エピック ソニー レコード

1.

2. Back & Front

2.

3. Front & Outside Spreads

6. MIMORI YUSA / PICTURE HOPE Video 1991 AD,D: Kenji Ishikawa DF: The Garden CL: Epic / Sony Records
遊佐未森 / ピクチャー ホープ ビデオ 1991 AD,D: 石川絢士 DF: ザ ガーデン CL: エピック ソニー レコード

7. MIMORI YUSA / HOPE CD 1990 AD,D,OBJECT DESIGN: Kenji Ishikawa D: Fumiko Hirano P: Yorihito Yamauchi OBJECT: Kazunori Shionoya (Space Product) DF: The Garden CL: Epic / Sony Records
遊佐未森 / ホープ CD 1990 AD,D,OBJECT DESIGN: 石川絢士 D: 平野文子 P: 山内順仁 OBJECT: 塩野谷 一徳 DF: ザ ガーデン CL: エピック ソニー レコード

8. MIMORI YUSA / MOSAIC CD 1991 AD: Kenji Ishikawa D: Yoko Kobayashi DF: The Garden CL: Epic / Sony Records
遊佐未森 / モザイク CD 1991 AD: 石川絢士 D: 小林陽子 DF: ザ ガーデン CL: エピック ソニー レコード

9. MIMORI YUSA / HITOMI SUISHO Promotional Music Box 1988 AD,D: Kenji Ishikawa DF: The Garden CL: Virgo Music
遊佐未森 / 瞳水晶 販促用オルゴール 1988 AD,D: 石川絢士 DF: ザ ガーデン CL: ヴァーゴ ミュージック

10. MIMORI YUSA / SORAMIMI DOKUHON Concert Program 1989,1990 CD: Takafumi Sotoma AD,D: Kenji Ishikawa D: Fumiko Hirano P: Yorihito Yamauchi DF: The Garden CL: Virgo Music
遊佐未森 / 空耳読本 コンサート パンフレット 1989,1990 CD: 外間隆史 AD,D: 石川絢士 D: 平野文子 P: 山内順仁 DF: ザ ガーデン CL: ヴァーゴ ミュージック

11. MIMORI YUSA / YUSA MIMORI CALENDAR Promotional Calendar 1990 AD,D: Kenji Ishikawa P: Yorihito Yamauchi DF: The Garden CL: Epic / Sony Records
遊佐未森 / 遊佐未森カレンダー 販促用カレンダー 1990 AD,D: 石川絢士 P: 山内順仁 DF: ザ ガーデン CL: エピック ソニー レコード

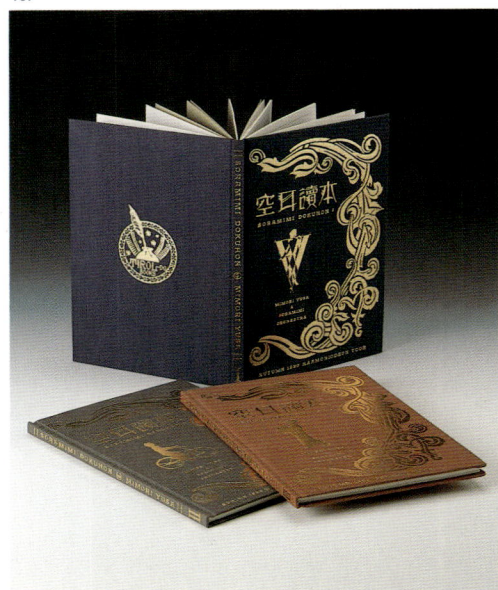

12.

13.

14.

12. **LAMP / SIGN OF THE LIGHT** Promotional Cassette 1991 AD,D: Kenji Ishikawa D: Yoko Kobayashi DF: The Garden CL: Virgo Music
ランプ / サイン オヴ ザ ライト 販促用カセット 1991 AD,D: 石川絢士 D: 小林陽子 DF: ザ ガーデン CL: ヴァーゴ ミュージック

13. **HARUOMI HOSONO / HOSONO HARUOMI POSTCARD** Promotional Postcard 1989 AD,D: Kenji Ishikawa DF: The Garden CL: Epic / Sony Records
細野晴臣 / 細野晴臣 ポストカード 販促用ポストカード 1989 AD,D: 石川絢士 DF: ザ ガーデン CL: エピック ソニー レコード

14. **HARUOMI HOSONO / OMNI SIGHT SEEING** Promotional Badge 1989 AD,D: Kenji Ishikawa DF: The Garden CL: Epic / Sony Records
細野晴臣 / オムニ サイト シーイング 販促用バッジ 1989 AD,D: 石川絢士 DF: ザ ガーデン CL: エピック ソニー レコード

15. **QUJILA "DRAGON" ORCHESTRA / IN MY SOUL** CD 1991 AD,D: Kenji Ishikawa D: Yoko Kobayashi P: Gen Murakoshi S: Mitsunori Aoyagi (Hamish) DF: The Garden CL: Epic / Sony Records
くじら ドラゴン オーケストラ / イン マイ ソウル CD 1991 AD,D: 石川絢士 D: 小林陽子 P: 村越 元 S: 青柳光則 DF: ザ ガーデン CL: エピック ソニー レコード

16. **MASAMI TSUCHIYA / HORIZON** CD 1988 AD,D,OBJECT DESIGN: Kenji Ishikawa D: Yukio Miyazaki P: Bruce Osborn OBJECT: Kengo Yoshida (Space Product) DF: The Garden CL: Epic / Sony Records
土屋昌巳 / ホライズン CD 1988 AD,D,OBJECT DESIGN: 石川絢士 D: 宮崎幸生 P: ブルース オズボーン OBJECT: 吉田健吾 DF: ザ ガーデン CL: エピック ソニー レコード

15.Back

15.Booklet / Back & Front

16.

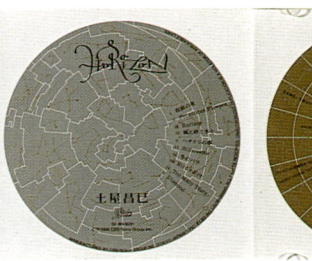
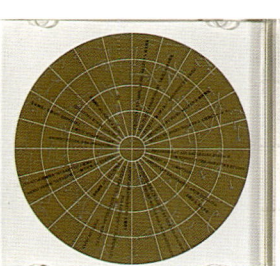

17. Back & Front

18. Back & Front

19. Back & Front

20. Back & Front

17. TOSHINORI KONDO IMA / SUNDOWN LP 1986
AD,D: Kenji Ishikawa P: Kenji Miura
DF: The Garden CL: Epic / Sony Records
近藤等則 IMA / サンダウン LP 1986
AD,D: 石川絢士 P: 三浦憲治
DF: ザ ガーデン CL: エピック ソニー レコード

18. VARIOUS ARTISTS / BETTENCHI LP 1986
AD,D: Kenji Ishikawa D: Michiyo Saito
DF: The Garden CL: Epic / Sony Records
ヴァリアス アーティスト / 別天地 LP 1986
AD,D: 石川絢士 D: 斉藤倫世
DF: ザ ガーデン CL: エピック ソニー レコード

19. BUBBLE GUM BROTHERS / SOUL SPIRIT PART II LP 1985
AD,D: Kenji Ishikawa P: Masa Ono
DF: The Garden CL: Epic / Sony Records
バブルガム ブラザーズ / ソウル スピリット パート II LP 1985
AD,D: 石川絢士 P: 小野麻早
DF: ザ ガーデン CL: エピック ソニー レコード

20. BUBBLE GUM BROTHERS / TROUBLE RUSH LP 1986
AD,D: Kenji Ishikawa P: Masa Ono
DF: The Garden CL: Epic / Sony Records
バブルガム ブラザーズ / トラブル ラッシュ LP 1986
AD,D: 石川絢士 P: 小野麻早
DF: ザ ガーデン CL: エピック ソニー レコード

21.Front B

21.Front A

22.Back & Front

21. RINSUKE TERUYA, BUTEN ONAHA / UCHINA YUNTAKU ＜OKINAWA NO WARAI-GEI＞ LP 1981 AD,D: Kenji Ishikawa DF: The Garden CL: Sony Records
照屋林助、小那覇舞天 / うちなーゆんたく＜沖縄の笑い芸＞ LP 1981 AD,D: 石川絢士 DF: ザ ガーデン CL: ソニー レコード

22. KILLING TIME / SKIP LP 1987 AD,D: Kenji Ishikawa P: Masa Ono DF: The Garden CL: Epic / Sony Records
キリング タイム / スキップ LP 1987 AD,D: 石川絢士 P: 小野麻早 DF: ザ ガーデン CL: エピック ソニー レコード

23. FRANK ZAPPA / FRANK ZAPPA NO ○△□ LP (Belt) 1983 AD,D: Kenji Ishikawa DF: The Garden CL: Sony Records
フランク ザッパ / フランク ザッパの○△□ LP用オビ 1983 AD,D: 石川絢士 DF: ザ ガーデン CL: ソニー レコード

24. I. R. S / I. R. S GREATEST HITS LP (Belt) 1983 AD,D: Kenji Ishikawa DF: The Garden CL: Sony Records
I. R. S / I. R. S グレイテスト ヒッツ LP用オビ 1983 AD,D: 石川絢士 DF: ザ ガーデン CL: ソニー レコード

25. FUKKATSU! VIOLIN ENKA LP 1983 AD,D: Kenji Ishikawa DF: The Garden CL: Sony Records
復活! ヴァイオリン演歌 LP 1983 AD,D: 石川絢士 DF: ザ ガーデン CL: ソニー レコード

26. RED ROCKERS / GOOD OF GOLD Concert Program 1984 AD,D: Kenji Ishikawa DF: The Garden CL: Sony Records
レッド ロッカーズ / グッド オヴ ゴールド コンサート パンフレット 1984 AD,D: 石川絢士 DF: ザ ガーデン CL: ソニー レコード

27. AFRIKA BAMBAATAA & SOULSONIC FORCE / LOOKING FOR THE PERFECT BEAT LP 1985 AD,D: Kenji Ishikawa DF: The Garden CL: Sony Records
アフリカ バンバーター & ソウルソニック フォース / ルッキング フォー ザ パーフェクト ビート LP 1985 AD,D: 石川絢士 DF: ザ ガーデン CL: ソニー レコード

28. WHODINI / ESCAPE LP 1985 AD,D: Kenji Ishikawa DF: The Garden CL: Sony Records
フーディーニ / エスケープ LP 1985 AD,D: 石川絢士 DF: ザ ガーデン CL: ソニー レコード

23.

24.

25. Back
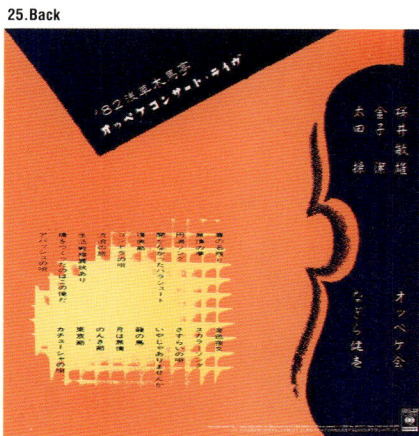

25. Front
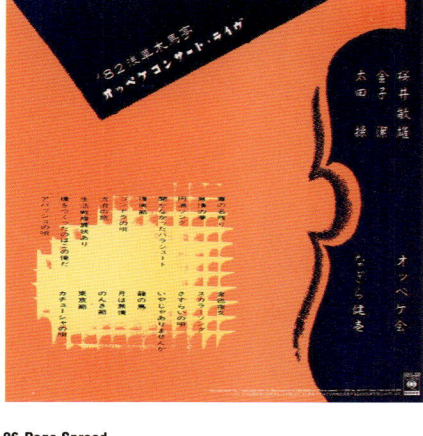

26. Page Spread

27. Back
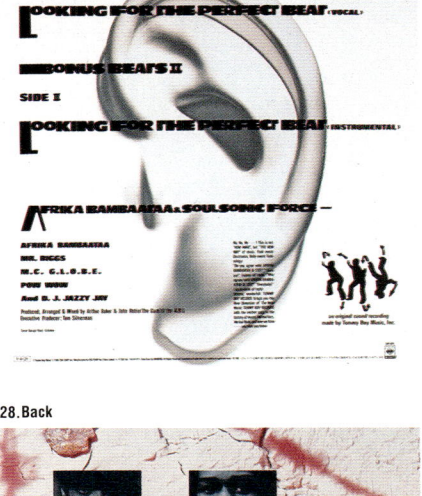

27. Front

28. Back

28. Front
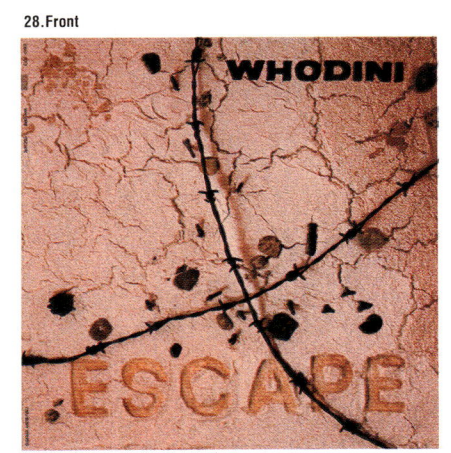

29.

29. CHARA / SWEET Promotional Kit 1991 AD: Kenji Ishikawa D,I: Yoko Kobayashi DF: The Garden CL: Epic / Sony Records
チャラ / スウィート 販促用キット 1991 AD: 石川絢士 D,I: 小林陽子 DF: ザ ガーデン CL: エピック ソニー レコード

30. STEP / LA REVOLUTION Promotional Poster 1987 AD,D: Kenji Ishikawa D: Yukio Miyazaki P: Kenji Miura OBJECT: Kengo Yoshida (Space Product)
DF: The Garden CL: Epic / Sony Records
ステップ / ラ レヴォリューション 販促用ポスター 1987 AD,D: 石川絢士 D: 宮崎幸生 P: 三浦憲治 OBJECT: 吉田健吾
DF: ザ ガーデン CL: エピック ソニー レコード

31. SHOKO SUZUKI / THE GATE OF WIND CD 1990 AD,D: Kenji Ishikawa D: Fumiko Hirano P: Yorihito Yamauchi OBJECT: Kengo Yoshida (Space Product)
DF: The Garden CL: Epic / Sony Records
鈴木祥子 / 風の扉 CD 1990 AD,D: 石川絢士 D: 平野文子 P: 山内順仁 OBJECT: 吉田健吾 DF: ザ ガーデン CL: エピック ソニー レコード

32. SHOKO SUZUKI / THE SONGS Promotional CD 1990 AD,D: Kenji Ishikawa D: Fumiko Hirano P: Yorihito Yamauchi OBJECT: Kengo Yoshida (Space Product)
DF: The Garden CL: Epic / Sony Records
鈴木祥子 / ザ ソングズ 販促用 CD 1990 AD,D: 石川絢士 D: 平野文子 P: 山内順仁 OBJECT: 吉田健吾 DF: ザ ガーデン CL: エピック ソニー レコード

30.

31. Back & Front

32. Booklet / Page Spread

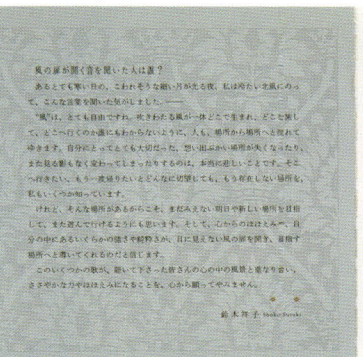 

33. Booklet / Back & Front

33. Booklet / Page Spread

33. TOMOKO TANE / KISS OF LIFE CD 1991
AD: Kenji Ishikawa D: Yoko Kobayashi, Akiko Hori P: Yorihito Yamauchi S: Mitsunori Aoyagi (Hamish) DF: The Garden CL: Sony Records
種 ともこ / キス オヴ ライフ CD 1991 AD: 石川絢士 D: 小林陽子、堀 昭子 P: 山内順仁 S: 青柳光則 DF: ザ ガーデン CL: ソニー レコード

33. Back

33. Package / Inside

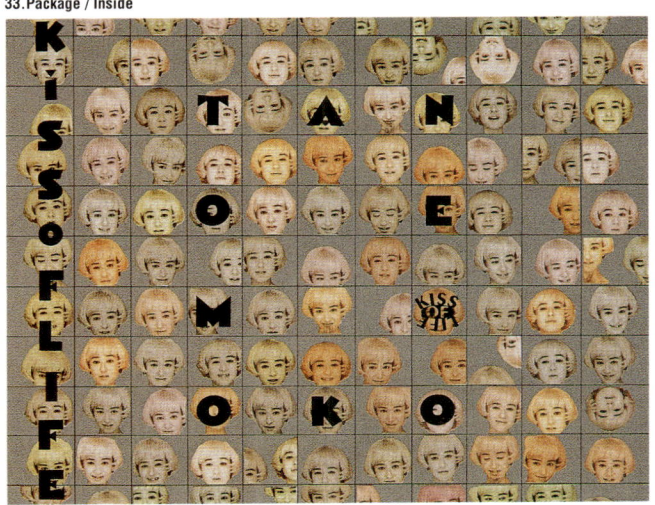

34. KAORI KANO
FILLED WITH GENUINE EMOTION
Promotional Kit 1991
AD,D: Kenji Ishikawa
D: Yoko Kobayashi
P: Gen Murakoshi
DF: The Garden
CL: Sony Records
かの香織
ほんものがいっぱい
販促用キット 1991
AD,D: 石川絢士
D: 小林陽子
P: 村越 元
DF: ザ ガーデン
CL: ソニー レコード

34.Package

34.CD Cover / Inside Spread

34.

34.Video Cover / Front

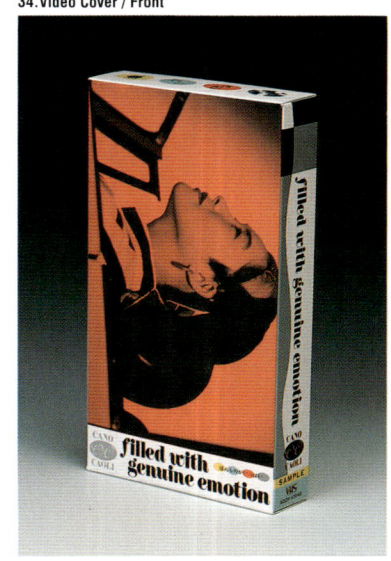

34.Video Cover / Back

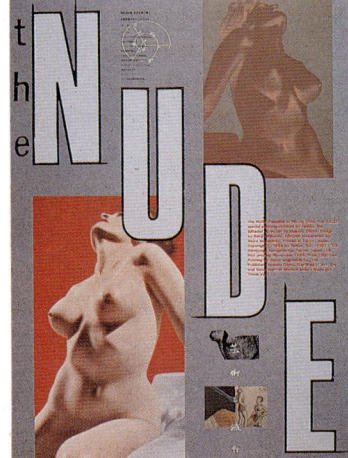

35. DANCE TO THE HEAVEN Event Poster 1986
AD,D: Kenji Ishikawa DF: The Garden CL: Epic / Sony Records
ダンス トゥ ザ ヘヴン イヴェント ポスター 1986
AD,D: 石川絢士 DF: ザ ガーデン
CL: エピック ソニー レコード

36. THE NUDE Promotional Poster 1984
CD: Makoto Orui AD,D: Kenji Ishikawa DF: The Garden CL: Fiction
ザ ヌード 販促用ポスター 1984
CD: 大類 信 AD,D: 石川絢士 DF: ザ ガーデン CL: フィクション

Photography / Anthony Oliver

David Crow

My personal project, *Trouble* is the vehicle for expressing the areas of graphic design which most interest me. I strive to produce stimulating images which are coded with layers of meaning and cross cultural inferences as well as techniques. I have a particular fascination with the way aspects of everyday life are presented by the media as a 'spectacle' which seldom resembles everyday life as we experience it. This is the primary focus of *Trouble*.
To this end I enjoy the process of displacing everyday objects, images and words to give them new, more surprising meanings than those common sense may dictate. I hope always to be able to treat the viewer, as well as the client, with respect and try to work with subject matter which has integrity as an integral quality.

　私のパーソナルなプロジェクト『Trouble』は、自分が最も興味を持っている分野＝グラフィック・デザインを表現するための媒体だ。そこでは自分のテクニックを発表するだけでなく、デザインの持つ意味や異種文化のことまで様々な要素が盛り込まれた、刺激的なイメージをつくりだしたいと考えている。
　私は、実生活では味わえない"スペクタクル"というメディアを通じて表現される日常生活に、非常に興味があるのだ。そしてそれは『Trouble』の中心テーマでもある。このテーマに向かうために、自分の実生活での品や、イメージ、言葉をいったん排除し、"日常生活"の常識的な部分よりも、ずっと新鮮な驚きを与えてもらうよう、心がけている。
　私は、私の作品を観てくれる人やクライアントに敬意をもって接し、完全で、クオリティの高い作品を常に提供していきたいと思っている。

Born Galashiels, Scotland, 1962. Studied Graphic Design at Manchester Polytechnic. Since then has worked mainly in the music industry firstly as a designer at *Assorted Images* design studio then at *Island Records* and currently as a freelance designer. Published personal magazine project Trouble as a quarterly magazine of no fixed format. This is available in a limited edition by subscription.

1962年、スコットランドのガラシールズで誕生。マンチェスター工芸学校でグラフィック・デザインを学ぶ。その後「Assorted Images」というデザイン・グループのデザイナーを経て、アイランド・レコードのデザイナーとして音楽業界で仕事をしてきたが、現在はフリーランスで活躍中。パーソナルな雑誌プロジェクト『Trouble』に取り組み、季刊誌として出版、一定のフォーマットに定まらない誌面づくりに励む。この雑誌は限定発売で、予約購読者のみに配布している。

1. Hoarding 1991 AD: David Crow P: Anthony Oliver DF: Trouble
広告板 1991 AD: デヴィッド クロウ P: アンソニー オリヴァー DF: トラブル

2. TEA Promotional Poster 1990 D: David Crow DF: Trouble
TEA 宣伝用ポスター 1990 D: デヴィッド クロウ DF: トラブル

3. THE FIRST SIGN OF TROUBLE Promotional Poster D: David Crow DF: Trouble
ザ ファースト サイン オヴ トラブル 宣伝用ポスター D: デヴィッド クロウ DF: トラブル

4. TROUBLE ＜HIJACK＞ Magazine 1990 D: David Crow DF: Trouble
トラブル ＜ハイジャック＞ 雑誌 1990 D: デヴィッド クロウ DF: トラブル

2.

3.

THE FIRST SIGN OF TROUBLE

4.

5.

5.,6. MASTERLUX THE BAPTIST Personal Work 1991
AD: David Crow DF: Trouble
マスターラックス ザ バプティスト 個人作品 1991
AD: デヴィッド クロウ DF: トラブル

6.

7.

8.

9.

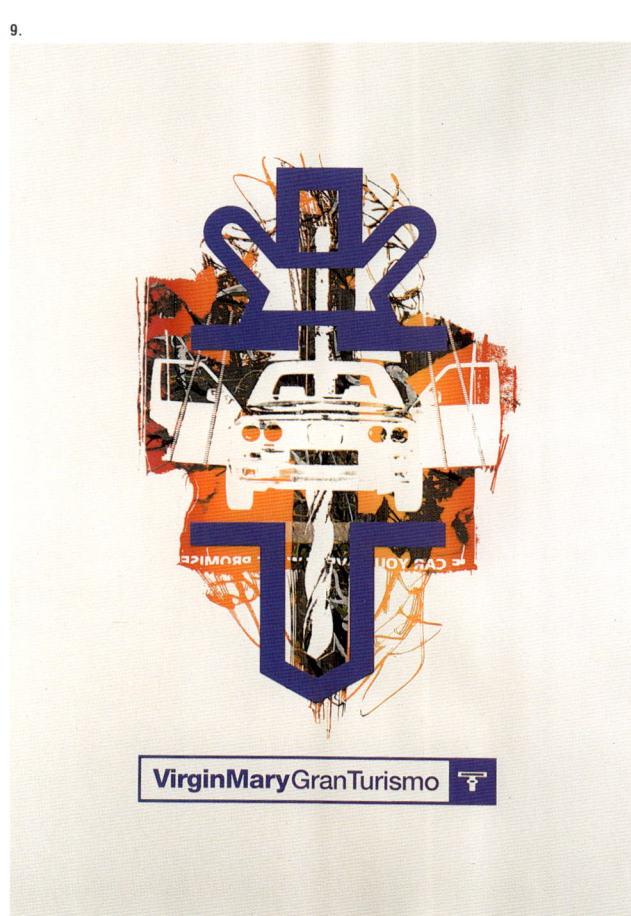

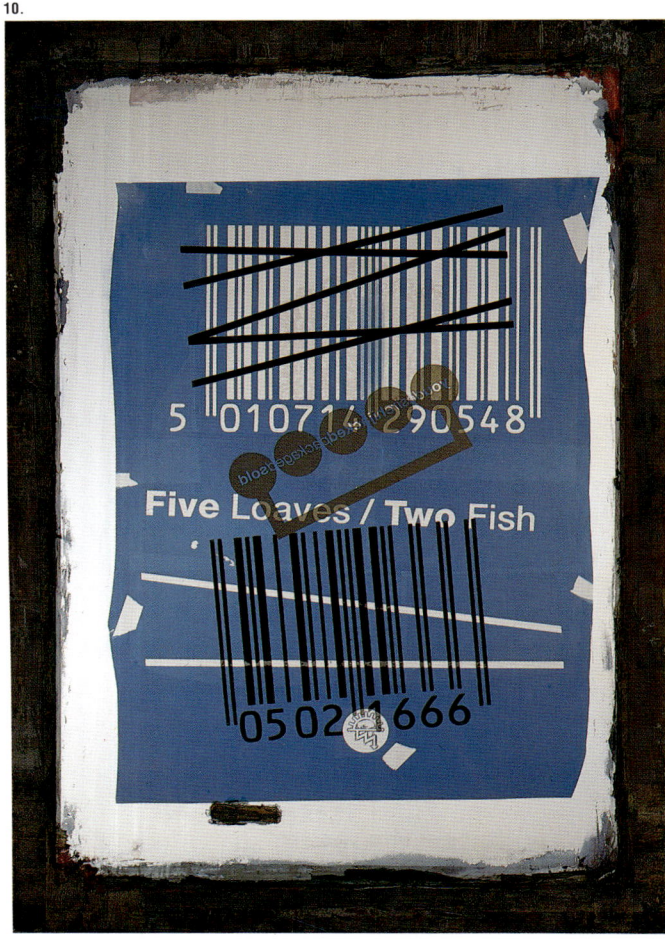

10.

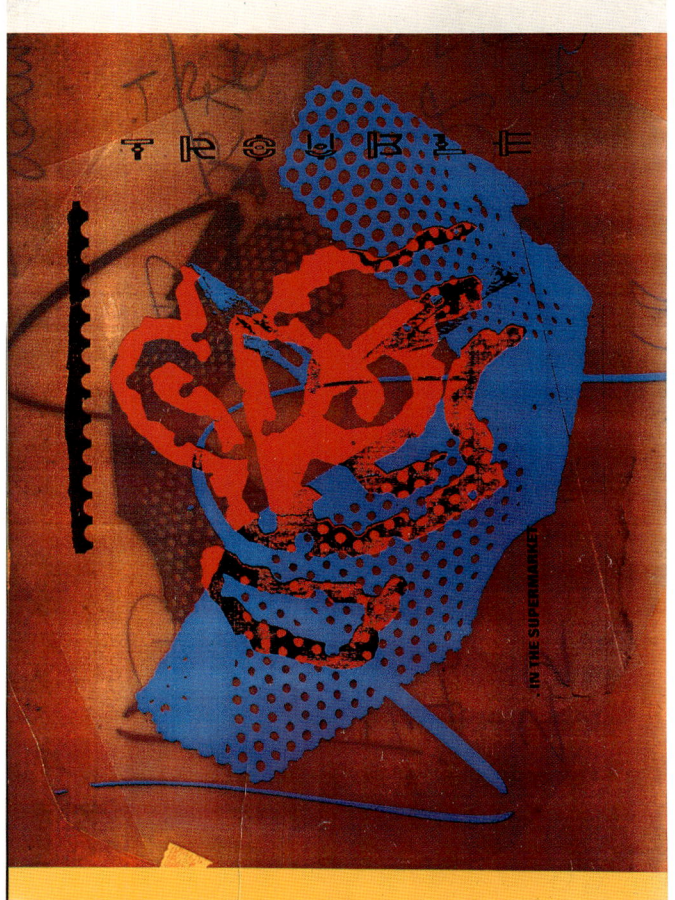

11.

12.

10. MIRACLE Personal Work 1991
AD: David Crow DF: Trouble
ミラクル 個人作品 1991
AD: デヴィッド クロウ DF: トラブル

11. TROUBLE ＜IN THE SUPERMARKET＞ Magazine
D,I: David Crow DF: Trouble
トラブル ＜イン ザ スーパーマーケット＞ 雑誌
D,I: デヴィッド クロウ DF: トラブル

12. TROUBLE ＜TOAST RACK＞ Magazine (T-shirt) 1990
D: David Crow DF: Trouble
トラブル ＜トースト ラック＞ 雑誌（Tシャツ）1990
D: デヴィッド クロウ DF: トラブル

13. YOU Personal Work 1991 AD: David Crow DF: Trouble
ユー 個人作品 1991 AD: デヴィッド クロウ DF: トラブル

14. TROUBLE <IN THE SUPERMARKET>
Magazine
D,I,CW: David Crow
CW: Rick Walker
DF: Trouble
トラブル <イン ザ スーパーマーケット>
雑誌
D,I,CW: デヴィッド クロウ
CW: リック ウォーカー
DF: トラブル

14. Cover / Back & Front

14.

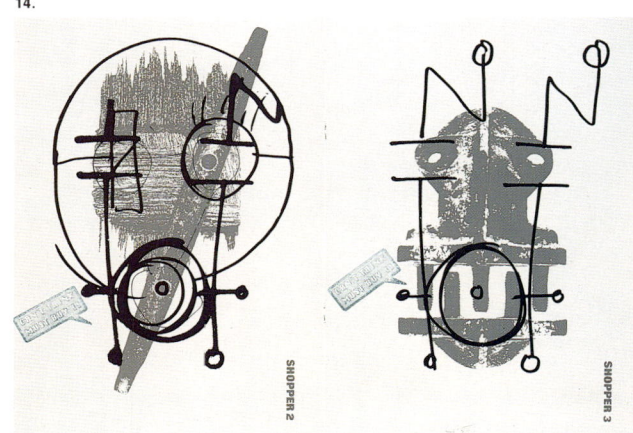

14.

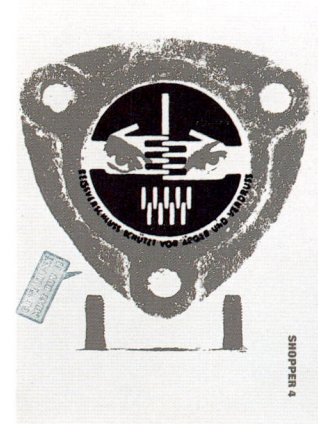

14.

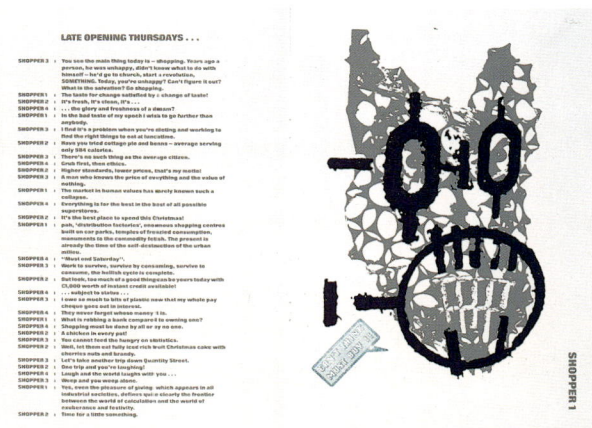

15. Cards

WITH REMOVABLE SILVER INK

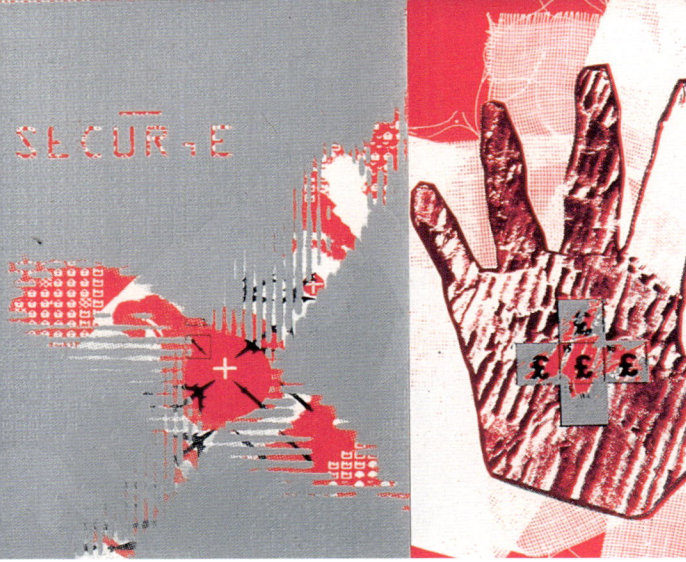

15. Package / Outside

15. Package / Inside

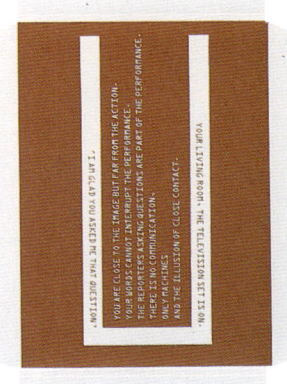

15. TROUBLE ＜ISSUE TWO＞
Magazine (Pack of Cards) 1987
D: David Crow **DF:** Trouble
トラブル ＜イシュー－2＞
雑誌（カードセット）1987
D: デヴィッド クロウ **DF:** トラブル

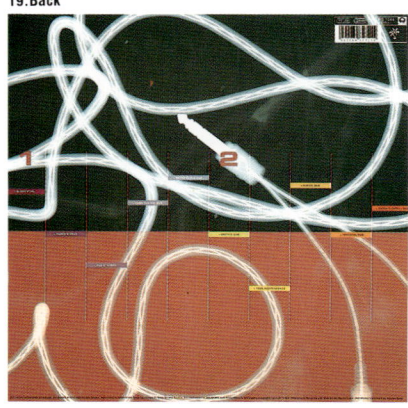

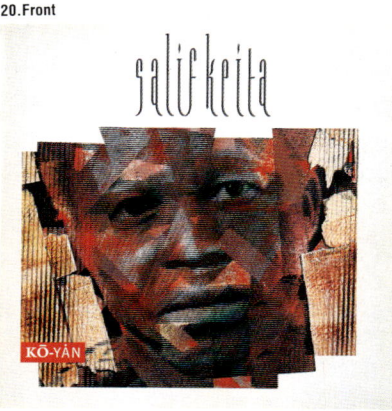
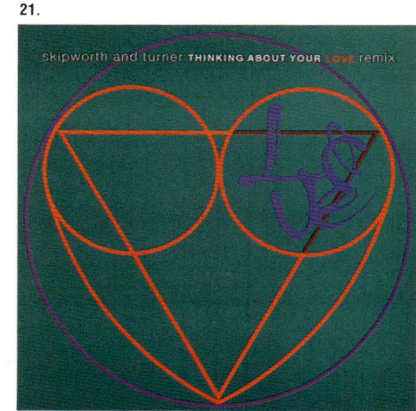

16. PLUTONIC / TUBULAR BELLS LP 1990 D,I: David Crow CL: CBS Records
プルトーニック / チュービュラー ベルズ LP 1990 D,I: デヴィッド クロウ CL: CBSレコード

17. ENNIO MORRICONE / THE ENDLESS GAME LP 1989 D,I: David Crow CL: Virgin Records
エンニオ モリコーネ / ジ エンドレス ゲーム LP 1989 D,I: デヴィッド クロウ CL: ヴァージン レコード

18. COURTNEY PINE / SONGS FROM OUR UNDERGROUND LP 1990 AD,D,I: David Crow P: Kevin Davies I: Dirk Van Doren CL: Island Records
コートニー パイン / ソングズ フロム アワー アンダーグラウンド LP 1990 AD,D,I: デヴィッド クロウ P: ケヴィン デイヴィス I: ダーク ヴァン ドレン CL: アイランド レコード

19. JAH SHAKA / DUB SYMPHONY LP 1990 AD,D: David Crow P: Non Destructive Testing, Adrian Boot CL: Island Records
ジャー シャカ / ダブ シンフォニー LP 1990 AD,D: デヴィッド クロウ P: ノン ディストラクティヴ テスティング、エイドリアン ブート CL: アイランド レコード

20. SALIF KEITA / KOYAN LP 1989 AD,D,I: David Crow TYPESTYLE: Garry Mouat CL: Island Records
サリフ ケイタ / コーヤン LP 1989 AD,D,I: デヴィッド クロウ TYPESTYLE: ゲイリー ムーアット CL: アイランド レコード

21. SKIPWORTH AND TURNER / THINKING ABOUT YOUR LOVE LP 1990 AD,D: David Crow CALLIGRAPH: Ruth Roland CL: Island Records
スキップワース アンド ターナー / シンキング アバウト ユア ラヴ LP 1990 AD,D: デヴィッド クロウ CALLIGRAPH: ラス ローランド CL: アイランド レコード

22. Back & Front

22. Back

22. ROLLING STONES
FLASHPOINT LP 1991
AD,D: David Crow, Garry Mouat
DF: M.C.O CL: Rolling Stones, Sony
ローリング ストーンズ
フラッシュ ポイント LP 1991
AD,D: デヴィッド クロウ、ゲイリー ムーアット
DF: M.C.O CL: ローリング ストーンズ、ソニー

23. METANOIA
Promotional Poster
D: David Crow CL: Metanoia
メタノイア
宣伝用ポスター
D: デヴィッド クロウ CL: メタノイア

23.

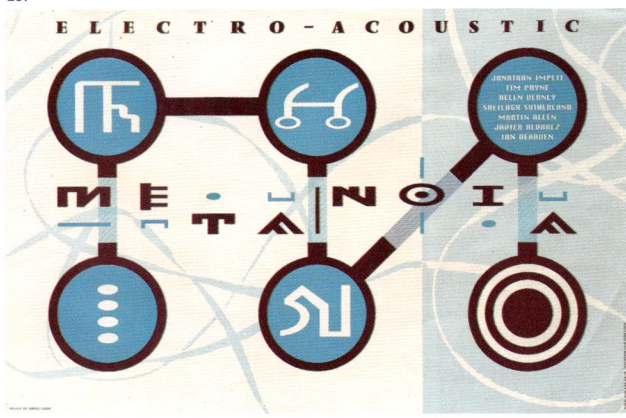

Photography / Steven Meisel

Hajime Tachibana

Creativity is wholesome.
Strength! Technique! Courage!
When one job is finished, move on to the next.
All creators are futurists:
Their ideas are certain to be realized in the future;
They see further than others,
Like a time machine traveler.
Too happy to stop.

モノ作りは健全だ。
力！ 技！ 度胸！
ひとつを仕上げてまた次へ。
モノを作っている人は皆、フューチャリストである。
そのアイデアは必ず未来で実現されるから。
皆より先に未来を見てる。
タイムマシンに乗っているようなものだ。
だから楽しくてやめられない。

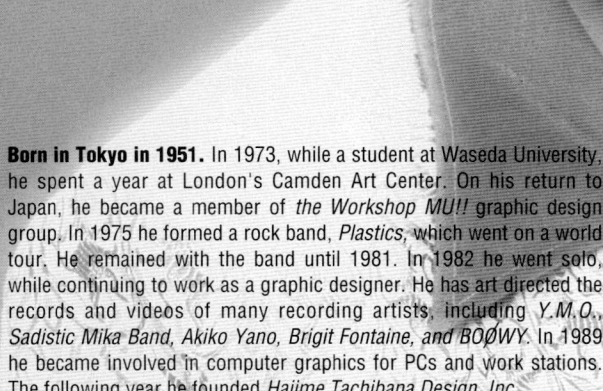

Born in Tokyo in 1951. In 1973, while a student at Waseda University, he spent a year at London's Camden Art Center. On his return to Japan, he became a member of *the Workshop MU!!* graphic design group. In 1975 he formed a rock band, *Plastics*, which went on a world tour. He remained with the band until 1981. In 1982 he went solo, while continuing to work as a graphic designer. He has art directed the records and videos of many recording artists, including *Y.M.O., Sadistic Mika Band, Akiko Yano, Brigit Fontaine,* and *BOØWY*. In 1989 he became involved in computer graphics for PCs and work stations. The following year he founded *Hajime Tachibana Design, Inc.*
He won *the 35th ADC (Art Director's Club) Award* in 1991 and released *BAMBI*, his first solo album in four years. In 1992 Yobisha published the first collection of his works, under the title *Introducing Hajime Tachibana Design*. His work has been exhibited at the Graphic Gallery in Ginza.

1951年、東京生まれ。1973年、早稲田大学在学中に1年間ロンドンに滞在、カムデン・アート・センターに学ぶ。翌年帰国後、グラフィック・グループ「ワークショップMU!!」に参加。1975年、バンド「プラスチックス」を結成。ワールド・ツアーを含め、1981年まで活動。1982年からソロ音楽家活動に入るが、そのかたわら芸術家活動も続け、Y.M.Oや矢野顕子、サディスティック・ミカ・バンド、ブリジット・フォンティーヌ、BO.ØWYなど、今日までに数多くのミュージシャンのレコード、ステージ、ビデオのアート・ディレクションを手がける。1989年、静止画としてのCG（コンピュータ・グラフィックス）を追求、パソコンからワーク・ステーションまでを幅広く活用。翌年、㈱立花ハジメデザインを設立。1991年、第35回ADC〈アート・ディレクターズ・クラブ〉最高賞を受賞。また音楽家活動としても、4年ぶりのソロ・アルバム『BAMBI』を発表。1992年、初めての画集『Introducing Hajime Tachibana Design』（用美社）を刊行、銀座グラフィック・ギャラリーにて初めての展覧会も行なう。

1. APE CALL FROM TOKYO
Exhibition Poster 1990
AD,D: Hajime Tachibana
CL: Toppan Printing
エイプ コール フロム トウキョウ
展覧会ポスター 1990
AD,D: 立花 ハジメ
CL: 凸版印刷

2. TOKYO ART DIRECTORS CLUB ANNUAL 1989
Design Annual Cover 1989
AD: Kaoru Kasai
I: Hajime Tachibana
CL: Bijutsu Shuppan-sha
ADC年鑑
年鑑 1989
AD: 葛西 薫
I: 立花 ハジメ
CL: 美術出版社

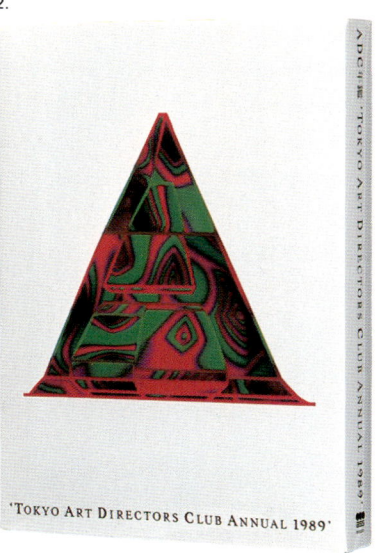

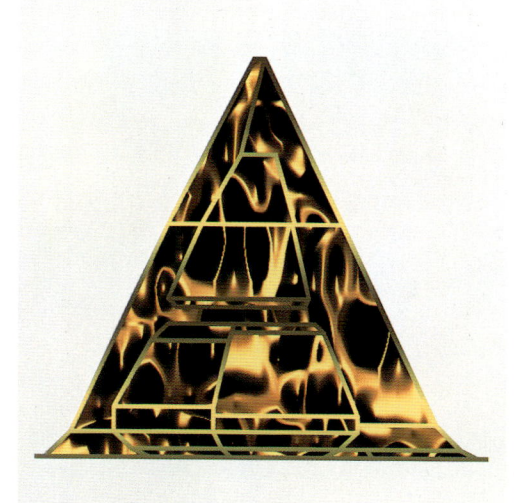

1.

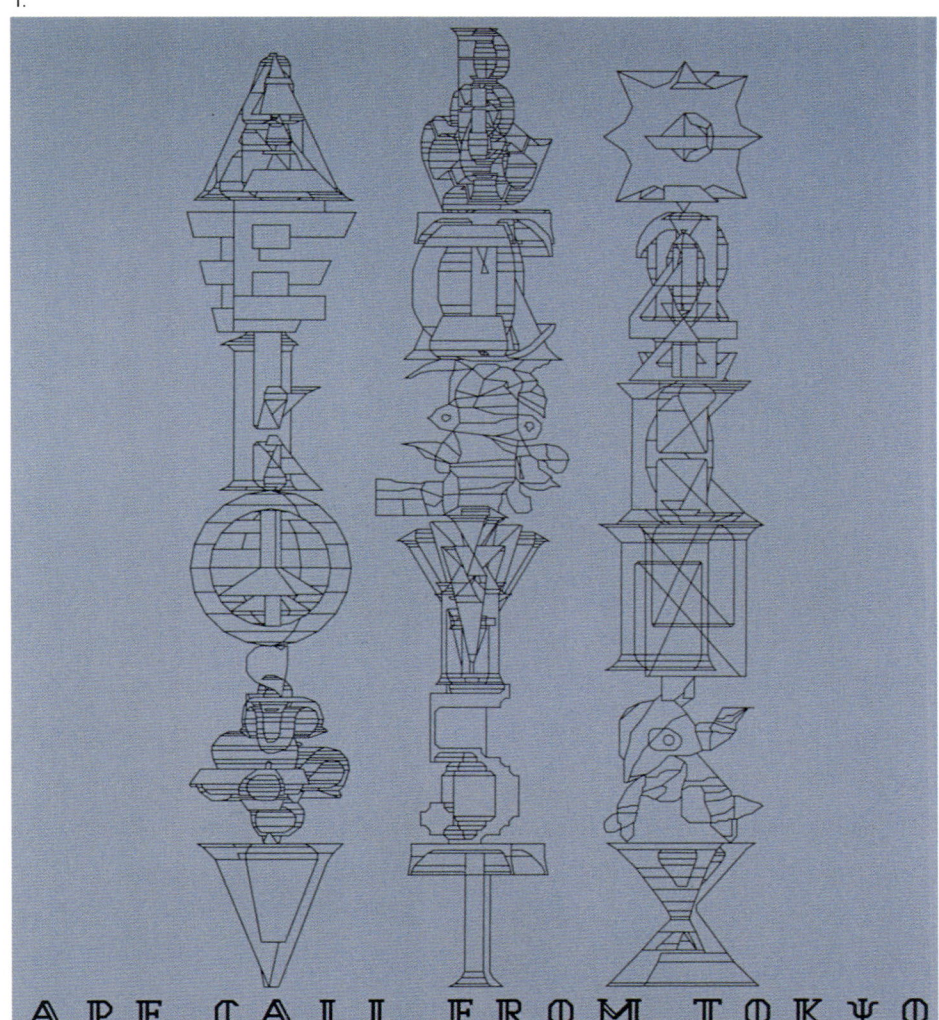

3.

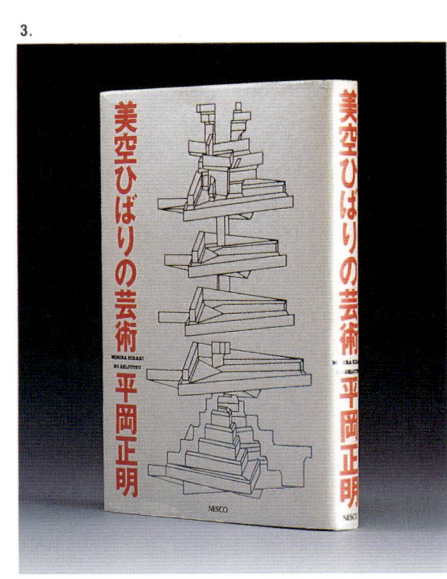

3.

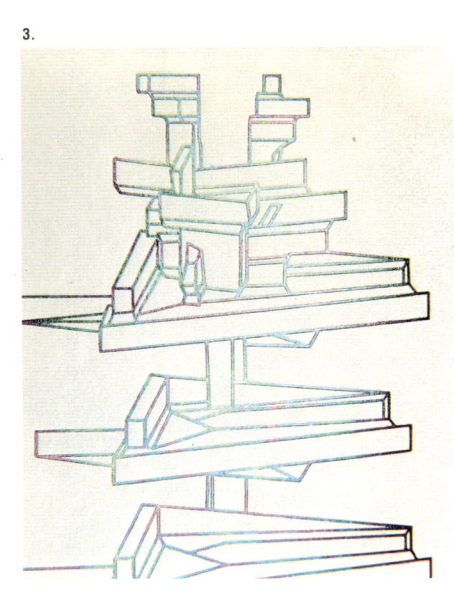

3. MASAAKI HIRAOKA
MISORA HIBARI NO GEIJUTSU
Book Cover 1990
CD: Michiyo Akiyama
AD,D: Hajime Tachibana
CL: Nesco Publishing
平岡正明
美空ひばりの芸術
単行本 1990
CD: 秋山 ミチヨ
AD,D: 立花 ハジメ
CL: ネスコ出版

4.

4. AKIKO YANO / BROOCH 7-inch Single Kit 1986 AD,D: Hajime Tachibana CL: Midi Records
矢野顕子 / ブローチ 7インチ シングル キット 1986 AD,D: 立花 ハジメ CL: ミディ レコード

5. AKIKO YANO / BROOCH 12-inch Single 1988 AD,D: Hajime Tachibana CL: Midi Records
矢野顕子 / ブローチ 12インチ シングル 1988 AD,D: 立花 ハジメ CL: ミディ レコード

6. AKIKO YANO / DEMAE CONCERT LD 1987 AD,D: Hajime Tachibana CL: Midi Records
矢野顕子 / 出前コンサート LD 1987 AD,D: 立花 ハジメ CL: ミディ レコード

5.Back

5.Front

6.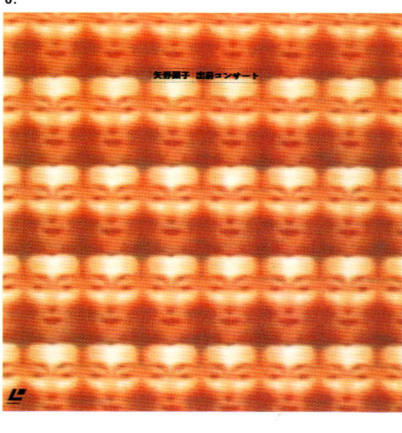

7.Back

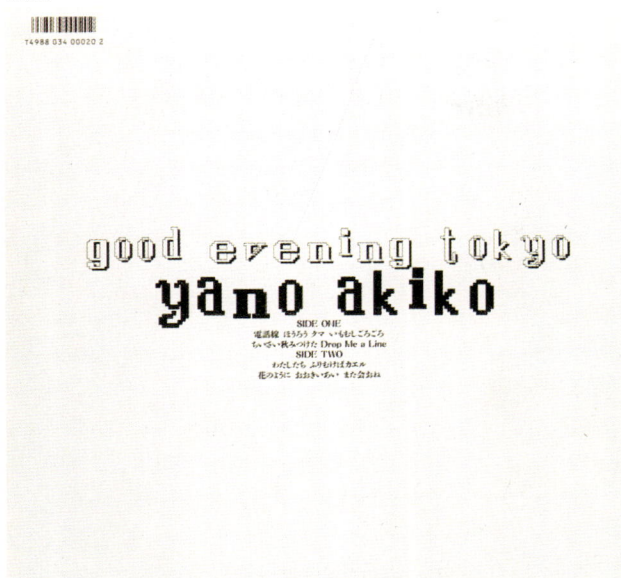

7.Front

8.

7. AKIKO YANO / GOOD EVENING TOKYO LP 1988
AD,D: Hajime Tachibana CL: Midi Records
矢野顕子 / グッド イーヴニング トウキョウ LP 1988
AD,D: 立花 ハジメ CL: ミディ レコード

8. HAJIME TACHIBANA / H LP 1982
AD,D: Hajime Tachibana P: Masayoshi Sukita CL: Alfa Records
立花 ハジメ / H LP 1982
AD,D: 立花 ハジメ P: 鋤田正義 CL: アルファ レコード

9. YUKIHIRO TAKAHASHI / TIME & PLACE LP 1983
AD,D: Hajime Tachibana CL: Alfa Records
高橋幸宏 / タイム & プレイス LP 1983
AD,D: 立花 ハジメ CL: アルファ レコード

10. TALKING HEADS / CITIES 12-inch Single 1981
AD: Plastics D: Hajime Tachibana CL: Sire Records
トーキング ヘッズ / シティーズ 12インチ シングル 1981
AD: プラスチックス D: 立花 ハジメ CL: サイアー レコード

11. RYUICHI SAKAMOTO / FIELD WORK 12-inch Single 1985
AD,D: Hajime Tachibana CL: Midi Records
坂本龍一 / フィールド ワーク 12インチ シングル 1985
AD,D: 立花 ハジメ CL: ミディ レコード

9.

10.

11.

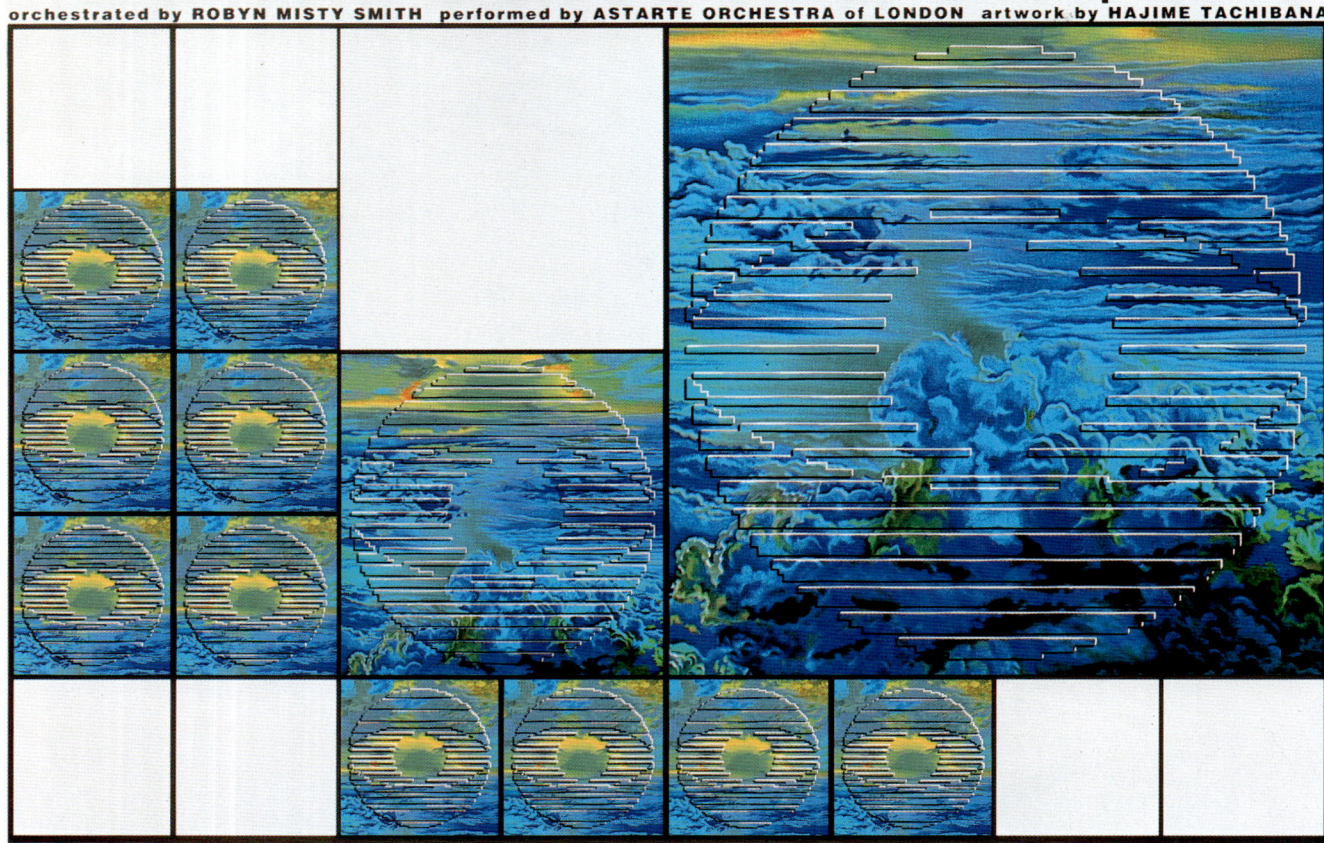

12. BOØWY / ORCHESTRATION BOØWY Promotional Poster 1990 AD,D: Hajime Tachibana CL: Toshiba EMI
ボウイ / オーケストレーション ボウイ 販促用ポスター 1990 AD,D: 立花 ハジメ CL: 東芝EMI

13. COMPLEX / ROMANTIC 1990 Personal Works (for CD and Poster) 1989
AD: Katsu Nagaishi D: Hajime Tachibana CL: Toshiba EMI
コンプレックス / ロマンティック 1990 個人作品（CD、ポスター用） 1989 AD: 永石 勝 D: 立花 ハジメ CL: 東芝EMI

14. TALKING HEADS / TALKING HEADS '79 JAPAN Concert Program 1979
AD,D: Hajime Tachibana, Toshio Nakanishi CL: Tom's Cabin
トーキング ヘッズ / トーキング ヘッズ '79 ジャパン コンサート パンフレット 1979
AD,D: 立花 ハジメ、中西俊夫 CL: トムズ キャビン

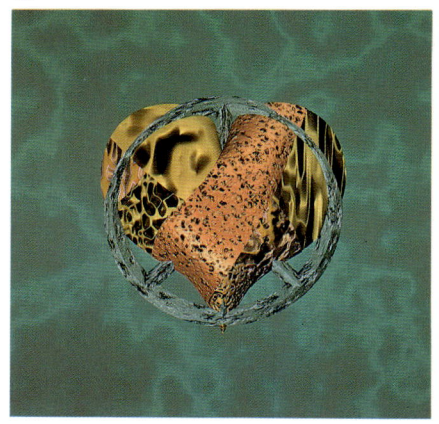

14. Cover / Back & Front

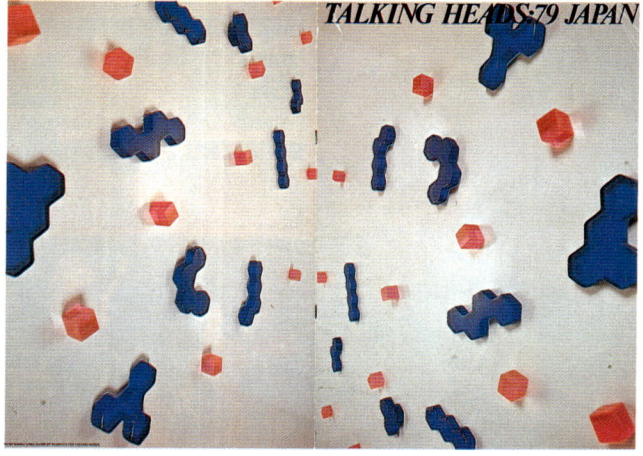

15. Back & Front

15. HAJIME TACHIBANA
HAJIMEYOKEREBA SUBETE YOSHI
CD 1990
AD,D: Hajime Tachibana
CL: Midi Records
立花 ハジメ
ハジメヨケレバスベテヨシ
CD 1990
AD,D: 立花 ハジメ
CL: ミディ レコード

16. HAJIME TACHIBANA
BARRICADE
12-inch Single 1985
AD,D: Hajime Tachibana
CL: Jun Men
立花 ハジメ
バリケード
12インチ シングル 1985
AD,D: 立花 ハジメ
CL: ジュン メン

15. Booklet / Back & Front

16. Back

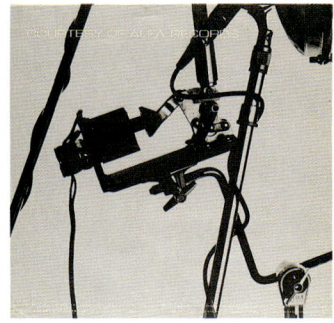

16. Label

16. Front

17. PLASTICS / FOREVER PLASTICO CD 1989 AD: Plastics D: Hajime Tachibana I: Toshio Nakanishi CL: Victor Musical Industries
プラスチックス / フォーエヴァー プラスチコ CD 1989 AD: プラスチックス D: 立花 ハジメ I: 中西俊夫 CL: ビクター音楽産業

18. HAJIME TACHIBANA / TAIYO SUN LP 1985 AD,D: Hajime Tachibana P: Kaoru Ijima CL: Midi Records
立花 ハジメ / 太陽さん LP 1985 AD,D: 立花 ハジメ P: 伊島 薫 CL: ミディ レコード

19. PLASTICS / PLASTICS Promotional Poster 1980 AD: Plastics D: Hajime Tachibana I: Toshio Nakanishi CL: Victor Musical Industries
プラスチックス / プラスチックス 販促用ポスター 1980 AD: プラスチックス D: 立花 ハジメ I: 中西俊夫 CL: ビクター音楽産業

20. HAJIME TACHIBANA / NICE TO MEET YOU, SORRY TO PART‥‥‥ LP 1985 AD,D: Hajime Tachibana P: Kaoru Ijima CL: Alfa Records
立花 ハジメ / 逢うは別れのハジメなり LP 1985 AD,D: 立花 ハジメ P: 伊島 薫 CL: アルファ レコード

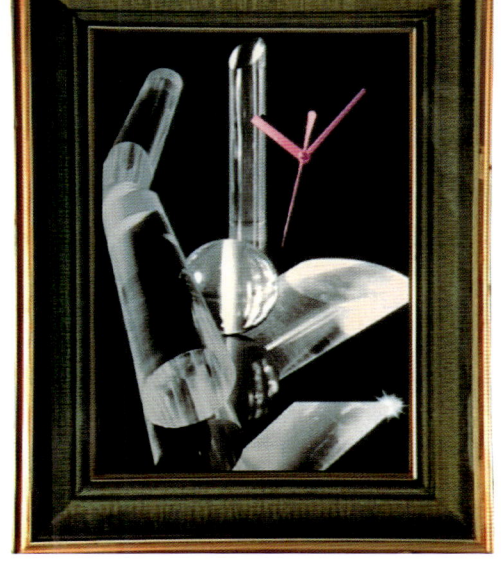

21. HAJIME TACHIBANA / BAMBI LP 1991 AD,D: Hajime Tachibana P: Steven Meisel CL: Toshiba EMI
立花 ハジメ／バンビ LP 1991 AD,D: 立花 ハジメ P: スティーヴン マイゼル CL: 東芝EMI

22. CRYSTAL CLOCK Magazine Illustration 1989 AD,D: Hajime Tachibana CL: Bijutsu-Techo
クリスタル クロック 個人作品（雑誌掲載用） 1989 AD,D: 立花 ハジメ CL: 美術手帖

23. HAJIME TACHIBANA / HAPPY 12-inch Single 1986 AD,D: Hajime Tachibana P: Kaoru Ijima CL: Midi Records
立花 ハジメ／ハッピー 12インチ シングル 1986 AD,D: 立花 ハジメ P: 伊島 薫 CL: ミディレコード

24. AIR-CON CLOCK Advertisement 1989 AD: Hajime Tachibana CL: Hitachi
エアコン クロック 広告 1989 AD: 立花 ハジメ CL: 日立製作所

25. ICE CREAM CLOCK Magazine Illustration 1989 AD,D: Hajime Tachibana CL: Shiseido
アイス クリーム クロック 個人作品（雑誌掲載用） 1989 AD,D: 立花 ハジメ CL: 資生堂

I/O

David James

Graphic Art is the bonding of aesthetics and ideas, of sign and symbol, of visual and spacial. Communication is its primary function, information its first concern. Inspiration is the process of creative freedom and the spirit of artistic endeavor. Visual language is the vocabulary of design, it transcends the one dimensionality of surface. Design is an organic gesture, an intuitive vision, a stimulus of the senses.

グラフィック・アートは、美意識とアイディア、サインとシンボル、それに視覚と空間が、それぞれ結び付いたものである。コミュニケーションは、その中心的な機能であり、情報はその最初の重要課題である。

インスピレーションは、自由を創り出すプロセスと、芸術を生みだそうとする姿勢によるものである。

視覚で語ることがデザインの表現様式であり、それは「表面」という次元を超越している。デザインは、意思表現の根本であり、直観的ヴィジョンであり、感覚の刺激である。

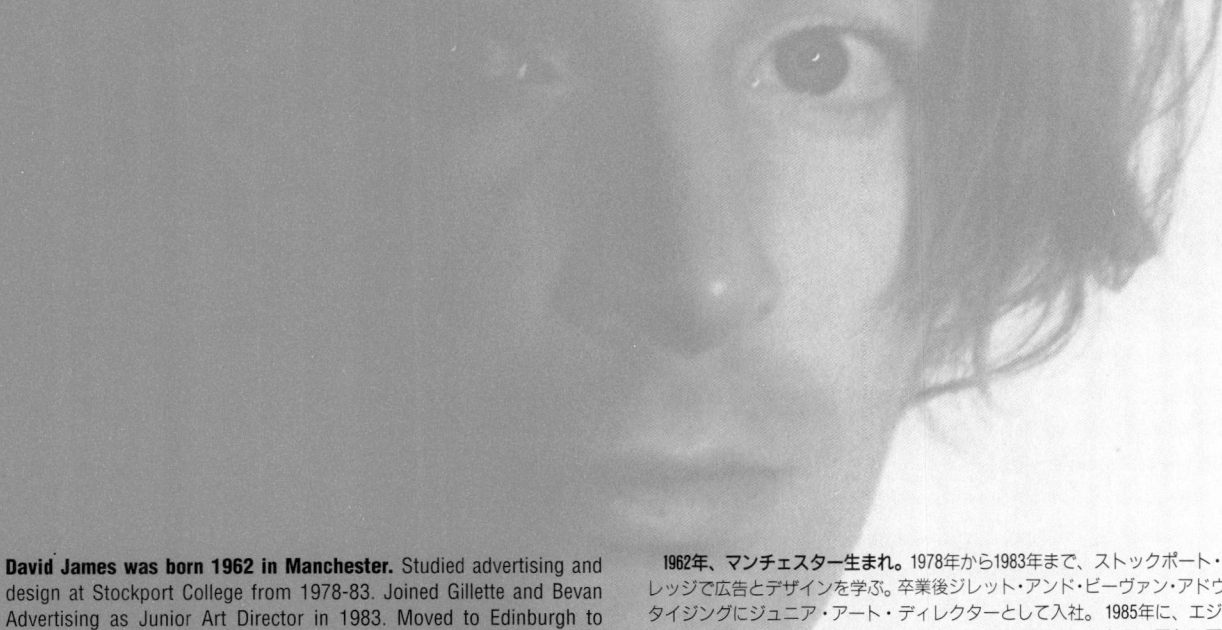

David James was born 1962 in Manchester. Studied advertising and design at Stockport College from 1978-83. Joined Gillette and Bevan Advertising as Junior Art Director in 1983. Moved to Edinburgh to become a designer with McIlroy Coates Design in 1985. Moved again in 1986 to London, working for the Fine White Line Design Company. Set up own design studio in 1987 concentrating on music, fashion and magazine design.

1962年、マンチェスター生まれ。1978年から1983年まで、ストックポート・カレッジで広告とデザインを学ぶ。卒業後ジレット・アンド・ビーヴァン・アドヴァタイジングにジュニア・アート・ディレクターとして入社。1985年に、エジンバラに移り、マッカロイ・コーツ・デザインのデザイナーになる。翌年に再びロンドンに戻り、ファイン・ホワイト・ライン・デザインに籍を置く。1987年に独立しスタジオを設立、以後、音楽やファッション、雑誌関係のデザインを中心に活動中。

1. Back & Front

2. Front

2. Inner Sleeve

2. Back

1. SOUL Ⅱ SOUL / KEEP ON MOVIN (REMIX) 12-inch Single 1989
AD,D: David James P: Jamie Morgan
PHOTOGRAPH MANIPULATION: Strechno Lab
DF: David James Associates CL: 10 Records
ソウル トゥー ソウル／キープ オン ムーヴィン（リミックス）12インチ シングル 1989
AD,D: デヴィッド ジェイムズ P: ジェイミー モーガン
PHOTOGRAPH MANIPULATION: ストレクノ ラブ
DF: デヴィッド ジェイムズ アソシエイツ CL: 10レコード

2. SOUL Ⅱ SOUL / SOUL Ⅱ SOUL CLUB CLASSICS VOL.1 LP 1989
AD,D: David James P: Jamie Morgan
DF: David James Associates CL: 10 Records
ソウル トゥー ソウル／ソウル トゥー ソウル クラブ クラシックス VOL.1 LP 1989
AD,D: デヴィッド ジェイムズ P: ジェイミー モーガン
DF: デヴィッド ジェイムズ アソシエイツ CL: 10レコード

3.

3.

3.

3.

3. MONIX POSTERS-4 1990 COLLECTION Promotional Posters 1990 AD,D: David James D: Gareth Hague P: Marcus Tomlinson CW: Monica Zipper DF: David James Associates CL: Monix
モニックス ポスターズ-4 1990 コレクション　販促用ポスター 1990 AD,D: デヴィッド ジェイムズ　D: ガレス ハグ　P: マーカス トムリンソン　CW: モニカ ジッパー
DF: デヴィッド ジェイムズ アソシエイツ　CL: モニックス

4. ROAD <ISSUE 1> Magazine 1990
AD,D: David James D: Gareth Hague
DF: David James Associates CL: Essay Designs
ロード <イシュー1> 雑誌 1990
AD,D: デヴィッド ジェイムズ D: ガレス ハグ
DF: デヴィッド ジェイムズ アソシエイツ CL: エッセイ デザインズ

4.Cover

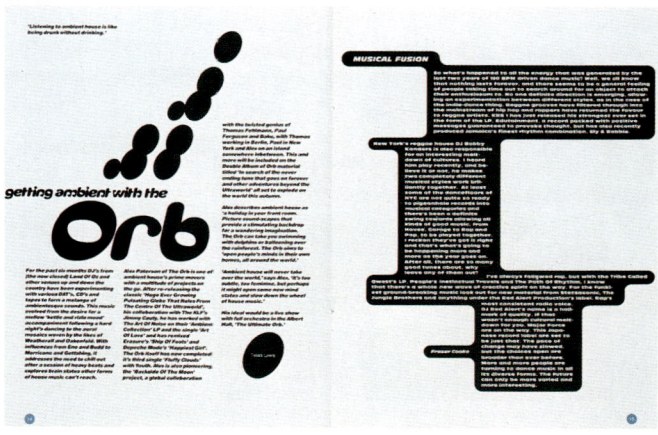

5.

5.

5.

5.

5. MOTO O 1989 COLLECTION Promotional Brochure 1988
PR: Moto O AD,D: David James AD,CW: Lee Farmer
P: Eddie Monsoon DF: David James Associates CL: Regis
モートO 1989 コレクション 販促用パンフレット 1988
PR: モートO AD,D: デヴィッド ジェイムズ AD,CW: リー ファーマー
P: エディ モンスーン DF: デヴィッド ジェイムズ アソシエイツ CL: レジス

5.Cover

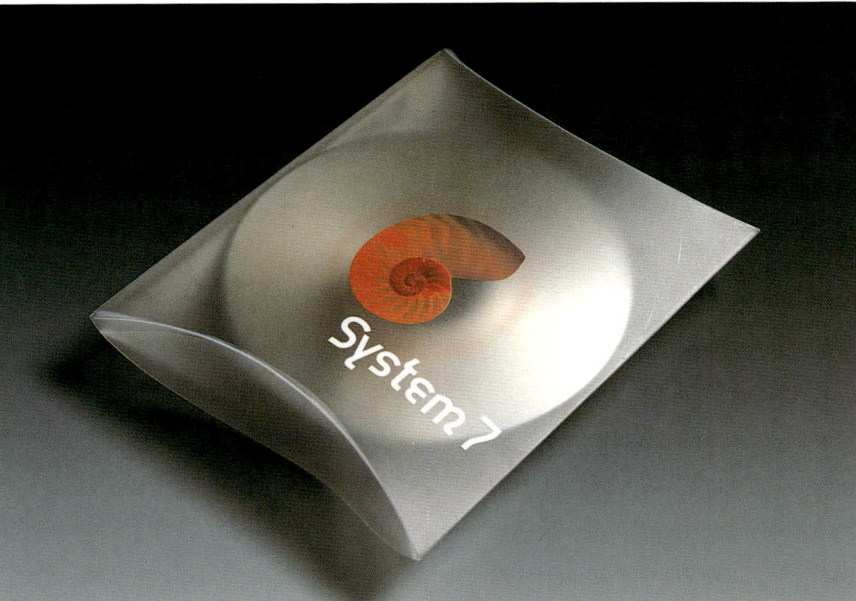

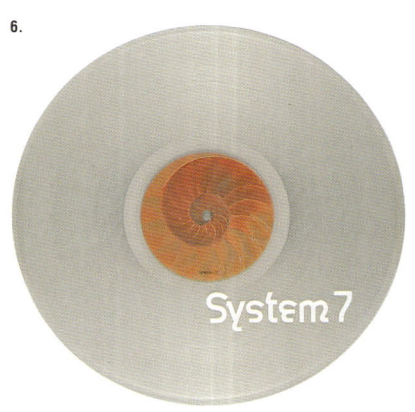

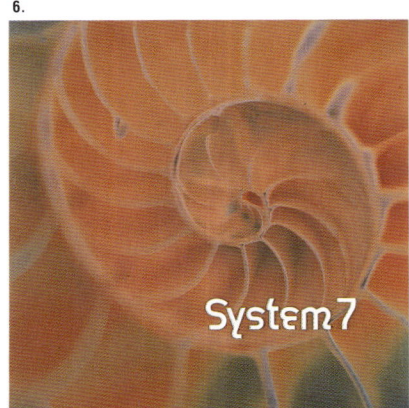 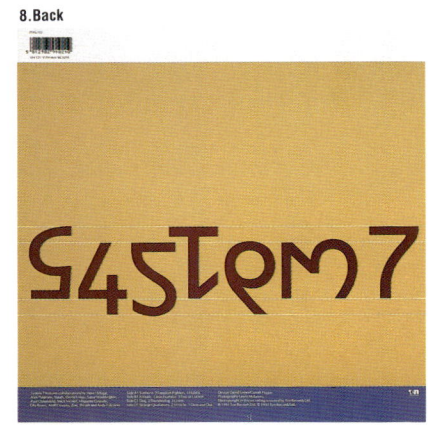 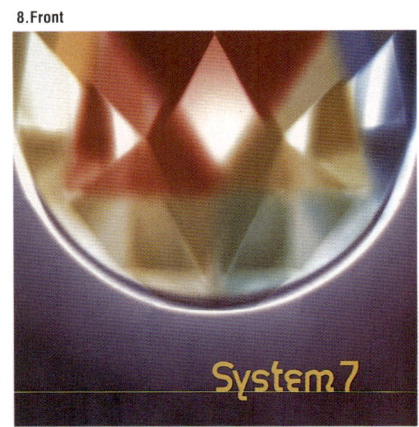

6. SYSTEM 7 / SYSTEM 7 12-inch Single 1991 AD,D: David James D: Gareth Hague P: Lewis Mulatero DF: David James Associates CL: AVL Records
システム セヴン / システム セヴン 12インチ シングル 1991 AD,D: デヴィッド ジェイムズ D: ガレス ハグ P: ルイス ムラテロ DF: デヴィッド ジェイムズ アソシエイツ CL: AVL レコード

7. SYSTEM 7 / SYSTEM 7 Promotional CD 1991 AD,D: David James P: Lewis Mulatero DF: David James Associates CL: 10 Records
システム セヴン / システム セヴン 販促用CD 1991 AD,D: デヴィッド ジェイムズ P: ルイス ムラテロ DF: デヴィッド ジェイムズ アソシエイツ CL: 10レコード

8. SYSTEM 7 / SYSTEM 7 LP 1991 AD,D: David James D: Gareth Hague P: Lewis Mulatero DF: David James Associates CL: 10 Records
システム セヴン / システム セヴン LP 1991 AD,D: デヴィッド ジェイムズ D: ガレス ハグ P: ルイス ムラテロ DF: デヴィッド ジェイムズ アソシエイツ CL: 10レコード

9. GARY CLAIL / BEEF Promotional Poster 1990 AD,D: David James D: Gareth Hague DF: Devid James Associates CL: Perfecto Records
ギャリー クレイル / ビーフ 販促用ポスター 1990 AD,D: デヴィッド ジェイムズ D: ガレス ハグ DF: デヴィッド ジェイムズ アソシエイツ CL: パーフェクト レコード

10. GARY CLAIL / BEEF 12-inch Single 1990 AD,D: David James AD: Paul Oakenfold D: Gareth Hague P: Herbert Giradet, N.Dickinson CW: Gary Clail
DF: David James Associates CL: Perfecto Records
ギャリー クレイル / ビーフ 12インチ シングル 1990 AD,D: デヴィッド ジェイムズ AD: ポール オーケンフォールド D: ガレス ハグ P: ハーバート ギラデ, N. ディッキンソン CW: ギャリー クレイル
DF: デヴィッド ジェイムズ アソシエイツ CL: パーフェクト レコード

11. THE SINDECUT / LIVE THE LIFE (REMIX) 12-inch Single 1991 AD,D: David James D: Gareth Hague DF: David James Associates CL: Virgin Records
ザ シンディカット / ライヴ ザ ライフ（リミックス） 12インチ シングル 1991 AD,D: デヴィッド ジェイムズ D: ガレス ハグ DF: デヴィッド ジェイムズ アソシエイツ CL: ヴァージン レコード

12. THE SINDECUT / WON'T CHANGE 12-inchngle 1991 AD,D: David James D: Gareth Hague P: Richard Burbridge DF: David James Associates CL: Virgin Records
ザ シンディカット / ウォント チェンジ 12インチ シングル 1991 AD,D: デヴィッド ジェイムズ D: ガレス ハグ P: リチャード バーブリッジ
DF: デヴィッド ジェイムズ アソシエイツ CL: ヴァージン レコード

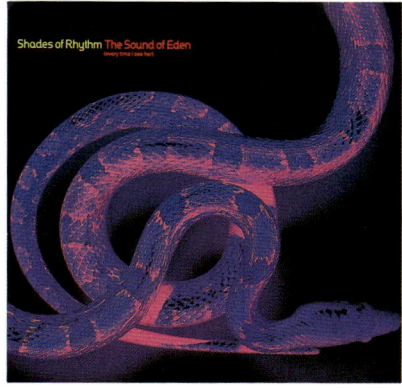
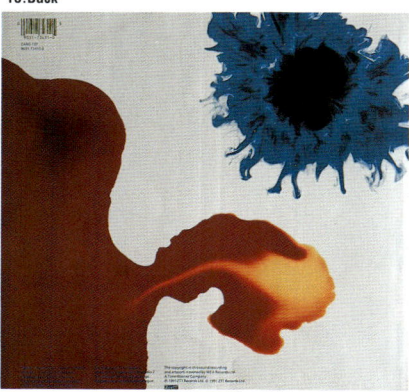

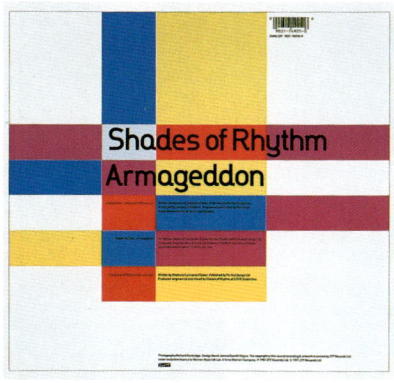

13. **SHADES OF RHYTHM / SWEET SENSATION** 12-inch Single 1991 **AD,D:** David James **D:** Gareth Hague **P:** Richard Burbridge **DF:** David James Associates **CL:** ZTT Records
シェイズ オヴ リズム / スウィート センセーション 12インチ シングル 1991 **AD,D:** デヴィッド ジェイムズ **D:** ガレス ハグ **P:** リチャード バーブリッジ **DF:** デヴィッド ジェイムズ アソシエイツ **CL:** ZTT レコード

14. **SHADES OF RHYTHM / THE SOUND OF EDEN** 12-inch Single 1991 **AD,D:** David James **D:** Gareth Hague **P:** Richard Burbridge **DF:** David James Associates **CL:** ZTT Records
シェイズ オヴ リズム / ザ サウンド オヴ エデン 12インチ シングル 1991 **AD,D:** デヴィッド ジェイムズ **D:** ガレス ハグ **P:** リチャード バーブリッジ **DF:** デヴィッド ジェイムズ アソシエイツ **CL:** ZTT レコード

15. **SHADES OF RHYTHM / HOMICIDE** 12-inch Single 1991 **AD,D:** David James **D:** Gareth Hague **P:** Richard Burbridge **DF:** David James Associates **CL:** ZTT Records
シェイズ オヴ リズム / ハマサイド 12インチ シングル 1991 **AD,D:** デヴィッド ジェイムズ **D:** ガレス ハグ **P:** リチャード バーブリッジ **DF:** デヴィッド ジェイムズ アソシエイツ **CL:** ZTT レコード

16.Back

16.Front

boy george

*tense nervous headache

17.Front & Back

18.

16. BOY GEORGE
TENSE NERVOUS HEADACHE
LP 1988
CD: Boy George
AD: Judy Blame
D: David James
P: Nick Knight
DF: David James Associates
CL: Virgin Records
ボーイ ジョージ
テンス ナーヴァス ヘッドエイク
LP 1988
CD: ボーイ ジョージ
AD: ジュディ ブレイム
D: デヴィッド ジェイムズ
P: ニック ナイト
DF: デヴィッド ジェイムズ アソシエイツ
CL: ヴァージン レコード

17. BOY GEORGE
TRIP
12-inch Single 1989
CD: Judy Blame
AD,D: David James
P: Nick Knight
DF: David James Associates
CL: Virgin Records
ボーイ ジョージ
トリップ
12インチ シングル 1989
CD: ジュディ ブレイム
AD,D: デヴィッド ジェイムズ
P: ニック ナイト
DF: デヴィッド ジェイムズ アソシエイツ
CL: ヴァージン レコード

18. NENEH CHERRY
BUFFALO STANCE
12-inch Single 1988
CD: Judy Blame
AD,D: David James
P: Eddie Monsoon
DF: David James Associates
CL: Circa Records
ネネ チェリー
バッファロー スタンス
12インチ シングル 1988
CD: ジュディ ブレイム
AD,D: デヴィッド ジェイムズ
P: エディ モンスーン
DF: デヴィッド ジェイムズ アソシエイツ
CL: サーカ レコード

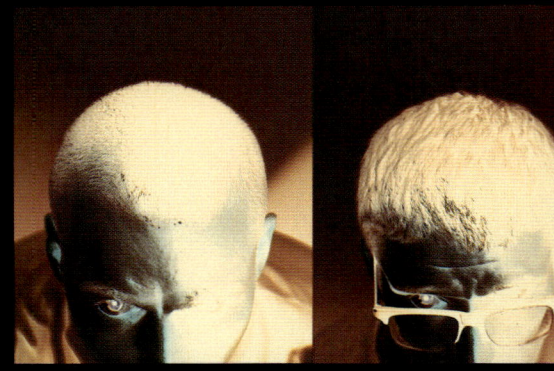

Photography / Kerry Wilson

Two

Before doing your design, rub the point of the Ball Point Pen on a piece of scrap paper until the ink flows smoothly. Put the Ball Point Pen (only) into one of the numbered holes of the wheel, with two fingers hold the ring down, with the other hand, hold the Ball Point Pen upright, and carefully move the Wheel around the inside of the Ring. Always keep the teeth of the Wheel and the Ring in contact with each other while drawing your designs. Start at hole number one on the ring and continue until your line meets where you started. Now you are ready to draw millions of fascinating designs!

図案を描く前に、ボールペンの先を、いらない紙の上でインクが滑らかに出るまでこすること。ボールペンだけを、回転盤の番号の付いた穴のひとつに入れる。2本の指でリングを下ろし、もう一方の手でボールペンをまっすぐに立てる。そして回転盤をリングの内側に沿って、注意深く動かす。図案を描いている間、回転盤の歯とリングが、密接にかみあっているかを常に確認しなくてはならない。リングの一番の穴から始め、線がスタート地点にぶつかるまで続ける。

これで君も、魅力的なデザインを描ける準備が整ったというわけだ。

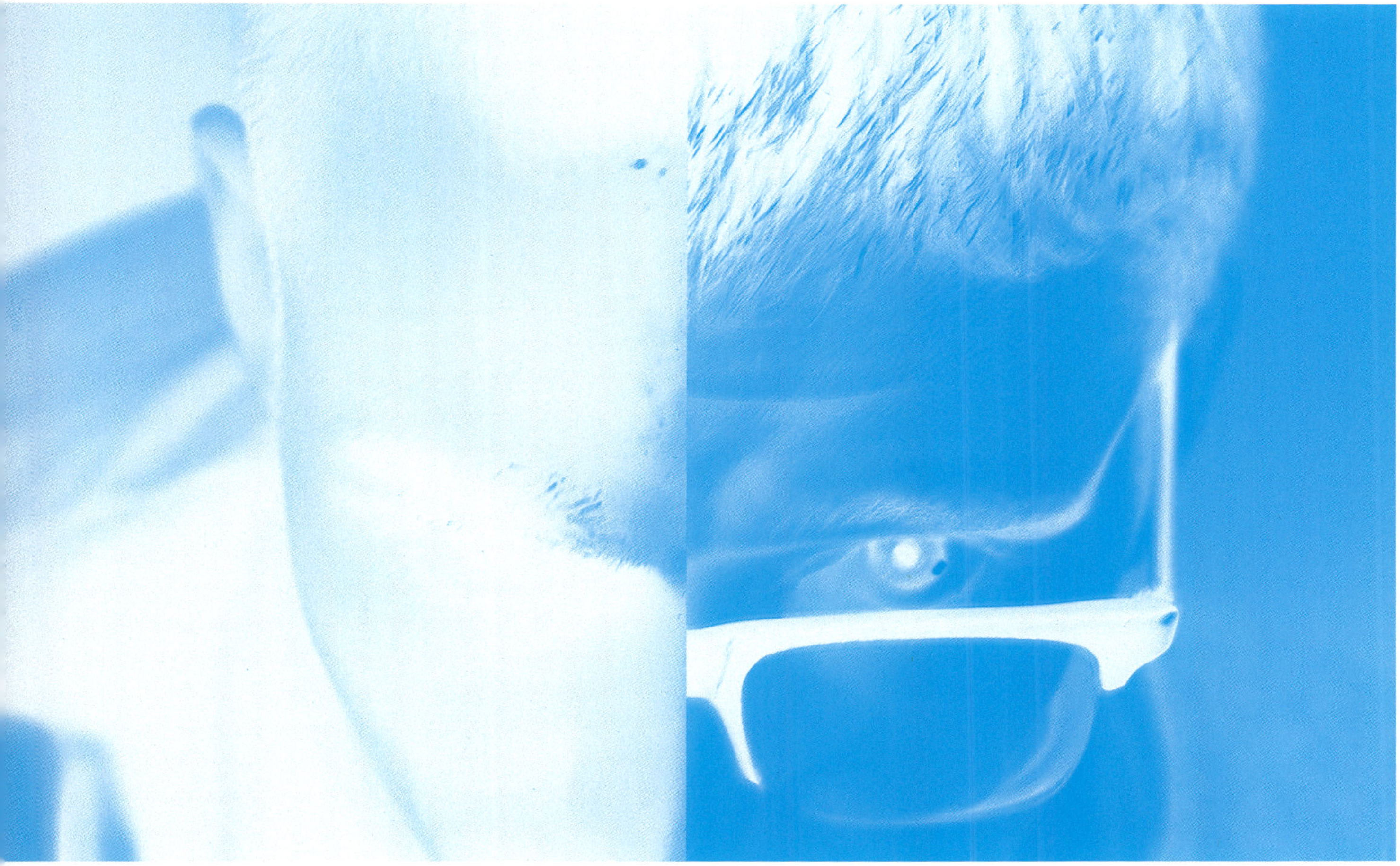

Since our formation in June 1990, we have worked with a broad spectrum of clients. The majority of these are record companies, which provide around 80% of our output. We also fulfill a role as art-directors and as such collaborate regularly with other designers on their projects.

1990年6月の結成以来、私たちはいろいろなクライアントと仕事をしてきた。大部分はレコード会社で、私たちの作品の約8割を占めている。またアート・ディレクターとしての仕事をする際には、他のデザイナーの企画にしたがって、彼らと定期的に話し合いながら、協力し合って仕事を進めて行く。

1. TWO PROMOTION Self-Promotion 1991 AD,D: David Hurren, Ian Hutchings (Two) DF: Two
トゥー プロモーション 宣伝用 個人作品 1991 AD,D: デヴィッド ハレン、イアン ハッチングス（トゥー） DF: トゥー

2.LP Back

2.LP Front

2. BANDERAS / RIPE LP,CD 1991 AD,D: Two P: Chris Nash DF: Two CL: London Records
バンデラス / ライブ LP,CD 1991 AD,D: トゥー P: クリス ナッシュ DF: トゥー CL: ロンドン レコード

2.CD Booklet / Back & Front

2.LP Lyrics / Outside Spread

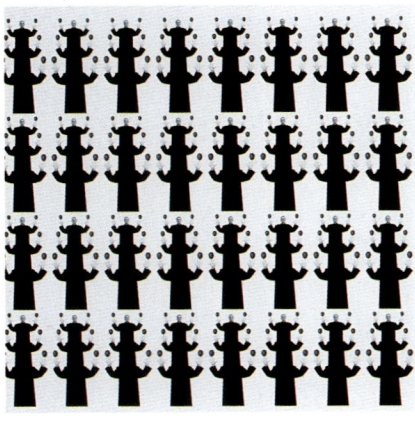
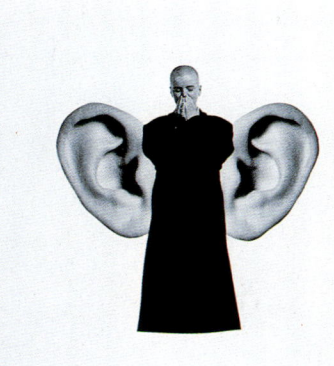

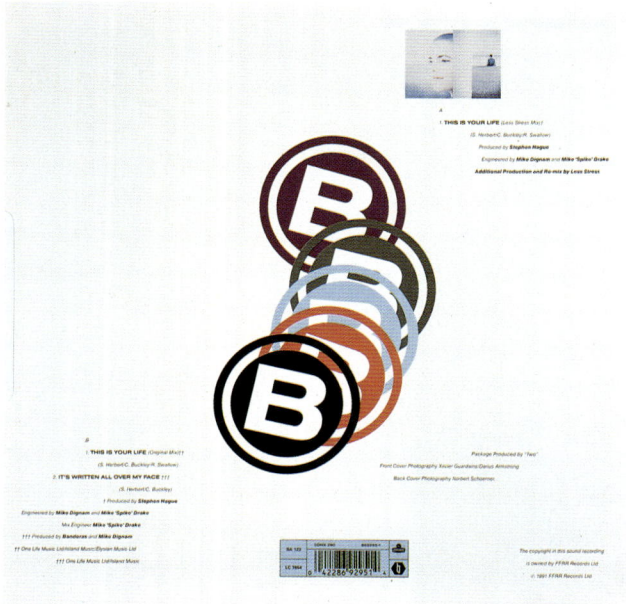

3. BANDERAS / SHE SELLS 7-inch Single 1991 AD,D: Two P: Chris Nash DF: Two CL: London Records
バンデラス / シー セルズ 7インチ シングル 1991 AD,D: トゥー P: クリス ナッシュ DF: トゥー CL: ロンドン レコード

4. BANDERAS / THIS IS YOUR LIFE 7-inch Single 1991 AD,D: Two P: Xavier Guardains DF: Two CL: London Records
バンデラス / ディス イズ ユア ライフ 7インチ シングル 1991 AD,D: トゥー P: ハヴィエア ガーデインズ DF: トゥー CL: ロンドン レコード

5. BANDERAS
THIS IS YOUR LIFE (REMIX)
12-inch Single 1991
AD,D: Two DF: Two CL: London Records
バンデラス
ディス イズ ユア ライフ (リミックス)
12インチ シングル 1991
AD,D: トゥー DF: トゥー CL: ロンドン レコード

6. BANDERAS
WORK IN PROGRESS
Promotional Kit 1990
AD,D: Two DF: Two CL: London Records
バンデラス
ワーク イン プログレス
販促用キット 1990
AD,D: トゥー DF: トゥー CL: ロンドン レコード

7. CATH CARROLL
Promotional Kit 1991
AD,D: Two P: Robert Mapplethorpe
DF: Two CL: Factory Records
キャス キャロル
販促用キット 1991
AD,D: トゥー P: ロバート メイプルソープ
DF: トゥー CL: ファクトリー レコード

7. Package / Outside Spread

8. HELTER SKELTER
ANGEL
12-inch Single(Poster-Wrap) 1991
AD,D: Two P: Lewis Mulatero
DF: Two CL: Island Records
ヘルター スケルター
エンジェル
12インチ シングル（ポスター パック）1991
AD,D: トゥー P: ルイス ムラテロ
DF: トゥー CL: アイランド レコード

9. LEWIS MULATERO
Promotional Kit 1991
AD,D: Two P: Lewis Mulatero
DF: Two CL: Lewis Mulatero
ルイス ムラテロ
販促用キット 1991
AD,D: トゥー P: ルイス ムラテロ
DF: トゥー CL: ルイス ムラテロ

9.Front

8.Front

8.Back

9.Back

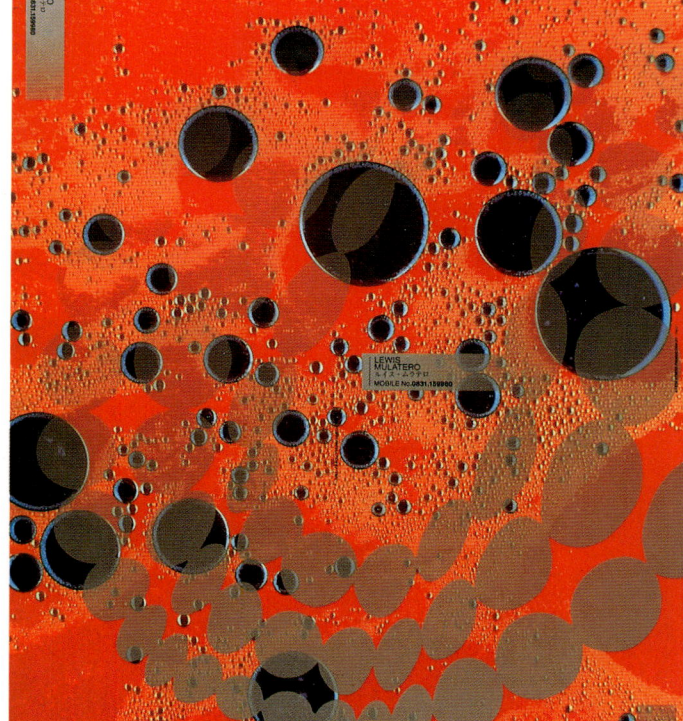

8.Inner Sleeve / Back

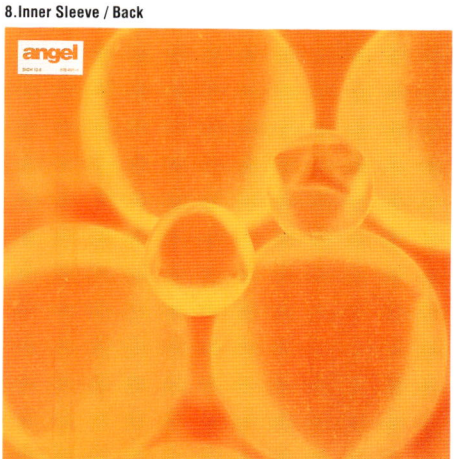

10.Back

10.Front

11.Back

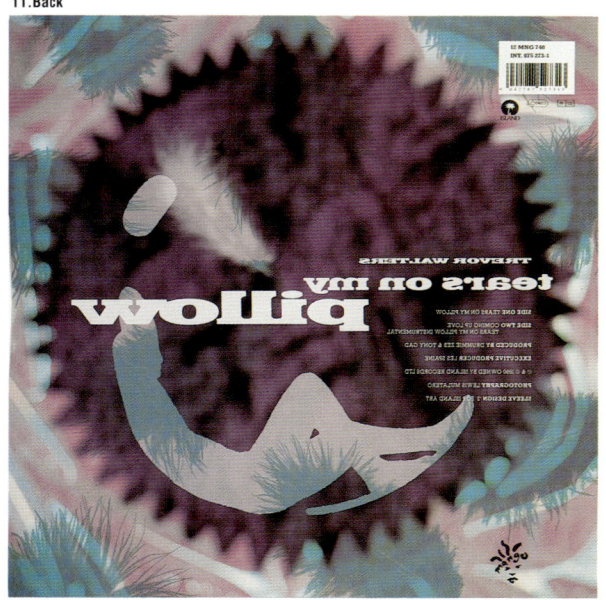

11.Front

10. BEAT SYSTEM / BEAT SYSTEM 12-inch Single 1991 AD,D: Two P: Lewis Mulatero DF: Two CL: Island Records
ビート システム / ビート システム 12インチ シングル 1991 AD,D: トゥー P: ルイス ムラテロ DF: トゥー CL: アイランド レコード

11. TREVOR WALTERS / TEARS ON MY PILLOW 12-inch Single 1990 AD,D: Two P: Lewis Mulatero DF: Two CL: Island Records
トレヴァー ウォルターズ / ティアーズ オン マイ ピロウ 12インチ シングル 1990 AD,D: トゥー P: ルイス ムラテロ DF: トゥー CL: アイランド レコード

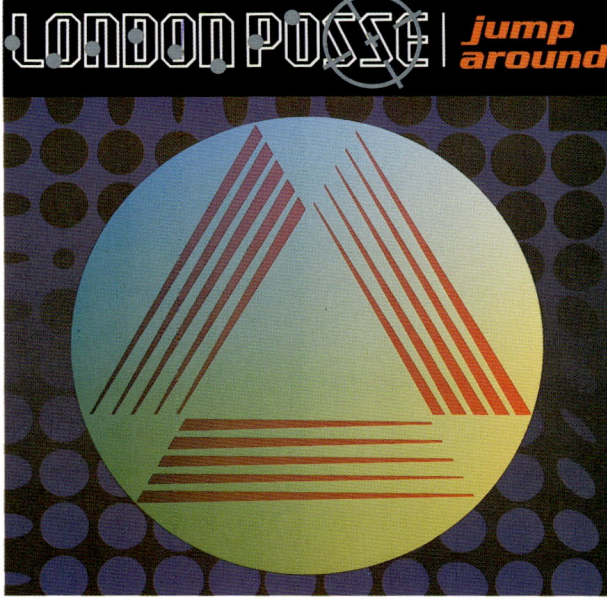

13.

12.

12.

14.

15.

12. SIMPLE MINDS / REAL LIFE Proposal for Images 1990
AD,D: Two P: Rocco Redondo DF: Two CL: Virgin Records
シンプル マインズ / リアル ライフ イメージ考案 1990
AD,D: トゥー P: ロッコ レドンド DF: トゥー CL: ヴァージン レコード

13. LONDON POSSE / JUMP AROUND 12-inch Single 1991
AD,D: Two DF: Two CL: Island Records
ロンドン ポシ / ジャンプ アラウンド 12インチ シングル 1991
AD,D: トゥー DF: トゥー CL: アイランド レコード

14. JANET-LEE DAVIS / PLEASURE SEEKERS 12-inch Single 1991
AD,D: Two P: Kerry Wilson DF: Two CL: Island Records
ジャネット-リー デイヴィス / プレジャー シーカーズ 12インチ シングル 1991
AD,D: トゥー P: ケリー ウィルソン DF: トゥー CL: アイランド レコード

15. BASSCUT / I'M NOT IN LOVE 12-inch Single 1991
AD,D: Two DF: Two CL: A.V.L
ベースカット / アイム ノット イン ラヴ 12インチ シングル 1991
AD,D: トゥー DF: トゥー CL: A.V.L

16.

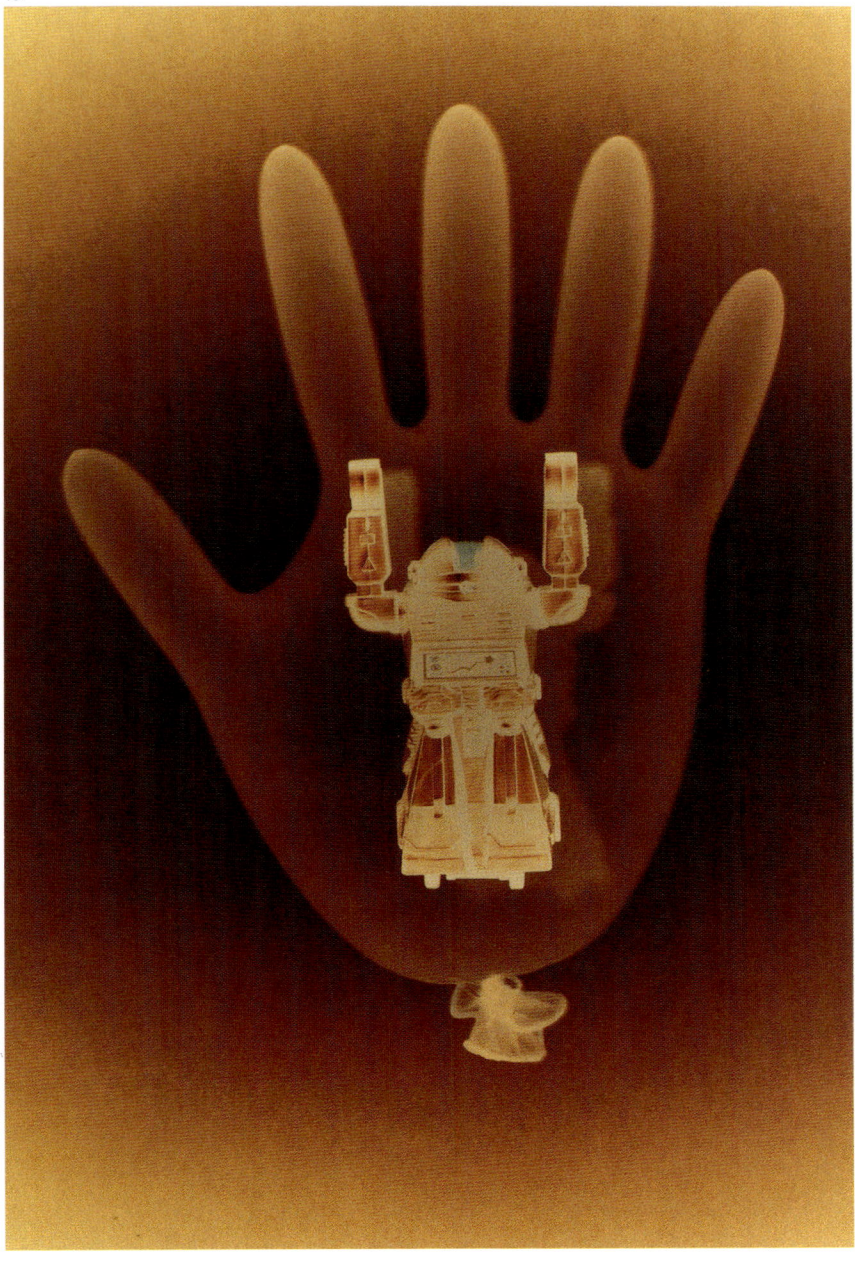

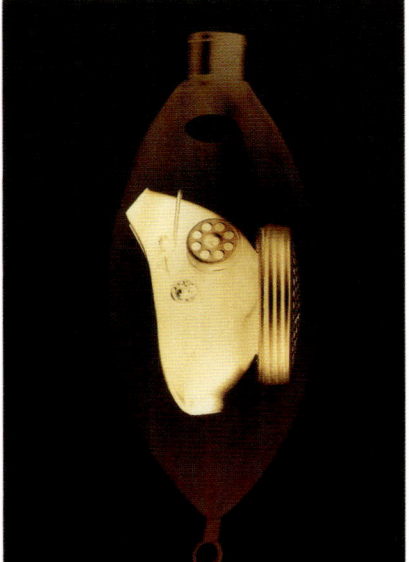

16. TWO PUBLICITY
Self-Promotion 1991
AD,D,P: Two DF: Two
トゥー パブリシティ
宣伝用 個人作品 1991
AD,D,P: トゥー DF: トゥー

Nobuaki Takahashi

Looking back, there is no unity in my work. When designing, I never go back to old ideas for inspiration. I'm the kind of person who gets bored easily, and when a design reaches the color-proof stage, I've already lost interest. Though I don't confine myself to particular musical genres or artists, most of my assignments for the music business have been for rock bands. I don't turn down jobs for commercial pop or jazz, and I don't even want to limit myself to music—I'm quite happy to do advertising—but being lazy, I don't expand the range of my work on my own initiative. I usually don't do presentations for clients: if I had to present several alternatives and ask them to choose the best, I would no longer feel responsible for the project. They just have to trust me to make the right choices. When I work, the thing I put my heart into is respecting the music's individuality and message and trying to convey it the best way possible. What I enjoy most about working with talented musicians is that it is always stimulating and gives me the chance to break out of the my own limitations.

こうして見ると、僕の作品には統一性がないですね。デザインをする上で、自分の過去の作品のアイディアを焼きなおして、繰り返して現在のスタイルを作るということはあまりやりません。むしろあきっぽい性格なので、いつも色校が出る頃にはもう、その作品にあきているのです。音楽のジャンルやアーティストの音楽性にもこだわりはありませんが、若い人向けのロック・ミュージシャンの仕事が多いです。歌謡曲やらジャズやら、別に音楽にこだわらずとも広告やら何やら、何でもやりたいのですが、めんどくさがりやなもので、自分から進んで仕事の幅を広げることができないのです。クライアントへのプレゼンもほとんどしませんが、信用してまかせてもらっています。何パターンもデザインを考えていると、しまいには無責任になってしまうと思うのです。何がベストなのか、判断するのは自分ですから。

僕が作品制作の際に心がけていることは、ミュージシャンの意向と個性を尊重すること、わかりやすくキャッチーであること、それでいて非凡であること、でしょうか？　才能あるミュージシャンと仕事していると、いつもいい刺激があって楽しいし、結果的に自分のせまいワクを飛び越えた仕事ができるので、みなさんに感謝してます。この場を借りてお礼を言います。

Nobuaki Takahashi was born in Dai-Yubari, Hokkaido, in 1956. After graduating from the Kuwasawa Design Institute in 1978, he joined *Epic/Sony Records*. He left the company in 1989 to found the *bahaty* Design Office.

1956年、北海道大夕張に生まれる。1978年、桑沢デザイン研究所を卒業、後にエピック・ソニー レコードに入社。1989年、エピック・ソニー レコードを退社し、フリーとしての活動を始める。同年、デザイン・オフィス「bahaty」を設立。

1. YOSHIYUKI OSAWA / SCRAP STORIES Promotional Poster 1987 AD,D: Nobuaki Takahashi P: Naoto Okawa S: Yuko Shimada SET: Big Art DF: bahaty CL: Epic / Sony Records
大沢 誉志幸 / スクラップ ストーリーズ 販促用ポスター 1987 AD,D: 高橋伸明 P: 大川直人 S: 島田優子 SET: ビッグ アート DF: バハティ CL: エピック ソニー レコード

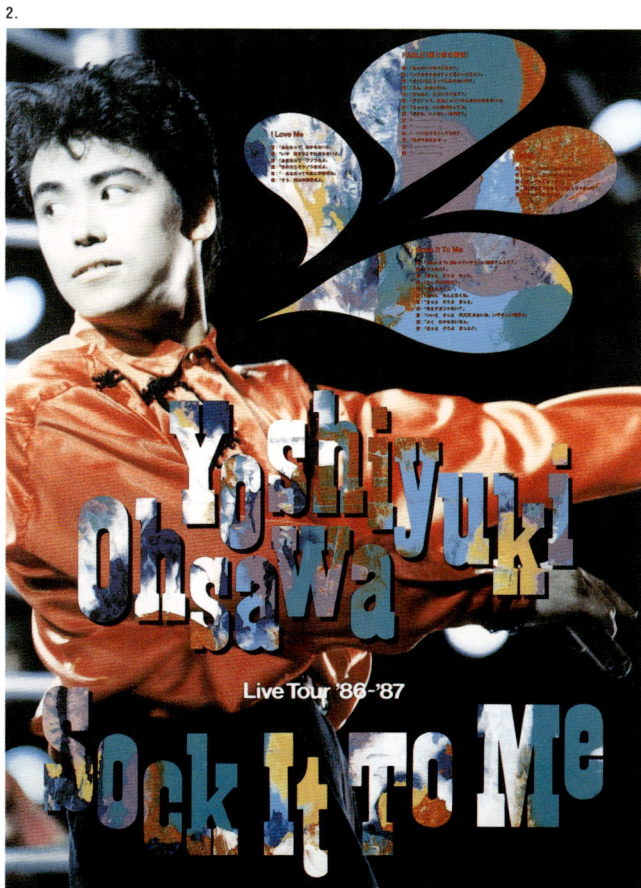

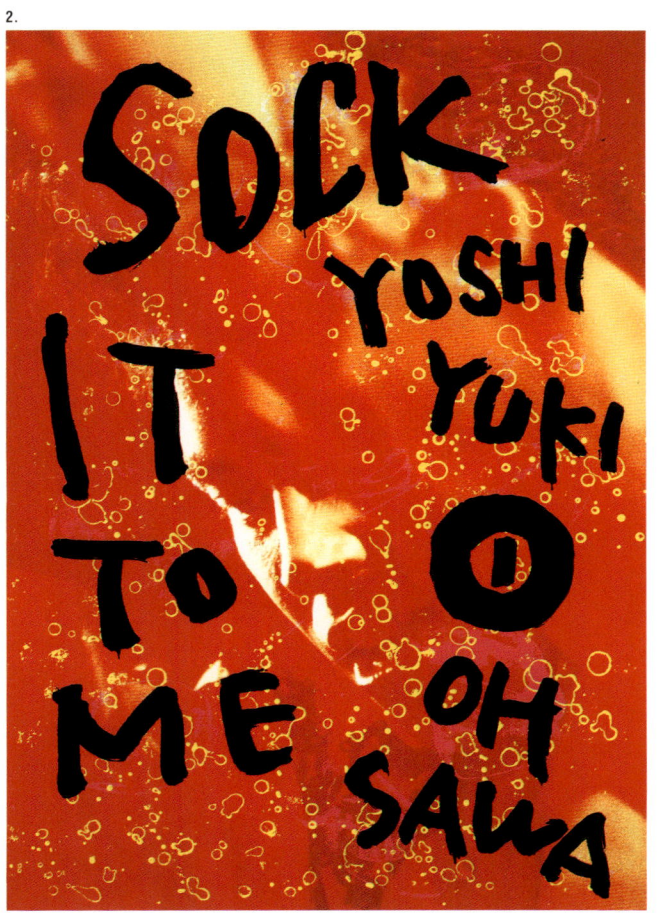

2. YOSHIYUKI OSAWA / SOCK IT TO ME Concert Poster 1986
AD,D: Nobuaki Takahashi DF: bahaty CL: Hip Land Music
大沢 誉志幸 / ソック イット トゥ ミー コンサート ポスター 1986
AD,D: 高橋伸明 DF: バハティ CL: ヒップ ランド ミュージック

3. YOSHIYUKI OSAWA / SOCK IT TO ME II Concert Poster 1987
AD,D: Nobuaki Takahashi DF: bahaty CL: Hip Land Music
大沢 誉志幸 / ソック イット トゥ ミー II コンサート ポスター 1987
AD,D: 高橋伸明 DF: バハティ CL: ヒップ ランド ミュージック

4.

4. YOSHIYUKI OSAWA / LIFE Promotional Poster 1986 AD,D: Nobuaki Takahashi P: Naoto Okawa OBJECT: Yoshihito Tada(Tada Bijutsu) DF: bahaty CL: Epic / Sony Records
大沢 誉志幸 / ライフ 販促用ポスター 1986 AD,D: 高橋伸明 P: 大川直人 OBJECT: 多田佳人 DF: バハティ CL: エピック ソニー レコード

5. YOSHIYUKI OSAWA / LIFE LP 1986 AD,D: Nobuaki Takahashi P: Naoto Okawa OBJECT: Yoshihito Tada(Tada Bijutsu) DF: bahaty CL: Epic / Sony Records
大沢 誉志幸 / ライフ LP 1986 AD,D: 高橋伸明 P: 大川直人 OBJECT: 多田佳人 DF: バハティ CL: エピック ソニー レコード

5.Inner Sleeve

5.Front

6.Lyrics

6.Front

6. YASUYUKI OKAMURA / YELLOW LP 1987
AD,D: Nobuaki Takahashi P: Naoto Okawa DF: bahaty CL: Epic / Sony Records
岡村靖幸 / イエロー LP 1987
AD,D: 高橋伸明 P: 大川直人 DF: バハティ CL: エピック ソニー レコード

7.Cover / Front & Outside Spreads

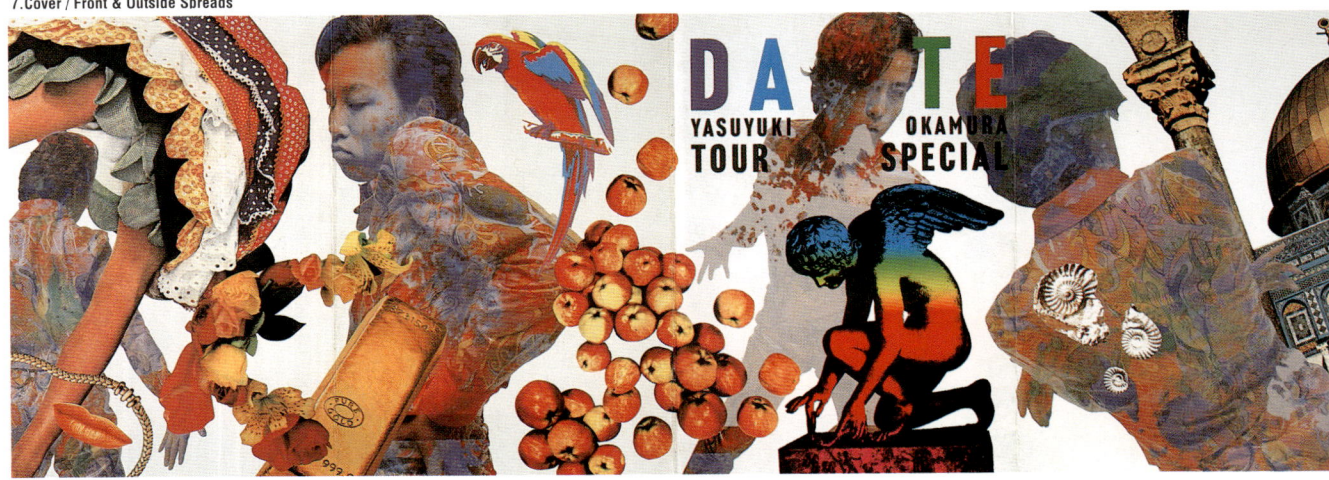

8.

8.

7. YASUYUKI OKAMURA / DATE
Concert Program 1989
AD,D: Nobuaki Takahashi P: Naoto Okawa
DF: bahaty CL: Pop Rock Company
岡村靖幸 / デート
コンサート パンフレット 1989
AD,D: 高橋伸明 P: 大川直人
DF: バハティ CL: ポップ ロック カンパニー

8. TMN / RHYTHM RED
Photography Collection 1990
AD,D,I: Nobuaki Takahashi P: Naoto Okawa
DF: bahaty CL: Sony Magazines
TMN / リズム レッド
写真集 1990
AD,D,I: 高橋伸明 P: 大川直人
DF: バハティ CL: ソニー マガジンズ

9. YASUYUKI OKAMURA / KATEI KYOSHI
CD 1990
AD,D,I: Nobuaki Takahashi DF: bahaty
CL: Epic / Sony Records
岡村靖幸 / 家庭教師
CD 1990
AD,D,I: 高橋伸明 DF: バハティ
CL: エピック ソニー レコード

9.Booklet / Back & Front

10.Booklet / Back & Front

10.Booklet / Page Spread

11.Booklet / Back & Front

10. YOSHIYUKI OSAWA / SERIOUS BARBARIAN Ⅱ CD 1989
AD,D: Nobuaki Takahashi P: Naoto Okawa, Nanako Sato
DF: bahaty CL: Epic / Sony Records
大沢 誉志幸 / シリアス バーバリアン Ⅱ CD 1989
AD,D: 高橋伸明 P: 大川直人、佐藤 奈々子
DF: バハティ CL: エピック ソニー レコード

11. YOSHIYUKI OSAWA / SERIOUS BARBARIAN Ⅲ ＜RAKUEN＞ CD 1991
AD,D: Nobuaki Takahashi P: Naoto Okawa
DF: bahaty CL: Epic / Sony Records
大沢 誉志幸 / シリアス バーバリアン Ⅲ ＜楽園＞ CD 1991
AD,D: 高橋伸明 P: 大川直人
DF: バハティ CL: エピック ソニー レコード

12. TM NETWORK
HUMAN SYSTEM LP 1988
AD,D: Nobuaki Takahashi
D: Katsutoshi Shiozaki P: Naoto Okawa
OBJECT: Yoshihito Tada(Tada Bijutsu)
DF: bahaty CL: Epic / Sony Records
TMネットワーク
ヒューマン システム LP 1988
AD,D: 高橋伸明
D: 塩崎勝利 P: 大川直人
OBJECT: 多田佳人
DF: バハティ
CL: エピック ソニー レコード

13. TO BE CONTINUED
TO BE CONTINUED… CD 1991
AD,D: Nobuaki Takahashi
D: Toshiki Yoshida P: Naoto Okawa
DF: bahaty
CL: Sony Records
トゥ ビー コンティニュード
トゥ ビー コンティニュード… CD 1991
AD,D: 高橋伸明
D: 吉田俊樹 P: 大川直人
DF: バハティ
CL: ソニー レコード

12.Front

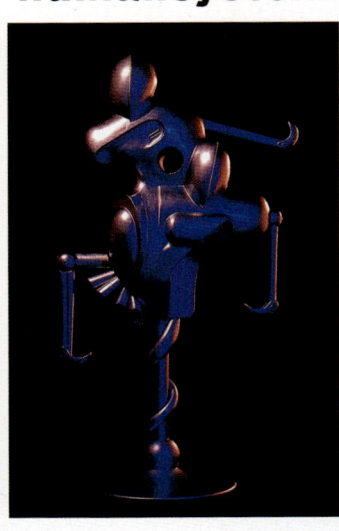

12.Back

13.Back & Front

13.

Self Control

Bang The Gong   Maria Club   Don't Let Me Cry   Self Control   All-Right All-Night
Fighting   Time Passed Me By   Spanish Blue   Fool On The Planet   Here, There & Everywhere

TM Network

14. TM NETWORK / SELF CONTROL
Promotional Poster 1987
AD,D: Nobuaki Takahashi P: Naoto Okawa
DF: bahaty CL: Epic / Sony Records
TMネットワーク / セルフ コントロール
販促用ポスター 1987
AD,D: 高橋伸明 P: 大川直人
DF: バハティ CL: エピック ソニー レコード

15. FENCE OF DEFENSE
Concert Poster 1991
AD,D: Nobuaki Takahashi P: Herbie Yamaguchi
DF: bahaty CL: FAN
フェンス オヴ ディフェンス
コンサート ポスター 1991
AD,D: 高橋伸明 P: ハービー 山口
DF: バハティ CL: ファン

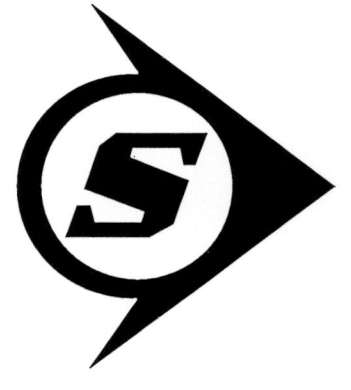

170

Ian Swift

I discovered graphic design by looking at magazines like *The Face, i-D* and *Blitz.* This urged me to look at typographic design rather than fine art. Following in the footsteps of Malcolm Garrett and Peter Saville, I secured a place at Manchester Polytechnic. In my final year I designed and produced *Fresh* handed down to me by David Crow. This gave me an outlet to explore typography in the Manchester tradition and my work was spotted by Neville Brody and he asked me to work on *The Face* magazine, and I joined as a junior designer, While still working on *The Face* I was asked by publisher Nick Logan to do some design work on a new publication called *Arena* - again working with Neville.
Not wanting to get branded as a magazine designer, and to broaden my horizons I took a job at Neville Brody's Studio as a senior designer and left *The Face*. This proved a valuable experience as I was working on all manner of projects - book covers, posters, record covers, corporate logos etc. After Neville Brody left Arena I took over as art director until '91 when I left to pursue other directions, At the moment *Straight No Chaser* is the main magazine that I design and probably the most influential work. I started designing *SNC* about two and a half years ago after meeting publisher Paul Bradshaw, I was very interested in producing magazines on *Apple Mac* computer which at that time was very rare. Through my work at *Straight No Chaser* I was introduced to Gilles Peterson who was starting up a record label called *Talkin Loud*. He asked me to design his logo which led to me designing all the sleeves. At this present moment *SNC* and *Talkin Loud* occupy most of my time, but other projects which are under way are a *Swifty* T-Shirt range; developing typefaces on the computer to publish and sell, and Film posters are an area of design I would like to get into.

ワシントン・アート・カレッジ在学中に、僕は『The Face』や『i-D』、『Blitz』といった雑誌を通して、デザインにめぐりあった。これがきっかけとなって、ファイン・アートの世界からタイポグラフィーへ矛先を変えたのだ。マルコム・ギャレットやピーター・サヴィルの後に継いでマンチェスター工芸学校に入学し、卒業した年に、デヴィッド・クロウに渡された雑誌『Fresh』でデザインとプロデュースを務めた。この雑誌のおかげでマンチェスターの伝統的なタイポグラフィーを経験することができ、僕の作品は、学校で講演をしていたネヴィル・ブロディの目にとまったのだった。ネヴィルが薦めてくれたこともあって、その後僕は『The Face』にジュニア・デザイナーとして参加、ここではデザインと印刷技術のことを、その業界でもトップの人たちから学ぶことができた。

『The Face』で仕事をしている時に、出版社のニック・ローガンから新雑誌『Arena』への参加を呼びかけられた。当初は双方の雑誌のデザインを両立させていたが、雑誌のデザイナーだけでなく、幅広く自分の可能性を広げたかったため『The Face』を退き、ネヴィル・ブロディ・デザインでシニア・デザイナーとして働きだした。ここでは、本のジャケットや、ポスター、レコード・ジャケット、CIロゴなどいろいろなものを手がけることができ、非常に大切な経験を得たのだ。また同時に、ネヴィルが手を引いてからの『Arena』のADを、1991年まで務めた。

1991年にフリーの活動を始めてからは、レコード・ジャケットの依頼を重点的に受けていたが、現在では雑誌『Straight No Chaser』(SNC) をメインに仕事をしている。この雑誌のデザインは、おそらく僕に最も影響を与えた仕事だと思う。2年半ほど前に、発行者のポール・ブラッドショーと出会ってからSNCのメンバーに加わったが、当時では非常にめずらしかったマッキントッシュ・コンピュータを使ってページ作りをすることに、とても興味を持った。またSNCの仕事を通して、『Talkin Loud』というレコード・レーベルを始めようとしていたジャイルス・ピーターソンにも出会えた。彼の依頼でレーベルのロゴマークを手がけ、しだいにほとんどのレコード・ジャケットをデザインできるようになったのだ。

SNCと『Talkin Loud』にほとんどの時間を費やしているような毎日だが、進行中のプロジェクトの中には、「A Swifty T-Shirt」という、コンピュータを使ったタイプ・フェイスを開発し、それをブランドとしてプリント販売する試みもある。今後は、映画のポスターのデザインにも取り組みたいと思っている。

Ian Swift was born in Merseyside. Liverpool in 1965. He graduated from Manchester Polytechnic in 1986 with a BA HONS in Graphic Design. His professional work experience includes designer for *The Face* magazine from 1986-1988 and designer and art director for *Arena* magazine from 1988-1990. His later years at *Arena* coincided with a position as senior designer at *Neville Brody Studio*. He presently freelances for clients such as *Straight No Chaser* magazine, *Talkin Loud* records and *Phonogram Records*.

イアン・スウィフトは1965年、マーシーサイド州リヴァプールに生まれる。1986年にマンチェスター工芸学校 (Ba Hons) を卒業後、1988年まで『The Face』のデザイナーを担当。1988年から1991年までは『Arena』のADとデザインに携わりながら、ネヴィル・ブロディ・デザインのシニア・デザイナーとして活躍する。現在は雑誌『Straight No Chaser』をはじめ、レコード・レーベル『Talkin Loud』やフォノグラムをクライアントに持つ、フリーのデザイナーとして活動中。

1. YOUNG DISCIPLES / GET YOURSELF TOGETHER
12-inch Single 1991
D: Ian Swift P: Chris Clunn
DF: Swifty Typographics CL: Talkin Loud Records
ヤング ディサイプルズ / ゲット ユアセルフ トゥゲザー
12インチ シングル 1991
D: イアン スウィフト P: クリス クラン
DF: スウィフティ タイポグラフィックス CL: トーキン ラウド レコード

2. YOUNG DISCIPLES / APPARENTLY NOTHIN'
12-inch Single 1991
D: Ian Swift P: Chris Clunn
DF: Swifty Typographics CL: Talkin Loud Records
ヤング ディサイプルズ / アパレントリー ナッシング
12インチ シングル 1991
D: イアン スウィフト P: クリス クラン
DF: スウィフティ タイポグラフィックス CL: トーキン ラウド レコード

3. YOUNG DISCIPLES / ROAD TO FREEDOM
LP 1991
D: Ian Swift P: Chris Clunn
DF: Swifty Typographics CL: Talkin Loud Records
ヤング ディサイプルズ / ロード トゥ フリーダム
LP 1991
D: イアン スウィフト P: クリス クラン
DF: スウィフティ タイポグラフィックス CL: トーキン ラウド レコード

2. Back

2. Front
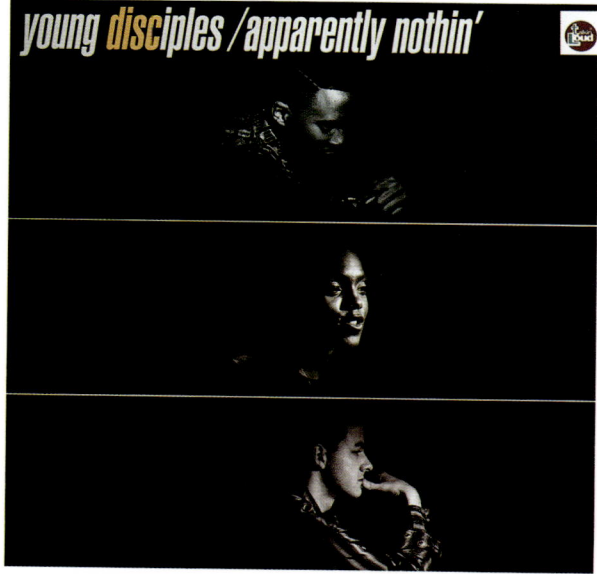

3. Back

3. Front
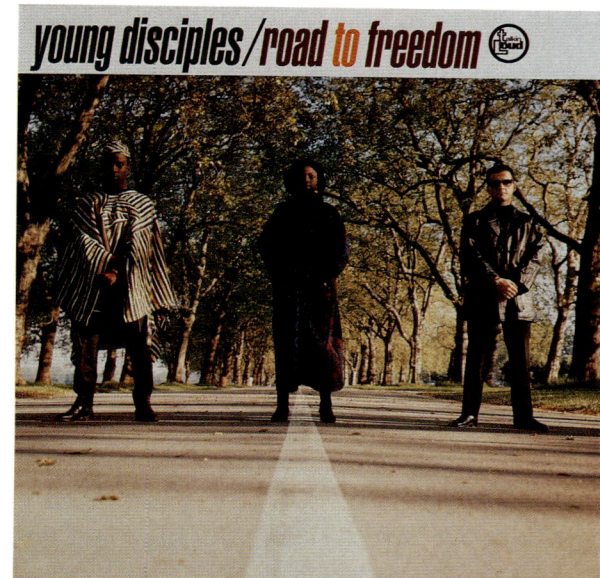

4. Front

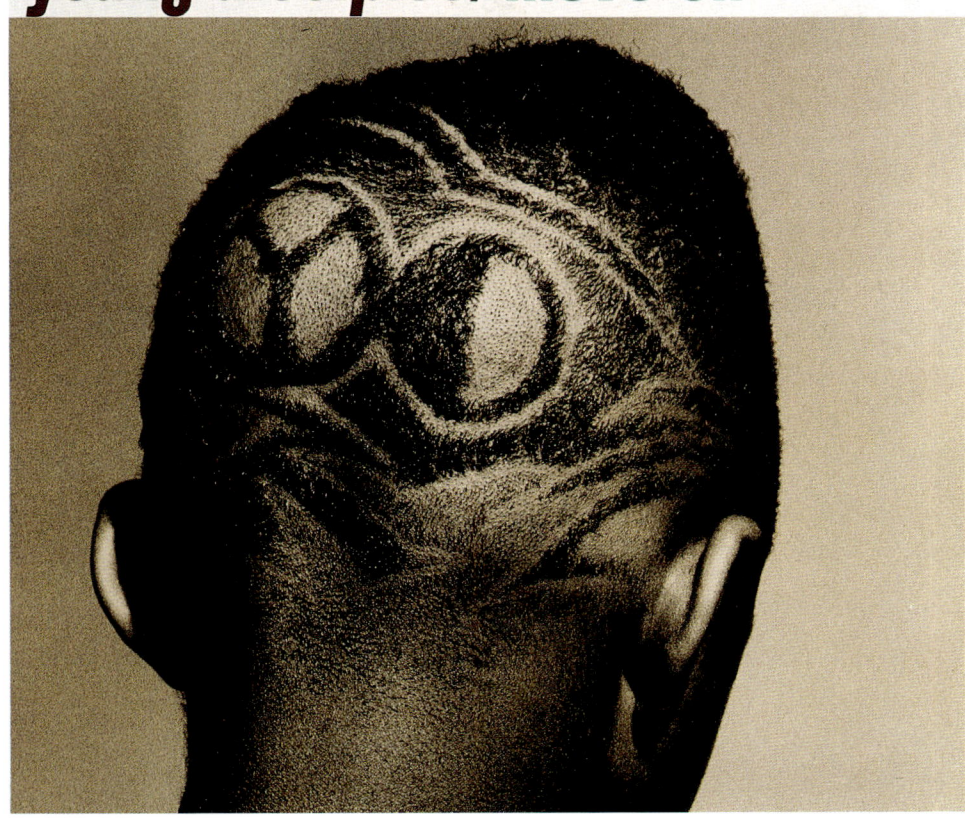

4. Back

4. YOUNG DISCIPLES
MOVE ON
12-inch Single 1991
D: Ian Swift P: Chris Clunn
DF: Swifty Typographics
CL: Talkin Loud Records
ヤング ディサイプルズ
ムーヴ オン
12インチ シングル 1991
D: イアン スウィフト **P:** クリス クラン
DF: スウィフティ タイポグラフィックス
CL: トーキン ラウド レコード

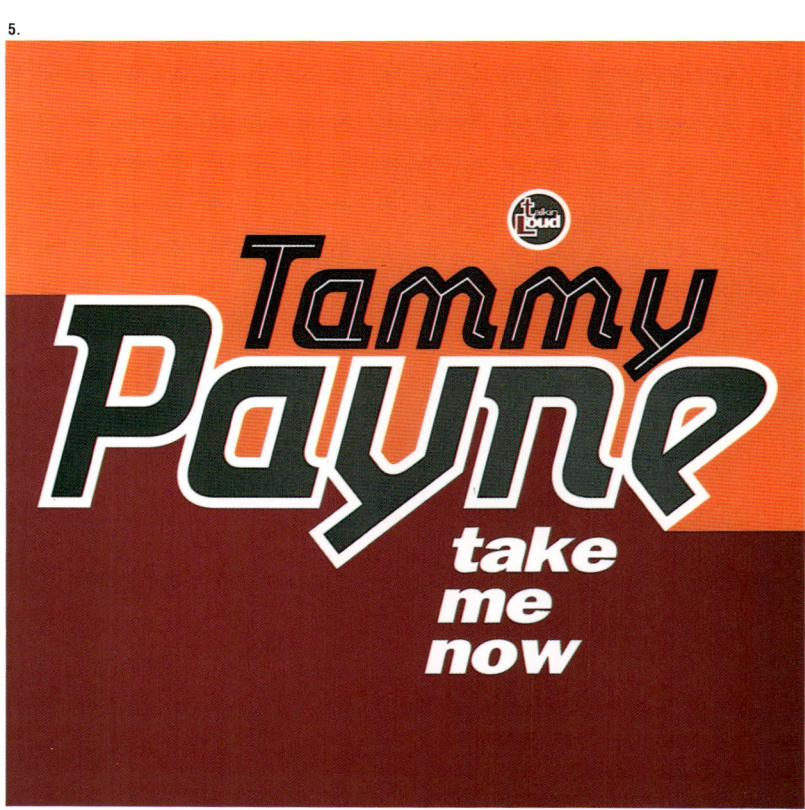

5. TAMMY PAYNE
TAKE ME NOW
12-inch Single 1991
D: Ian Swift
DF: Swifty Typographics
CL: Talkin Loud Records
タミー ペイン
テイク ミー ナウ
12インチ シングル 1991
D: イアン スウィフト
DF: スウィフティ タイポグラフィックス
CL: トーキン ラウド レコード

6. C.F.M. BAND
JAZZ IT UP
12-inch Single 1991
D: Ian Swift
I: Ian Wright
DF: Swifty Typographics
CL: Island Records
C.F.M.バンド
ジャズ イット アップ
12インチ シングル 1991
D: イアン スウィフト
I: イアン ライト
DF: スウィフティ タイポグラフィックス
CL: アイランド レコード

7. GALLIANO
NOTHING HAS CHANGED
12-inch Single 1991
D: Ian Swift
P: Chris Clunn
DF: Swifty Typographics
CL: Talkin Loud Records
ガリアーノ
ナッシング ハズ チェンジド
12インチ シングル 1991
D: イアン スウィフト
P: クリス クラン
DF: スウィフティ タイポグラフィックス
CL: トーキン ラウド レコード

6.Back

6.Front

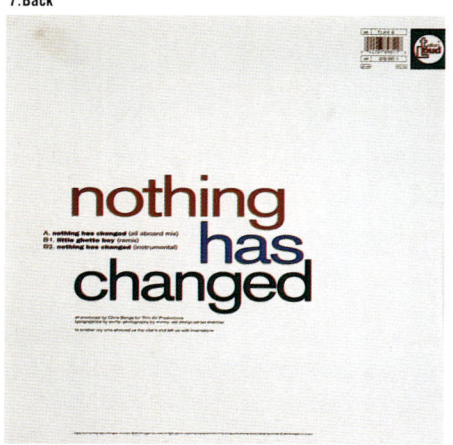

7.Back

7.Front

8.Front

8. GALLIANO / POWER + GLORY 12-inch Single 1991 D: Ian Swift I: Chris Long DF: Swifty Typographics CL: Talkin Loud Records
ガリアーノ / パワー＋グローリー 12インチ シングル 1991 D: イアン スウィフト I: クリス ロング DF: スウィフティ タイポグラフィックス CL: トーキン ラウド レコード

8.Back

9. MAZE 91 Promotional Poster 1991
D: Ian Swift CW: Jon Wozencroft DF: Swifty Typographics CL: Font Shop International
MAZE 91 販促用ポスター 1991
D: イアン スウィフト CW: ジョン ウォーゼンクラフト DF: スウィフティ タイポグラフィックス
CL: フォント ショップ インターナショナル

10. VIBRA-ZONE Logo 1991 D: Ian Swift DF: Swifty Typographics CL: Gilles Peterson
ヴィブラ-ゾーン ロゴマーク 1991
D: イアン スウィフト DF: スウィフティ タイポグラフィックス CL: ジャイルス ピーターソン

11. K-CREATIVE Logo 1991 D: Ian Swift DF: Swifty Typographics CL: Talkin Loud Records
K-クリエイティヴ ロゴマーク 1991
D: イアン スウィフト DF: スウィフティ タイポグラフィックス CL: トーキン ラウド レコード

12. RED＋HOT＋DANCE Logo 1991 D: Ian Swift DF: Swifty Typographics CL: Palace Pictures
レッド＋ホット＋ダンス ロゴマーク 1991
D: イアン スウィフト DF: スウィフティ タイポグラフィックス CL: パレス ピクチャーズ

13. PERCEPTION Logo 1991 D: Ian Swift DF: Swifty Typographics CL: Talkin Loud Records
パーセプション ロゴマーク 1991
D: イアン スウィフト DF: スウィフティ タイポグラフィックス CL: トーキン ラウド レコード

14. TALKIN LOUD PROMO BAG Record Sleeve 1990 D: Ian Swift DF: Swifty Typographics CL: Talkin Loud Records
トーキン ラウド プロモ バッグ レコード スリーヴ 1990
D: イアン スウィフト DF: スウィフティ タイポグラフィックス CL: トーキン ラウド レコード

15. PATRICK FORGE / A DIFFERENT BAG Flyer 1991 D: Ian Swift DF: Swifty Typographics CL: Patrick Forge
パトリック フォージ / ア ディファレント バッグ リーフレット 1991
D: イアン スウィフト DF: スウィフティ タイポグラフィックス CL: パトリック フォージ

16. INNER CITY BLUES Flyer 1991 D: Ian Swift DF: Swifty Typographics CL: Norman Jay
インナー シティ ブルース リーフレット 1991
D: イアン スウィフト DF: スウィフティ タイポグラフィックス CL: ノーマン ジェイ

17. CONTROVERSY Flyer 1990 D: Ian Swift DF: Swifty Typographics CL: Underworld Club
コントロヴァーシー リーフレット 1990
D: イアン スウィフト DF: スウィフティ タイポグラフィックス CL: アンダーワールド クラブ

18.

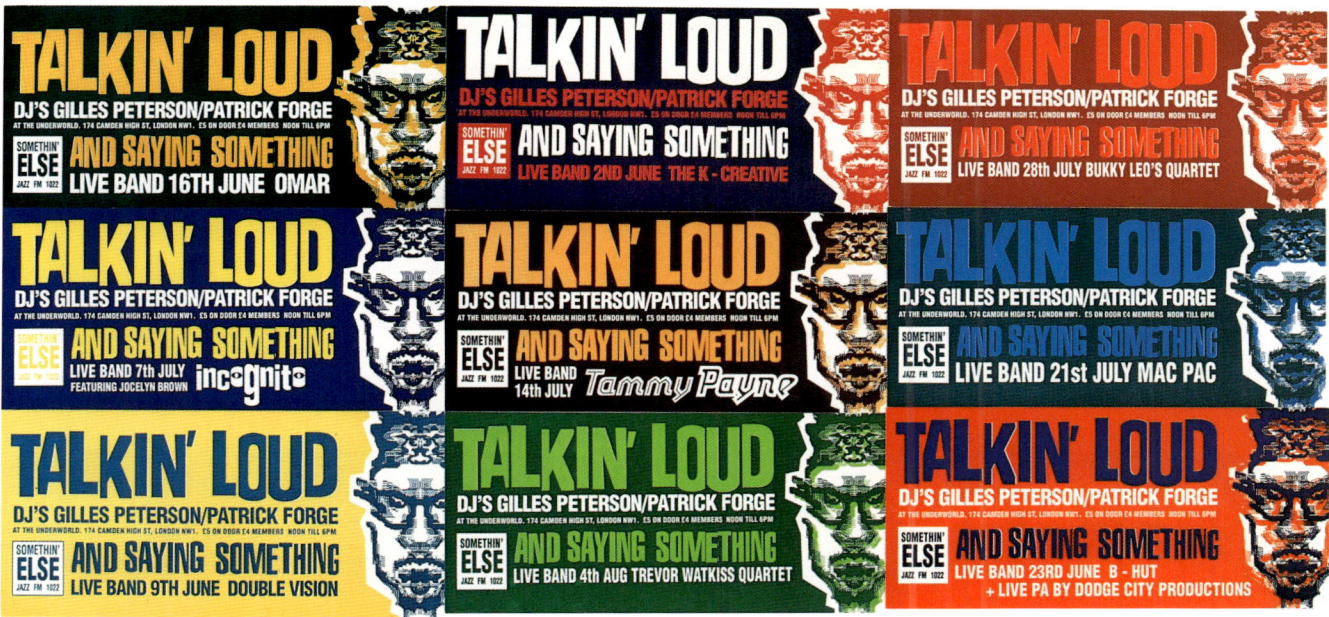

19.
20.
21.

18. TALKIN LOUD AND SAYING SOMETHING
Flyer 1991
D: Ian Swift I: Ian Wright
DF: Swifty Typographics CL: Underworld Club
トーキン ラウド アンド セイイング サムシング
リーフレット 1991
D: イアン スウィフト I: イアン ライト
DF: スウィフティ タイポグラフィックス CL: アンダーワールド クラブ

19. GALLIANO
Promotional T-Shirt 1991
D: Ian Swift DF: Swifty Typographics
CL: World Chief
ガリアーノ
販促用Tシャツ 1991
D: イアン スウィフト DF: スウィフティ タイポグラフィックス
CL: ワールド チーフ

20. GALLIANO / POWER + GLORY
Promotional T-Shirt 1991
D: Ian Swift I: Chris Long
DF: Swifty Typographics CL: World Chief
ガリアーノ / パワー＋グローリー
販促用Tシャツ 1991
D: イアン スウィフト I: クリス ロング
DF: スウィフティ タイポグラフィックス CL: ワールド チーフ

21. INCOGNITO
Promotional T-Shirt 1991
D: Ian Swift DF: Swifty Typographics
CL: Ricochet
インコグニート
販促用Tシャツ 1991
D: イアン スウィフト DF: スウィフティ タイポグラフィックス
CL: リコシェイ

22. Cover / Back & Front

22.

23.

23. Cover / Back & Front

24. Cover / Back & Front

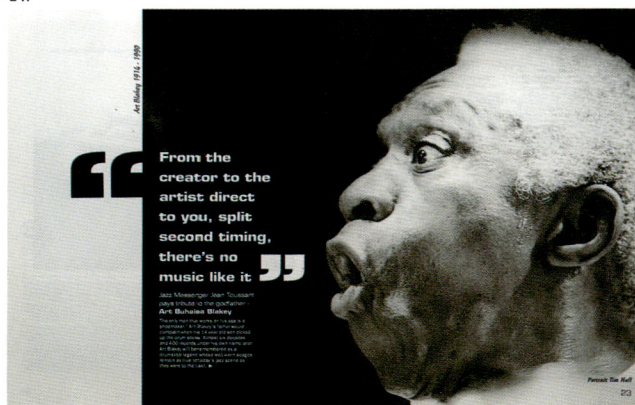

24.

22. STRAIGHT NO CHASER ＜NO.7＞　Magazine 1990　D: Ian Swift　P: Peter Williams　DF: Swifty Typographics　CL: Straight No Chaser
ストレート ノー チェイサー ＜NO.7＞　雑誌 1990　D: イアン スウィフト　P: ピーター ウィリアムズ　DF: スウィフティ タイポグラフィックス　CL: ストレート ノー チェイサー

23. STRAIGHT NO CHASER ＜NO.9＞　Magazine 1990　D: Ian Swift　P: Nick White　DF: Swifty Typographics　CL: Straight No Chaser
ストレート ノー チェイサー ＜NO.9＞　雑誌 1990　D: イアン スウィフト　P: ニック ホワイト　DF: スウィフティ タイポグラフィックス　CL: ストレート ノー チェイサー

24. STRAIGHT NO CHASER ＜NO.10＞　Magazine 1990　D: Ian Swift　P: Alex Shaftel　DF: Swifty Typographics　CL: Straight No Chaser
ストレート ノー チェイサー ＜NO.10＞　雑誌 1990　D: イアン スウィフト　P: アレックス シャフテル　DF: スウィフティ タイポグラフィックス　CL: ストレート ノー チェイサー

25.

25. Cover / Back & Front

26. Cover / Back & Front

25.

26.

27. Cover / Back & Front

25. STRAIGHT NO CHASER <NO.13> Magazine 1991 D: Ian Swift P: Chris Clunn DF: Swifty Typographics CL: Straight No Chaser
ストレート ノー チェイサー <NO.13> 雑誌 1991 D: イアン スウィフト P: クリス クラン DF: スウィフティ タイポグラフィックス CL: ストレート ノー チェイサー

26. STRAIGHT NO CHASER <NO.12> Magazine 1991 D: Ian Swift P: Chris Clunn DF: Swifty Typographics CL: Straight No Chaser
ストレート ノー チェイサー <NO.12> 雑誌 1991 D: イアン スウィフト P: クリス クラン DF: スウィフティ タイポグラフィックス CL: ストレート ノー チェイサー

27. STRAIGHT NO CHASER <NO.11> Magazine 1991 D: Ian Swift P: Nick White DF: Swifty Typographics CL: Straight No Chaser
ストレート ノー チェイサー <NO.11> 雑誌 1991 D: イアン スウィフト P: ニック ホワイト DF: スウィフティ タイポグラフィックス CL: ストレート ノー チェイサー

28. INCOGNITO
CRAZY FOR YOU
12-inch Single 1991
D: Ian Swift
P: Simon Fowler
DF: Swifty Typographics
CL: Talkin Loud Records
インコグニート
クレイジー フォー ユー
12インチ シングル 1991
D: イアン スウィフト
P: サイモン ファウラー
DF: スウィフティ タイポグラフィックス
CL: トーキン ラウド レコード

29. INCOGNITO
ALWAYS THERE
12-inch Single 1991
D: Ian Swift
P: Simon Fowler
DF: Swifty Typographics
CL: Talkin Loud Records
インコグニート
オールウェイズ ゼア
12インチ シングル 1991
D: イアン スウィフト
P: サイモン ファウラー
DF: スウィフティ タイポグラフィックス
CL: トーキン ラウド レコード

28.

29. Back

29. Front

30.

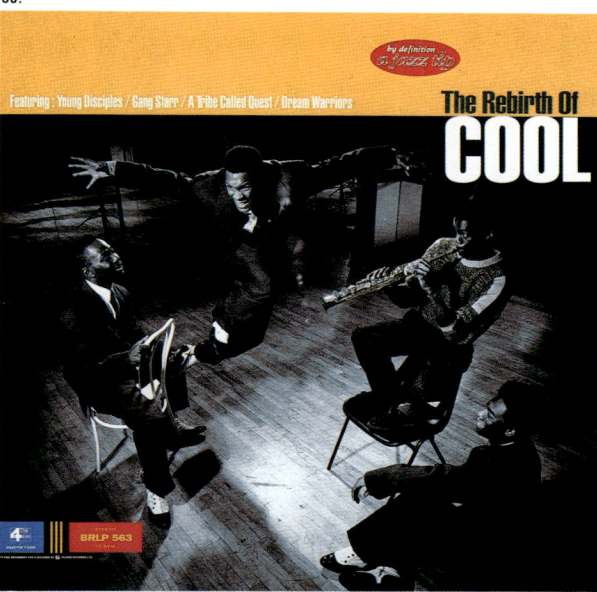

31.

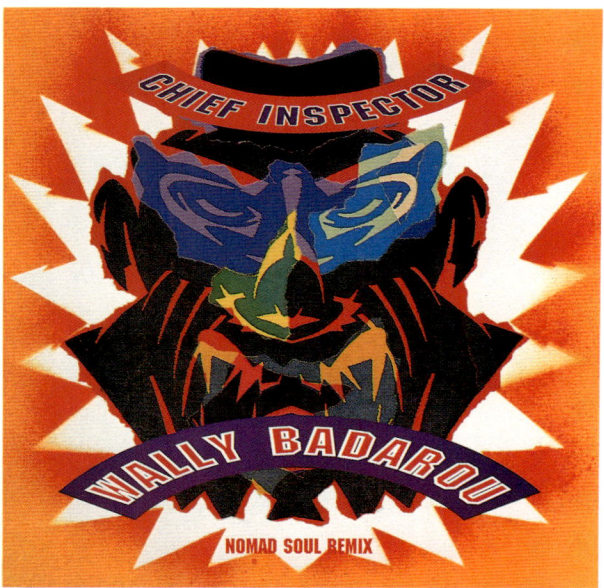

32. Back & Front

30. THE REBIRTH OF COOL (COMPILATION) LP 1991
D: Ian Swift, Ian Wright P: Nick White
DF: Swifty Typographics CL: Island Records
ザ リバース オヴ クール（コンピレーション） LP 1991
D: イアン スウィフト、イアン ライト P: ニック ホワイト
DF: スウィフティ タイポグラフィックス CL: アイランド レコード

31. WALLY BADAROU / CHIEF INSPECTOR 12-inch Single 1991
D: Ian Swift I: Ian Wright DF: Swifty Typographics CL: Island Records
ウォリー バダロウ / チーフ インスペクター 12インチ シングル 1991
D: イアン スウィフト I: イアン ライト
DF: スウィフティ タイポグラフィックス CL: アイランド レコード

32. TALKIN LOUD LP 1990
D: Ian Swift I: Ian Wright
DF: Swifty Typographics CL: Talkin Loud Records
トーキン ラウド LP 1990
D: イアン スウィフト I: イアン ライト
DF: スウィフティ タイポグラフィックス CL: トーキン ラウド レコード

Ken Sakaguchi

Ken Sakaguchi's work has many faces. Anger and aggressiveness, sorrow and foolishness, joy and pain, the din of the city, heartbeats on the streets, madness hiding within peace, life and death. In other words, humanity and everything arround it. Above all, he is trying to express the human condition—the feelings that occur as long as human beings breathe, walk, sleep and live on this planet. Regardless of the theme of the project: daily life, madness, anti-war, or the world, those who are looking straight at it or rather from side to side, are none other than him and us. This most original and universal theme is very close to something I want to express through music. It's rough and raw texture and stripped down style are similar to my own music. After a night working, drinking, and wandering about the city together, I realize that he and I are the same kind of people— we love people and want to live like humanely. I don't think there is another guy quite like him: so sincere and clumsy when it comes to living, sometimes laughing and crying so much that he gives a bad impression.

/ The Street Beats: Øki (Rock Musician)

サカグチケンの作品にはいくつもの顔がある。怒りや攻撃性、哀しさや愚かさ、喜びや切なさ、都市の騒音、路上に息づく鼓動、平穏の中に潜む狂気、そして生と死……。それは言い換えれば "人間" と、そしてそれを取りまき関わるおよそすべてのものだ。奴はどこまでも "人間" を表現しようとしている。"人間" がこの世界で呼吸をし、歩き、眠り、生きていく以上、必ず生まれてくる問題や感情を描こうとしている。

個々の作品のテーマが例えば "日常" であろうが "狂気" であろうが "反戦" であろうが "世界" であろうが、いずれにせよそれを見据え行動し、いや右往左往しているのは他でもない彼自身であり、俺たち自身だ。実はその最も根源的で普遍的なテーマは俺自身が音楽を通して表現しようとしている事と非常に近く、またその手法……ザラザラとしたむき出しの質感、装飾過多でないスタイルもとても俺の音楽と近いところがある。何度も一緒に作品を作り、また酒を飲み、夜の街を徘徊した上で、俺と彼は同じ匂いを持つ人間だという事を確認した。それは多分最も "人間を好きな" "人間らしく生きていきたい" タイプの人間であると言う事だ。

俺は彼ほど、生き方として誠実で不器用で時にみっともないほど泣き笑う、愛すべきナイスガイを他に知らない。

/The Street Beats : Øki (ロック・ミュージシャン)

Born in Kagawa prefecture in 1964. Graduated in design from Takamatsu College of technology. Besides his one-man shows, *The man who Designs Rock'n Roll, Come Bleed for Our Rights,* and *Dead Start,* he has exhibited at many national and international exhibitions, including *the N.Y.ADC, the Lahati Poster Biennale, Blue International Graphic Biennale,* and *the Toyama Triennale.* He has also worked closely with musicians, and has worked as a commercial art director. He set up *Sakaguchi Ken Factory* in 1990.

1964年香川県生まれ。高松工芸高校デザイン科卒業。『ロックをデザインする男』、『カム・ブリード・フォー・アワ・ライツ』、『デッド・スタート』などのワンマンショーの他、N.Y.ADC国際展、ラハチポスタービエンナーレ、ブルー／国際グラフィックビエンナーレ、トリエンナーレトヤマなど国内外の展覧会多数。交流の深いミュージシャンたちとのジョイント・ワークの他、コマーシャル分野でもアート・ディレクターとして活動。1990年、サカグチケン ファクトリーを設立。

1.

2.

1. THE ROCK BAND / THE ROCK BAND Concert Poster 1987
AD,D: Ken Sakaguchi **P:** Toru Kinoshita **DF:** Sakaguchi Ken Factory **CL:** Music Planters
ザ ロック バンド / ザ ロック バンド コンサート ポスター 1987
AD,D: サカグチ ケン **P:** 木下 透 **DF:** サカグチケン ファクトリー **CL:** ミュージック プランターズ

2. THE ROCK BAND / THE ROCK BAND Logo 1987
AD,D: Ken Sakaguchi **DF:** Sakaguchi Ken Factory **CL:** The Rock Band
ザ ロック バンド / ザ ロック バンド ロゴマーク 1987
AD,D: サカグチ ケン **DF:** サカグチケン ファクトリー **CL:** ザ ロック バンド

3. ANARCHY / DERACINES
Exhibition Poster 1983
AD: Ken Sakaguchi
P: Shinichi Minami
DF: Sakaguchi Ken Factory
CL: Anarchy
アナーキー / デラシネ
展覧会ポスター 1983
AD: サカグチ ケン
P: 南 慎一
DF: サカグチケン ファクトリー
CL: アナーキー

4. ANARCHY / ANARCHY
Exhibition Poster 1983
AD,D,I: Ken Sakaguchi
P: Shinichi Minami
DF: Sakaguchi Ken Factory
CL: Anarchy
アナーキー / アナーキー
展覧会ポスター 1983
AD,D,I: サカグチ ケン
P: 南 慎一
DF: サカグチケン ファクトリー
CL: アナーキー

5. THE ROCK BAND / THE ROCK BAND
Concert Poster 1987
AD,D: Ken Sakaguchi
DF: Sakaguchi Ken Factory
CL: Music Planters
ザ ロック バンド / ザ ロック バンド
コンサート ポスター 1987
AD,D: サカグチ ケン
DF: サカグチケン ファクトリー
CL: ミュージック プランターズ

6. IT'S NOT A DESPAIR THAT FLOWS
Event Poster 1990
AD,D: Ken Sakaguchi
P: Toru Kinoshita
CW: Takayuki Oki
DF: Sakaguchi Ken Factory
湧き出てくるのは絶望じゃない
イヴェント ポスター 1990
AD,D: サカグチ ケン
P: 木下 透
CW: 沖 隆行
DF: サカグチケン ファクトリー

7. MAKE SURE EVERYTHING BEFORE ME
Event Poster 1990
AD,D: Ken Sakaguchi
P: Toru Kinoshita
CW: Takayuki Oki
DF: Sakaguchi Ken Factory
目の前のすべてを確かめたい
イヴェント ポスター 1990
AD,D: サカグチ ケン
P: 木下 透
CW: 沖 隆行
DF: サカグチケン ファクトリー

8. THE SADDEST CITY IN THE WORLD
Event Poster 1989
AD,D: Ken Sakaguchi
P: Kazuhiro Kitaoka
CW: Takayuki Oki
DF: Sakaguchi Ken Factory
世界一悲しい街
イヴェント ポスター 1989
AD,D: サカグチ ケン
P: 北岡一浩
CW: 沖 隆行
DF: サカグチケン ファクトリー

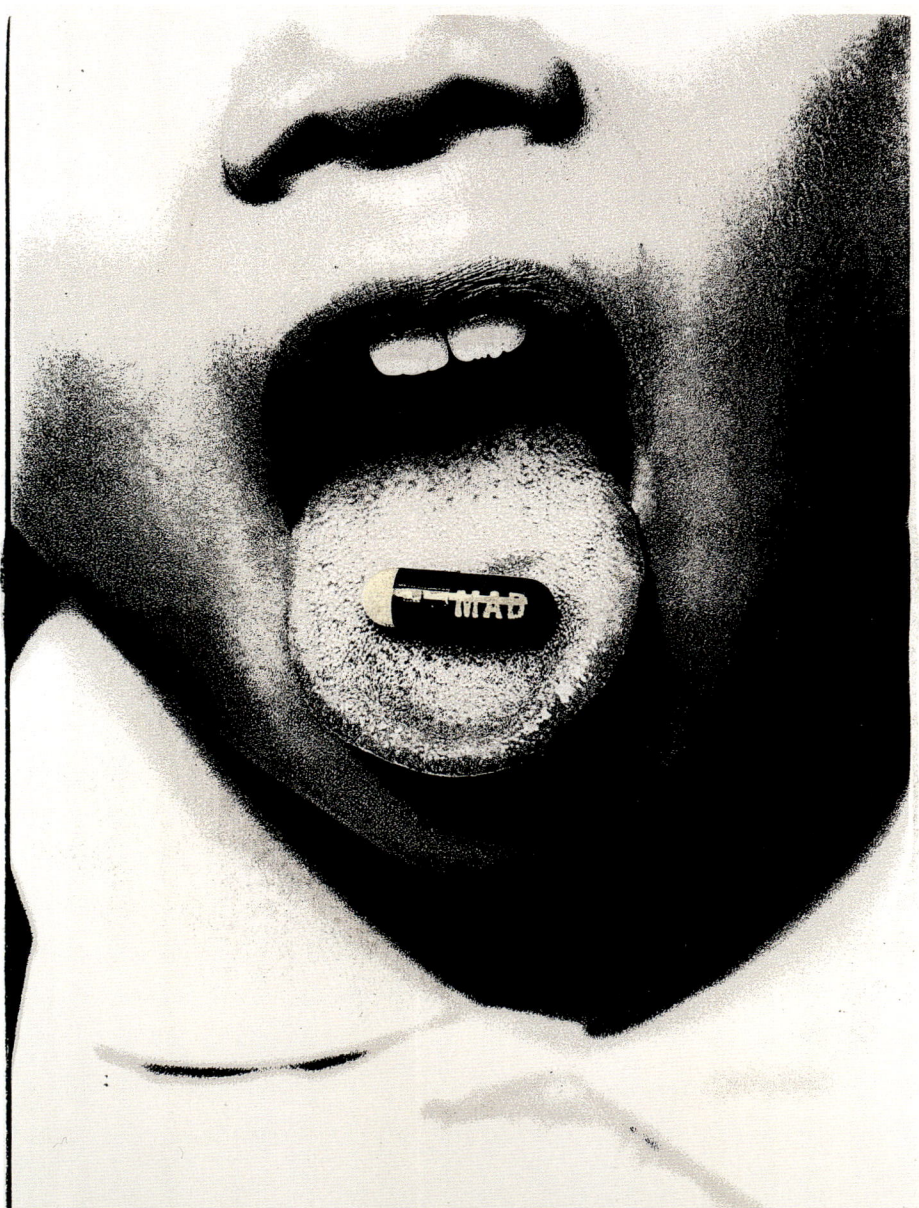

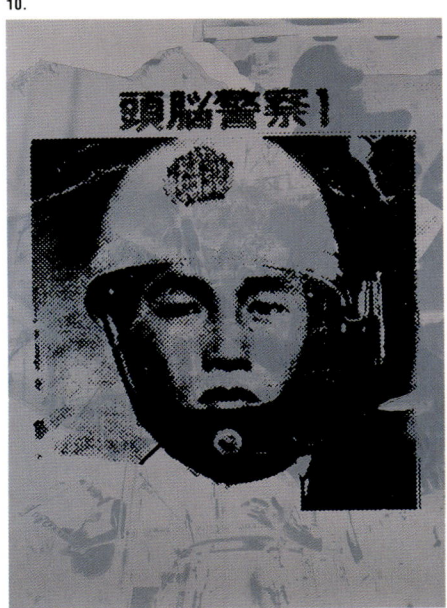

9. DEDICATED TO THE MAD CAPSULE MARKET'S
Exhibition Poster 1991
AD,D: Ken Sakaguchi
P: Kazuhiro Kitaoka
DF: Sakaguchi Ken Factory
THE MAD CAPSULE MARKET'Sに捧ぐ
展覧会ポスター 1991
AD,D: サカグチ ケン
P: 北岡一浩
DF: サカグチケン ファクトリー

10. BRAIN POLICE
BRAIN POLICE 1991
Exhibition Poster 1991
AD,D: Ken Sakaguchi
DF: Sakaguchi Ken Factory
頭脳警察
頭脳警察 1991
展覧会ポスター 1991
AD,D: サカグチ ケン
DF: サカグチケン ファクトリー

11. BRAIN POLICE
NINTH SYMPHONY
Exhibition Poster 1991
AD,D: Ken Sakaguchi
P: Hiro Ito
DF: Sakaguchi Ken Factory
頭脳警察
歓喜の歌
展覧会ポスター 1991
AD,D: サカグチ ケン
P: ヒロ伊藤
DF: サカグチケン ファクトリー

12. THE MAD SUN
<DEDICATED TO BUCK-TICK>
Exhibition Poster 1991
AD,D: Ken Sakaguchi
P: Atsushi Ueda
DF: Sakaguchi Ken Factory
狂った太陽 <バクチクに捧ぐ>
展覧会ポスター 1991
AD,D: サカグチ ケン
P: 植田 敦
DF: サカグチケン ファクトリー

13. BUCK-TICK
TABOO CD 1989
CD: Junichi Tanaka, Buck-Tick
AD,D: Ken Sakaguchi
P: Kazuhiro Kitaoka
DF: Sakaguchi Ken Factory
CL: Victor Musical Industries
バクチク
タブー CD 1989
CD: 田中淳一、バクチク
AD,D: サカグチ ケン
P: 北岡一浩
DF: サカグチケン ファクトリー
CL: ビクター音楽産業

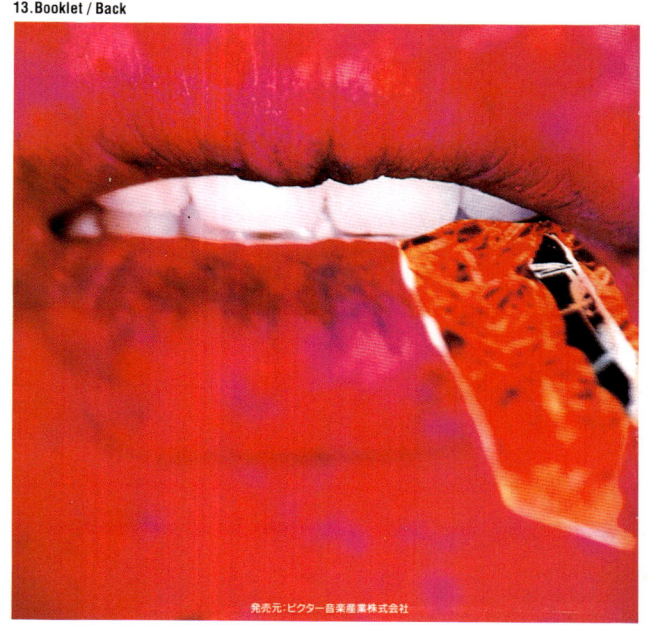

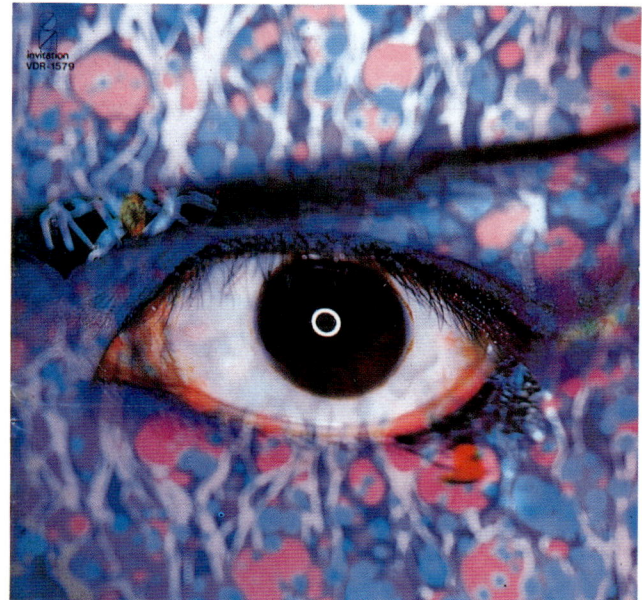

14.

15.

16.

14. THE IMAGE OF HISASHI IMAI IN SABBAT
Promotional Poster 1989
AD,D: Ken Sakaguchi
P: Katsuhiro Ichikawa
DF: Sakaguchi Ken Factory
SABBATにおける今井寿のイメージ
販促用ポスター 1989
AD,D: サカグチ ケン
P: 市川勝弘
DF: サカグチケン ファクトリー

15. BUCK-TICK
M・A・D LD 1991
CD: Buck-Tick
AD,D: Ken Sakaguchi
P: Atsushi Ueda
DF: Sakaguchi Ken Factory
CL: Victor Musical Industries
バクチク
M・A・D LD 1991
CD: バクチク
AD,D: サカグチ ケン
P: 植田 敦
DF: サカグチケン ファクトリー
CL: ビクター音楽産業

16. BUCK-TICK
FLOWER OF EVIL
CD 1990
CD: Junichi Tanaka, Buck-Tick
AD,D: Ken Sakaguchi
D: Keiko Yamamoto
P: Bruno Dayan
DF: Sakaguchi Ken Factory
CL: Victor Musical Industries
バクチク
悪の華
CD 1990
CD: 田中淳一、バクチク
AD,D: サカグチ ケン
D: 山本恵子
P: ブルーノ ダイアン
DF: サカグチケン ファクトリー
CL: ビクター音楽産業

17. **COME BLEED FOR OUR RIGHTS**
Exhibition Poster 1991
AD,D: Ken Sakaguchi
DF: Sakaguchi Ken Factory
自分のために血を流せ！
展覧会ポスター 1991
AD,D: サカグチ ケン
DF: サカグチケン ファクトリー

18. **ROCK SAVES THIS TOWN SHIMABARA**
Event Poster 1991
AD,D,P: Ken Sakaguchi
MODEL: Odd Bowz
DF: Sakaguchi Ken Factory
ロック セイヴス ディス タウン シマバラ
イヴェント ポスター 1991
AD,D,P: サカグチ ケン
MODEL: 横道坊主
DF: サカグチケン ファクトリー

19. **THE MAN WHO DESIGNS ROCK'N ROLL**
Exhibition Poster 1989
AD,D: Ken Sakaguchi
P: Toru Kinoshita
CW: Tatsuya Hayashida
DF: Sakaguchi Ken Factory
ロックをデザインする男
展覧会ポスター 1989
AD,D: サカグチ ケン
P: 木下 透
CW: 林田辰也
DF: サカグチケン ファクトリー

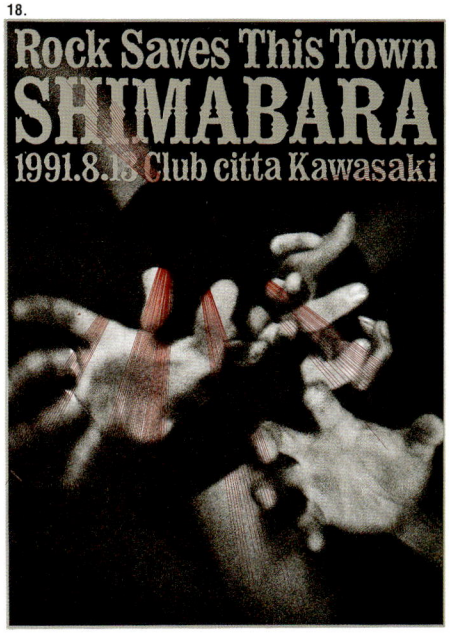

20. 5 COLORS' DEATH Personal Work 1990 AD: Ken Sakaguchi DF: Sakaguchi Ken Factory
5色の死 個人作品 1990 AD: サカグチ ケン DF: サカグチケン ファクトリー

Photography / Kayt Jones

Terry Jones

My design attitude is to mirror a moment in time. I see my role as a conductor. I try to feel the energy and channel its direction to produce, by impulse and intuition, a message. My work is to communicate, using whatever resources I have at hand at the time I produce any work. I like to use old and new technology without the restriction of understanding how it works. I like to react to spontaneous, controlled accidents while in the search of momentary perfect solutions. Often my work is with people who have specific skills, my role as catalyst is to conceive ideas, through the interaction of people, technology and time to produce an image, for magazines, television or any other media. "Instant" is an illusion, an "Instant" is a frozen image in the space of a lifetime.

私のデザインに対する姿勢と言えば、その時々の瞬間をありのままに表現するということだ。自分の役目はオーケストラでいえばコンダクターのようであり、人々が作品のエネルギーを感じとって、衝撃や直観でメッセージを伝えられるようにこころがけている。そのためには、手元にある材料を使ってコミュニケーションすることが必要。古いテクノロジーであれ、最新のテクノロジーであれ、性能のよしあしに関わらず使ってみたい。また完璧なアイディアを探している間に、自然と頭に浮かんでくる事柄にも、反応していきたいと思っている。触媒としての私の役目は、特殊技術を持っている人達と仕事をすることを活かして、雑誌やテレビなどのメディア作りをするために、人々やテクノロジーや時間の相互作用を通したアイディアを考えることである。

「Instant」は、幻覚だ。「Instant」は、人生という空間における凍結したイメージなのだ。

Terry Jones was born in 1945 in Great Britain. After leaving College in 1966 he worked in a design studio in London. In 1970 he became Art Director of *Vanity Fair* before moving to *Vogue* in 1972. Jones left *Conde Nast* in 1977 to start his own studio. Informat Design and Instant Design producing many books, record sleeves, fashion catalogues, videos, television graphics and magazines. Between art directing for various clients like *Charro, Chipie, Fiorucci, Mexx, sportswear Europe* and *Esprit*, Terry Jones started publishing *i-D* magazine in August, 1980. In 1984 a partnership was made with Tony Elliott of *Time Out London* and *i-D* became a wealthy magazine. In September, 1991, UPU started to publish *i-D Japan* with the art direction of Terry Jones. Instant Design exhibitions have been held in London, England; Genoa, Italy; and Tokyo, Japan.

1945年9月2日、イギリスに生まれる。コマーシャル・アートとデザインを学ぶために、4年間、ウェスト・オヴ・イングランド・カレッジ・オヴ・アートに進学。1966年に大学卒業後、ロンドンでデザイン・スタジオの仕事に就く。1970年から『Vanity Fair』のアート・ディレクターを担当、1972年に『Vogue』に移る。5年間『British Vogue』のアート・ディレクターを務めた後、コンドナストを辞めて自分のスタジオを設立。「Informat Design」と「Instant Design」によって、多くの本、レコードジャケット、ファッション・カタログ、ビデオ、テレヴィジョン・グラフィック、雑誌などを手掛けてきた。

『Vogue』や『Donna』などの雑誌や、Charro、Chipie、Fiorucci、Mexxなどの広告代理店、それにEuropeやEspritなどのスポーツウェアのアート・ディレクションを務めるかたわら、1980年8月に「i-D」を創刊。1984年にはTime Out Londonのトニー・エリオットの協力を得て、内容豊かな雑誌に成長していく。また1991年9月から、UPUのアプローチにより「i-D」の日本版「i-D Japan」がスタート。「Instant Design」の展覧会は、すでにロンドン、ジェノバ、東京で開催されている。

1. ARTS BALL Event Poster 1962
CD: Terry Jones DF: Informat Design
CL: West of England College of Art Student Union
アーツ ボール イヴェント ポスター 1962
CD: テリー ジョーンズ DF: インフォーマット デザイン
CL: ウェスト オヴ イングランド カレッジ オヴ アート ステューデント ユニオン

2. CURCUIT MAGAZINE Magazine 1963
CD,D: Terry Jones D: Richard Hollis
CL: West of England College of Art Student Union
サーキット マガジン 雑誌 1963
CD,D: テリー ジョーンズ D: リチャード ハリス
CL: ウェスト オヴ イングランド カレッジ オヴ アート ステューデント ユニオン

3. VOGUE Magazine 1974
AD: Terry Jones P: Bill Cunningham, Norman Parkinson
CL: Conde Naste, Vogue UK
ヴォーグ 雑誌 1974
AD: テリー ジョーンズ P: ビル カニンガム、ノーマン パーキンソン
CL: コンド ナスト、ヴォーグ UK

4. VANITY FAIR Magazine 1970
AD: Terry Jones P: Frank Horvat CL: Vanity Fair
ヴァニティー フェア 雑誌 1970
AD: テリー ジョーンズ P: フランク ホーヴァット CL: ヴァニティー フェア

5. GREED OR GREEN Self-Promotion
AD: Terry Jones DF: Instant Design
グリード オア グリーン 宣伝用 個人作品
AD: テリー ジョーンズ DF: インスタント デザイン

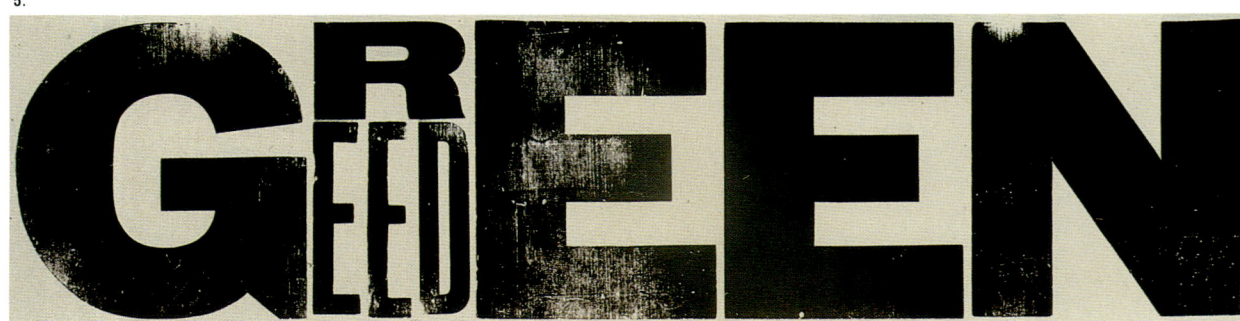

6.

6.Cover / Back & Front

6.

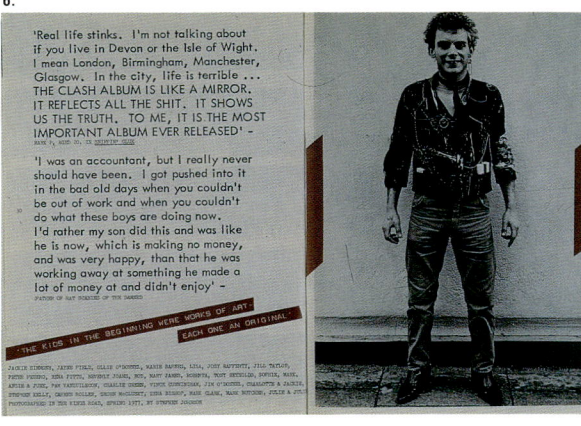

6. NOT ANOTHER PUNK BOOK Punk Rock Book 1978
AD: Terry Jones
P: Norma Moreceau, Dennis Morris, Steve Johnston
CL: Aurum Press
ノット アナザー パンク ブック 単行本 1978
AD: テリー ジョーンズ
P: ノーマ モレシャウ、デニス モリス、スティーヴ ジョンストン
CL: オーラム プレス

7. VOGUE Magazine 1974, 1976
AD: Terry Jones
P: David Bailey, Willie Christie
CL: Conde Nast
ヴォーグ 雑誌 1974, 1976
AD: テリー ジョーンズ
P: デヴィッド バレイ、ウィリー クリスティ
CL: コンド ナスト

6.

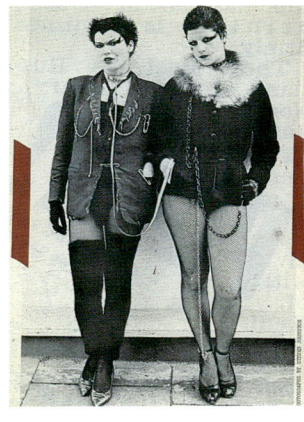

7.

7.

8. WEAR CARE
Self-Promotion 1990
AD: Terry Jones
D: Alan Kitching
DF: Instant Design
ウェアー ケアー
宣伝 個人作品 1990
AD: テリー ジョーンズ
D: アラン キッチング
DF: インスタント デザイン

9. FIORUCCI
Logo 1982
D: Terry Jones
DF: Instant Design
CL: Fiorucci
フィオルッチ
ロゴマーク 1982
D: テリー ジョーンズ
DF: インスタント デザイン
CL: フィオルッチ

10. FIORUCCI
Promotional Poster 1984
AD: Terry Jones
P: Nick Knight
DF: Instant Design
CL: Fiorucci
フィオルッチ
販促用ポスター 1984
AD: テリー ジョーンズ
P: ニック ナイト
DF: インスタント デザイン
CL: フィオルッチ

11. FIORUCCI PORTFORIO
Promotional Brochure 1988
AD: Terry Jones
P: Marcus Thomlinson
CL: Fiorucci Gypsy Jeans
フィオルッチ ポートフォリオ
販促用パンフレット 1988
AD: テリー ジョーンズ
P: マーカス トムリンソン
CL: フィオルッチ ジプシー ジーンズ

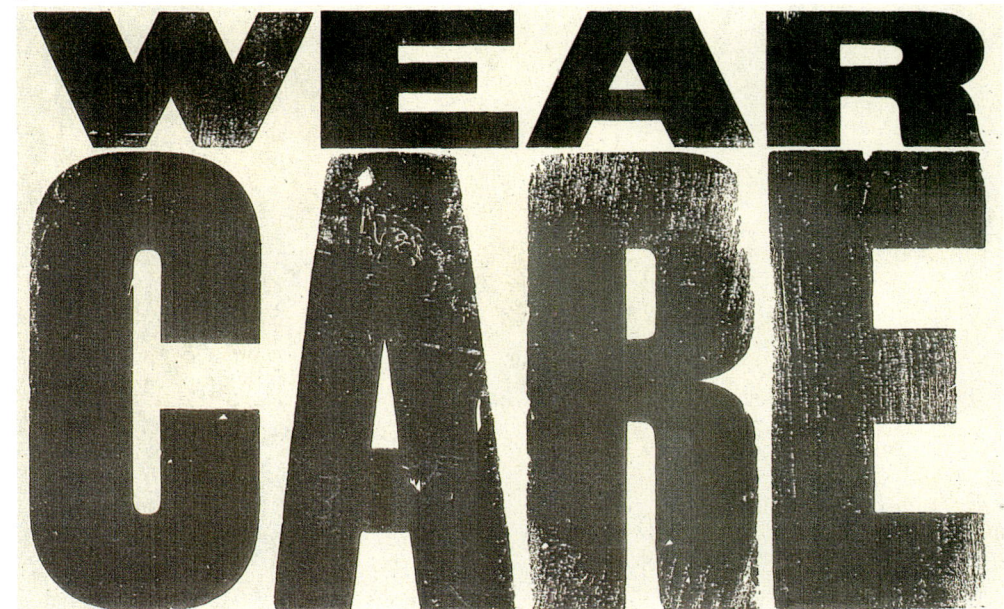

8.

9.

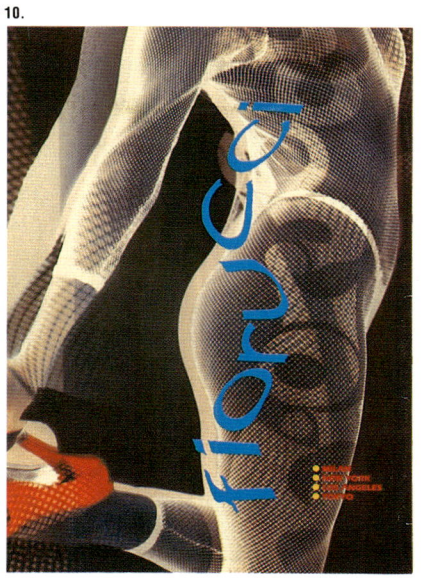

10.

11.

11.

12.

12.

13.

13.

14.

12. MEXX MAGAZINE Promotional Magazine 1987,1988
AD: Terry Jones P: Chico Bialas
DF: Instant Design CL: Mexx
メックス マガジン 販促用 雑誌 1987、1988
AD: テリー ジョーンズ P: チコ ビアラス
DF: インスタント デザイン CL: メックス

13. FIORUCCI CATALOGUE Promotional Brochure 1983,1984
AD: Terry Jones P: Oliviero Toscani
DF: Instant Design CL: Fiorucci
フィオルッチ カタログ 販促用パンフレット 1983、1984
AD: テリー ジョーンズ P: オリヴィエロ トスカーニ
DF: インスタント デザイン CL: フィオルッチ

14. SPORTSWEAR Magazine 1979
AD: Terry Jones P: Oliviero Toscani
CL: Sportswear Europe
スポーツウェア 雑誌 1979
AD: テリー ジョーンズ P: オリヴィエロ トスカーニ
CL: スポーツウェア ヨーロッパ

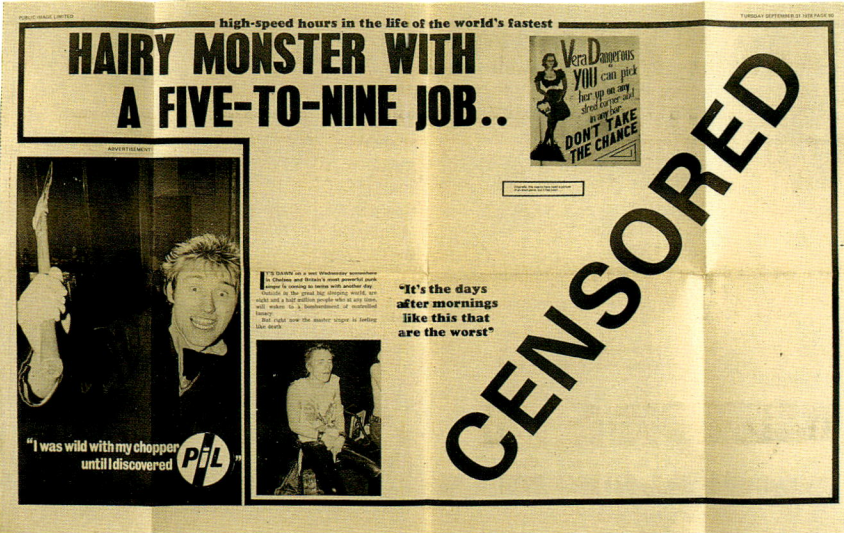

15. PIL / PUBLIC IMAGE 7-inch Single 1978
AD: Terry Jones P: Dennis Morris
DF: Zebulon
PIL / パブリック イメージ 7インチ シングル 1978
AD: テリー ジョーンズ P: デニス モリス
DF: ゼブロン

16. LKJ Promotional Poster 1978
AD: Terry Jones P: Dennis Morris
DF: Zebulon CL: Island Records
LKJ 販促用ポスター 1978
AD: テリー ジョーンズ P: デニス モリス
DF: ゼブロン CL: アイランド レコード

17. BIALAS LETTERHEAD
Business Stationery 1978
AD: Terry Jones CL: Chico Bialas
ビアラス レターヘッド
ビジネス ステーショナリー 1978
AD: テリー ジョーンズ CL: チコ ビアラス

18. PIL Logo 1979
D: Terry Jones DF: Zebulon
CL: Virgin Records
PIL ロゴマーク 1979
D: テリー ジョーンズ DF: ゼブロン
CL: ヴァージン レコード

19.

20.

21.

21.Cover

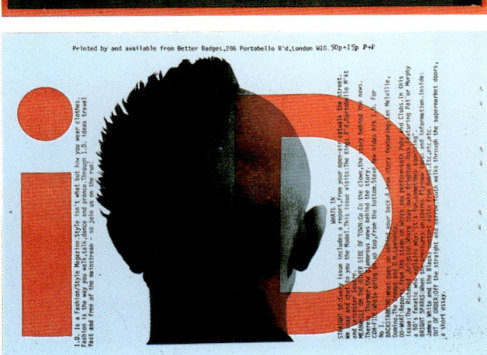

22.
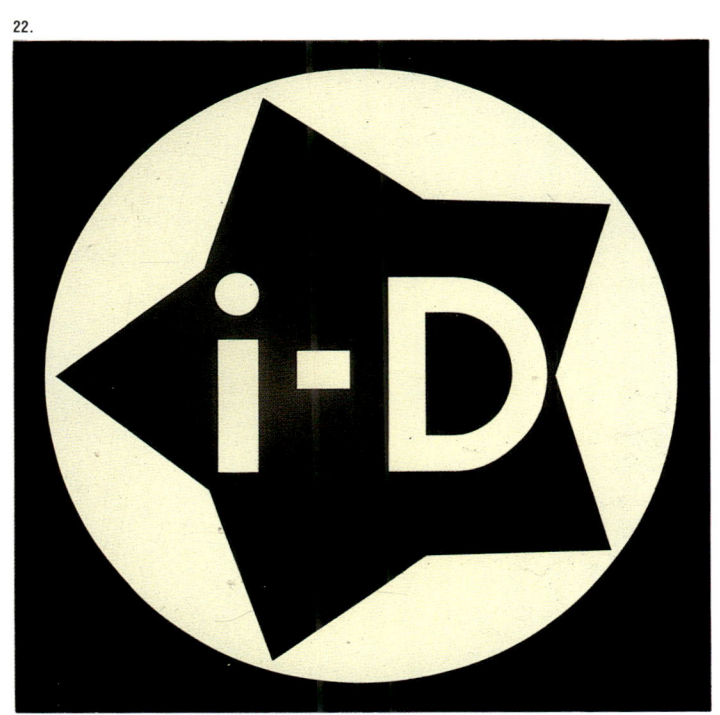

19. i-D COVER Magazine 1980-1988
AD: Terry Jones CL: i-D
i-D (アイディー) カヴァー 雑誌 1980-1988
AD: テリー ジョーンズ CL: i-D

20. i-D ＜EARTH ISSUE＞ Magazine 1989
AD: Terry Jones P: Phil Bickenberg CL: i-D
i-D ＜アース イシュー＞ 雑誌 1989
AD: テリー ジョーンズ P: フィル ビッケンバーグ CL: i-D

21. i-D ＜ISSUE 1＞ Magazine 1980
AD: Terry Jones P: Steve Johnston CL: i-D
i-D ＜創刊号＞ 雑誌 1980
AD: テリー ジョーンズ P: スティーヴ ジョンストン CL: i-D

22. i-D STAR LOGO Logo 1980
CD: Terry Jones DF: Instant Design CL: i-D
i-D スター ロゴ ロゴマーク 1980
CD: テリー ジョーンズ DF: インスタント デザイン CL: i-D

23. i-D ＜BIBLE 2＞ Magazine 1988
CD: Terry Jones DF: Instant Design CL: i-D
i-D ＜バイブル 2＞ 雑誌 1988
CD: テリー ジョーンズ DF: インスタント デザイン CL: i-D

24. INSTANT DESIGN Exhibition Brochure 1986
AD: Terry Jones DF: Instant Design
CL: Commune di Genoa
インスタント デザイン 展覧会パンフレット 1986
AD: テリー ジョーンズ DF: インスタント デザイン
CL: コミュン ディ ジェノア

25. BANK NOTES Nightclub Drink Ticket 1988
D: Terry Jones DF: Instant Design
CL: The Bank Club
バンク ノーツ クラブ用ドリンク チケット 1988
D: テリー ジョーンズ DF: インスタント デザイン
CL: ザ バンク クラブ

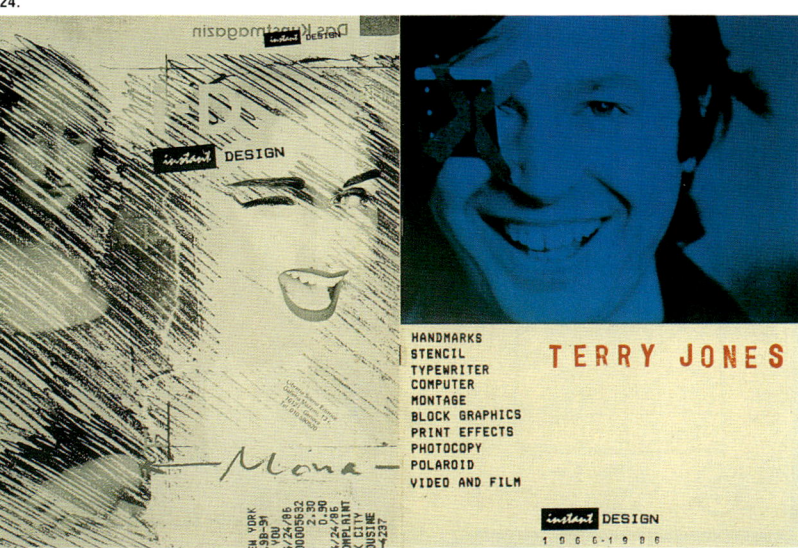

26.

26. TERRY JONES / WINK
Personal Work (for Magazine) 1988
AD: Terry Jones DF: Instant Design
CL: Picabia
テリージョーンズ / ウィンク
個人作品（雑誌掲載用）1988
AD: テリー ジョーンズ　DF: インスタント デザイン
CL: ピカビア

27. TERRY JONES / WINK
Collection of Works 1989
CD: Terry Jones DF: Instant Design
CL: ADT Press
テリージョーンズ / ウィンク
作品集 1989
CD: テリー ジョーンズ　DF: インスタント デザイン
CL: ADTプレス

28. i-D ENCYCLOPEDIA
Book Cover 1989
CD: Terry Jones AD: Steve Male
P: Nick Knight CL: Penguin Books
i-D エンサイクロペディア
単行本 1989
CD: テリー ジョーンズ　AD: スティーヴ メイル
P: ニック ナイト　CL: ペンギン ブックス

27.

27.Cover

28.

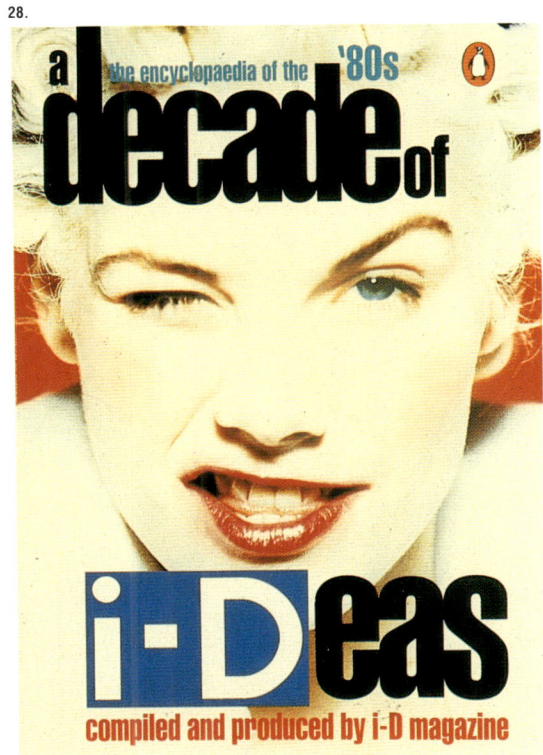

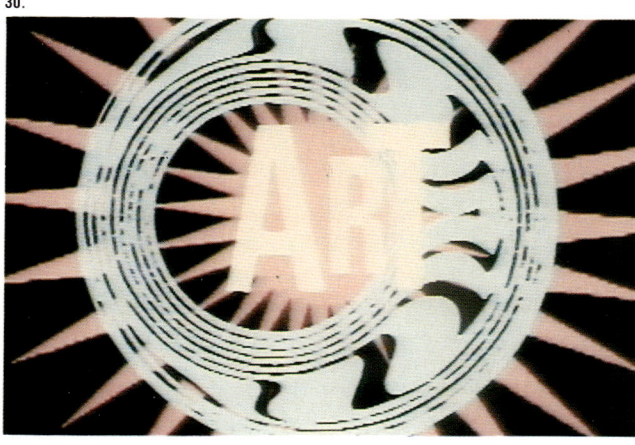

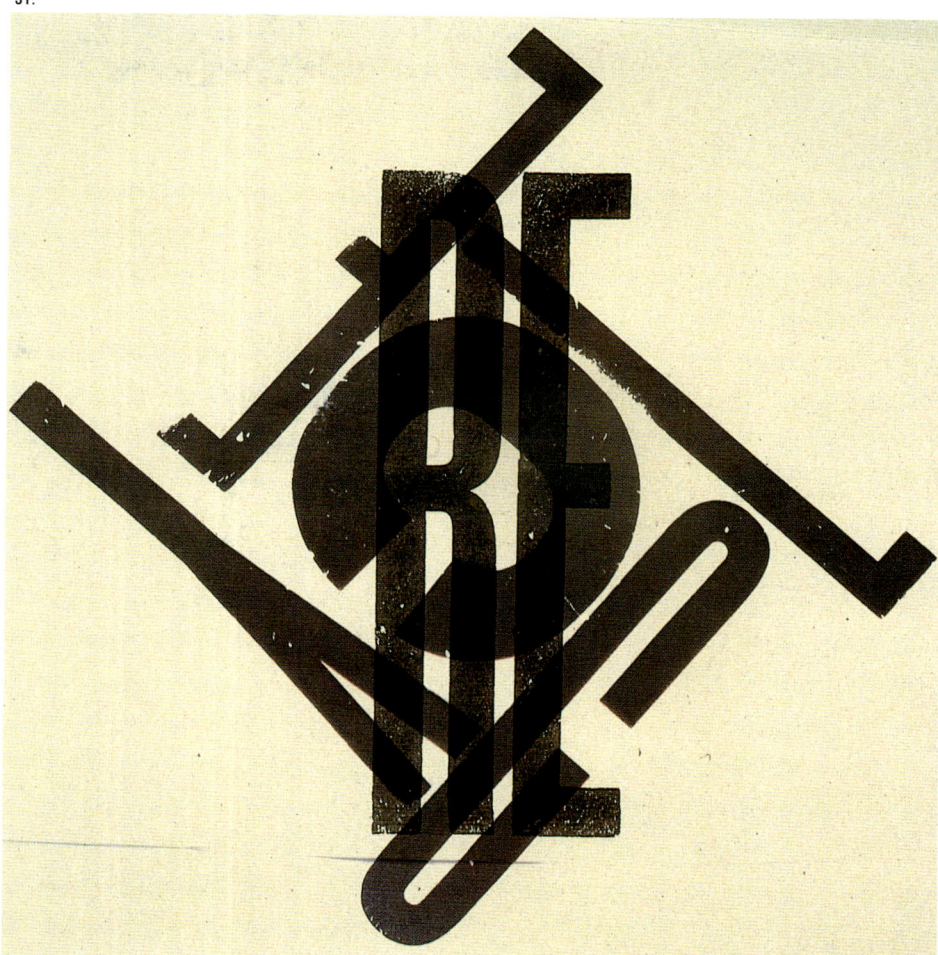

29. SUPER CHANNEL GRAPHICS
Identity for TV Program
CD: Terry Jones DF: Instant Design
CL: Super Channel TV
スーパー チャンネル グラフィックス
TV番組 タイトル映像
CD: テリージョーンズ DF: インスタント デザイン
CL: スーパー チャンネルTV

30. 01 FOR LONDON
TV Program Graphics 1987
CD: Terry Jones DF: Instant Design
CL: Mentorn Films
01 フォー ロンドン
TV番組 タイトル映像 1987
CD: テリー ジョーンズ DF: インスタント デザイン
CL: メンターン フィルムス

31. RECYCLE
Self- Promotion 1990
CD: Terry Jones D: Alan Kitching
DF: Instant Design
リサイクル
宣伝用 個人作品 1990
CD: テリー ジョーンズ D: アラン キッチング
DF: インスタント デザイン

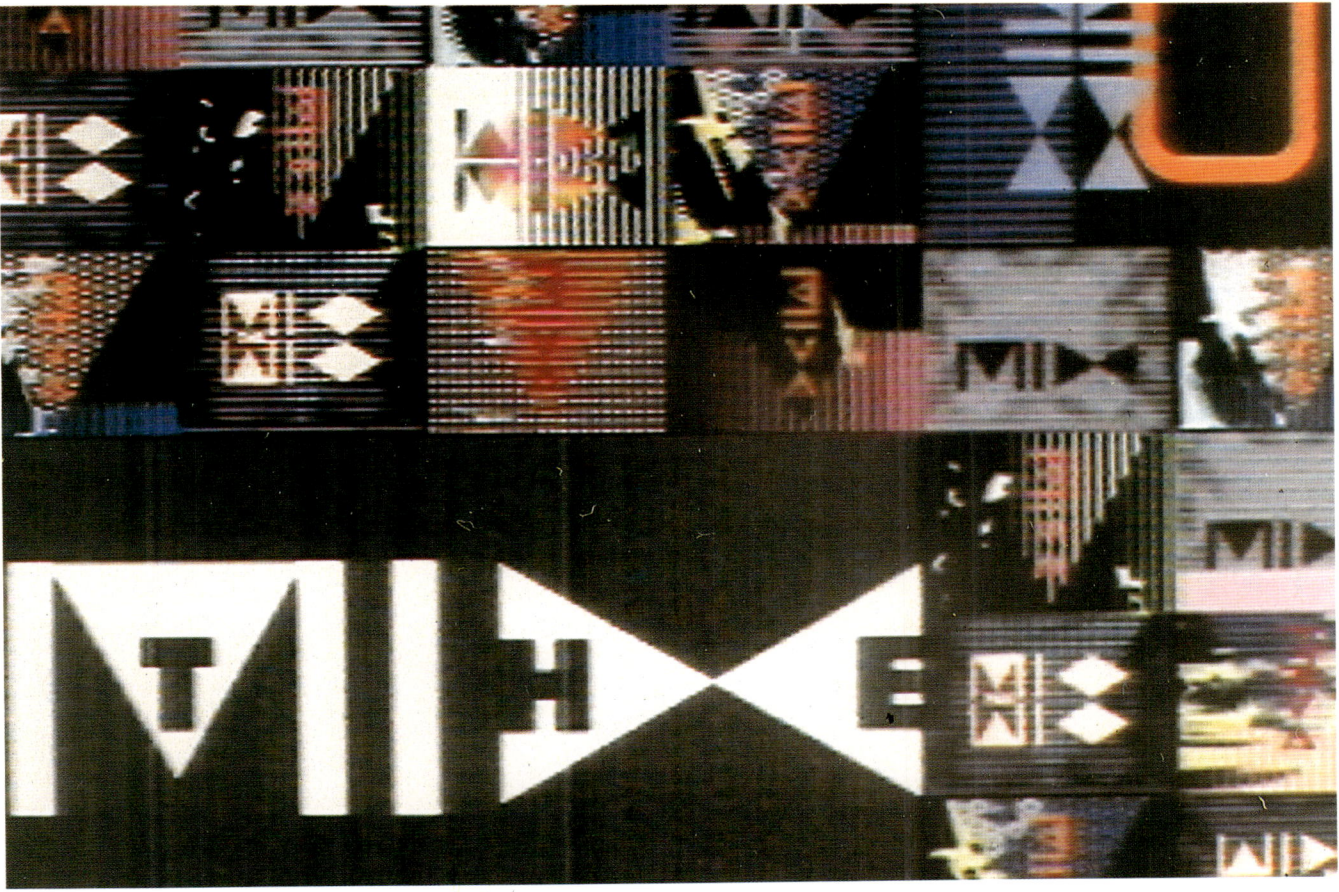

32. THE MIX Identity for TV Program 1989 CD: Terry Jones CL: Super Channel TV
ザ ミックス TV番組 タイトル映像 1989 CD: テリー ジョーンズ CL: スーパー チャンネル TV

33. REPORTAGE LOGO Logo for TV Program 1988 D: Terry Jones DF: Instant Design CL: BBC Television
ルポルタージュ ロゴ TV番組 ロゴマーク 1988 D: テリー ジョーンズ DF: インスタント デザイン CL: BBCテレヴィジョン

34. SUPER CHANNEL GRAPHICS Identity for TV Program CD: Terry Jones DF: Instant Design CL: Super Channnel TV
スーパー チャンネル グラフィックス TV番組 タイトル映像 CD: テリー ジョーンズ DF: インスタント デザイン CL: スーパー チャンネルTV

35. ESPRIT Advertisement 1990 AD: Terry Jones P: Peggy Sirota DF: Instant Design CL: Esprit
エスプリ 広告 1990 AD: テリー ジョーンズ P: ペギー シロタ DF: インスタント デザイン CL: エスプリ

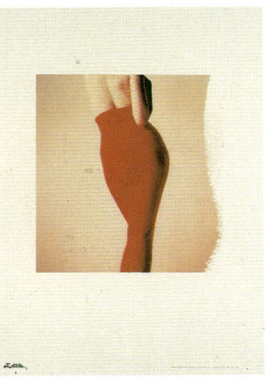

36. CHIPIE Advertisement 1989 AD: Terry Jones P: Brian Griffin DF: Instant Design CL: Chipie
シピー 広告 1989 AD: テリー ジョーンズ P: ブライアン グリフィン DF: インスタント デザイン CL: シピー

37. MR JOE Advertisement 1988 AD: Terry Jones P: Nick Knight DF: Soncini Ginepro CL: Mr Joe
ミスター ジョー 広告 1988 AD: テリー ジョーンズ P: ニック ナイト DF: ソンシニ ジネプロ CL: ミスター ジョー

38. THE TREE Book Cover AD: Terry Jones P: Frank Horvat CL: Aurum Press
ザ トゥリー 単行本 AD: テリー ジョーンズ P: フランク ホーヴァット CL: オーラム プレス

39. ROCK DANS LES ANNÉES '80
Title for TV Program 1980
CD: Terry Jones
DF: Instant Design
CL: NBdC Television
ロック ダン レザンヌ '80
TV番組 タイトル映像 1980
CD: テリー ジョーンズ
DF: インスタント デザイン
CL: NBdCテレヴィジョン

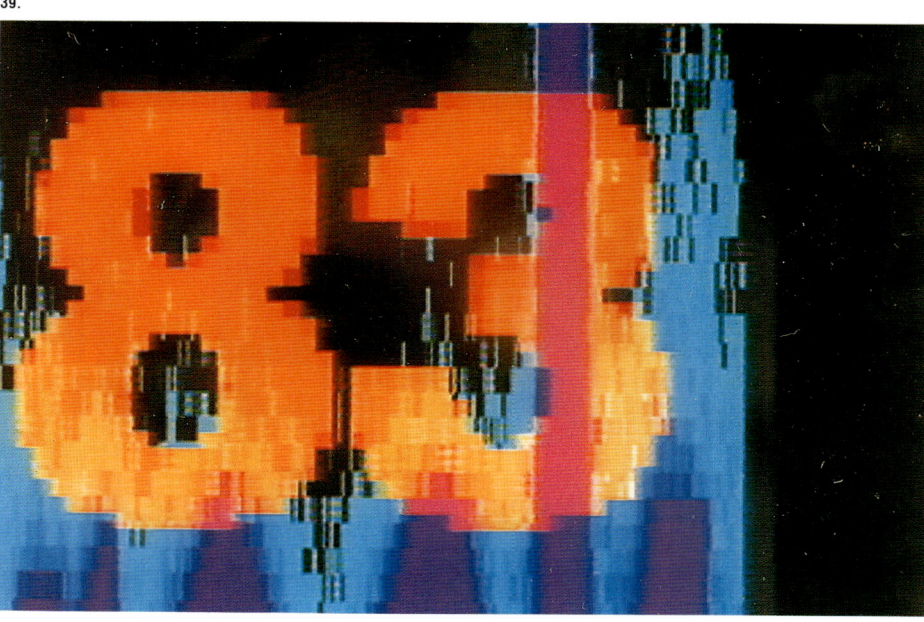

40. i-D TWO ＜PILOT ISSUE＞ Magazine 1991 CD: Terry Jones AD: Shozo Shinoda CL: UPU
i-D トゥー ＜創刊 0号＞ 雑誌 1991 CD: テリー ジョーンズ AD: 篠田昌三 CL: UPU

41. WE ARE WHAT WE BR (EAT) H Advertisement 1991 AD: Terry Jones P: Franklyn Rodgers CL: UPU, Nissan
ウィ アー ホワット ウィ ブレス 広告 1991 AD: テリー ジョーンズ P: フランクリン ロジャース CL: UPU、日産グループ

42. i-D JAPAN ＜ISSUE 1＞ Magazine 1991 AD,P: Terry Jones P: Nobuyoshi Araki, Takashi Honma, Sachio Ono CL: UPU
i-D ジャパン ＜創刊号＞ 雑誌 1991 AD,P: テリー ジョーンズ P: 荒木経惟、ホンマ タカシ、小野幸生 CL: UPU

43. i-D JAPAN ＜ISSUE 1＞　Magazine 1991　AD: Terry Jones　P: Takashi Honma　CL: UPU
i-D ジャパン ＜創刊号＞　雑誌 1991　AD: テリー ジョーンズ　P: ホンマ タカシ　CL: UPU

Acknowledgements

graphic beat: the soft mix vol.1

a collaboration of music and graphics

london tokyo

Acknowledgements

This book could not have been made without the talent and labor of a great many people outside of P·I·E BOOKS. We would like to express our sincerest gratitude and appreciation to:

Yasutaka Kato at Sony Records for his cheerful and valuable advice on both the planning and production of this book.
Helen Rees from the Design Museum for writing the foreword.
Ryuichi Sakamoto, Oscar winning musician and **Norika Sora** from KAB who contributed their own unique perspectives on the visual arts as they apply to music.
Hirotsugu Shibata at Parco for helped us plan the foreword.
Akio Ninbari at Sony Records for his invaluable advice on establishing an editorial framework.
Tsuyoshi Yamamoto at Parco for his role in procurring the artwork by Malcolm Garrett.
Akiko Sanada at Bijutsu Shuppan-sha for generously providing artwork by Hajime Tachibana.
write Away and **Minos Agency** for the translations.
Inori Hagiwara for her expertise in the translations of the English and Japanese text.
Douglas Allsopp, **Eric Chaline** and **Malcolm Wong** for their erudite counsel on the production of the English text.
Everyone at **Window** for their help with French pronunciation.
Naomi Sakuma and **Sachiko Ishii** for their patient support on the design work.
Pamela Virgilio for her astute advice on many of the design considerations regarding this project.
Noriko Yamada and **Nobuko Nakagawa** for their vital hand in preparing the credits for the artwork.
All the folks down at **WAVE DTP Lab.**, **PROP** and **TM Planning** for preparing beautiful camera ready copy.
Tetsuya Ando at UPU and **Keiko Nakano** at Parco who provided inspiration for the book cover.
All the producers that helped us along the way, as well as the people in creative production and designers for their insightful editorial advice.
Last but not least, everyone who those supported and encouraged the designers we are featured in this book. Thank you all very much.

P·I·E BOOKS

この本を作るにあたり、本当にたくさんの人たちの力添えをいただきました。彼らに助けてもらったことを強く感謝するとともに、彼らとともにひとつの企画をこうして形にできたことを、とても嬉しく思っています。この場を借りて、心から感謝の意を表します。

本の企画、進行に親身になってアドヴァイスしてくださった、
ソニーレコードの**加藤靖隆氏**。
序文という形で、音楽とデザインの関係を提示してくださった、
デザイン・ミュージアムの**ヘレン・リースさん**、
ミュージシャンの**坂本龍一氏**。
坂本氏と共に、力強い意見を聞かせてくださった、
KABの空里香さん。
序文作りに並々ならぬお世話をいただいた、
パルコの**柴田廣次氏**。
作品掲載についてアドヴァイスをいただいた、
ソニーレコードの**仁張明男氏**。
マルコム・ギャレットの作品提供に一役かってくださった、
パルコの**山本剛氏**。
立花ハジメのページに快く作品協力してくださった、
美術出版社の**真田暁子さん**。
翻訳を引き受けてくださった、
ライトアウェイ、ミノス翻訳センターの方々。
英文、和文作りで知恵をかしてくださった、
萩原いのりさん。
英文作りで適切なアドヴァイスをいただいた、
ダグラス・オルソップ氏、エリック・シャリン氏、マルコム・ウォング氏。
フランス語の発音についてご教示いただいた、**ウィンドウの方々**。
デザイン作業において根気よく手伝ってくれた、
佐久間尚美さん、石井佐知子さん。
またアドヴァイスをいただいた、**パメラ・ヴァジリオさん**。
作品クレジット作りに大変ご協力をいただいた、**山田典子さん、中川信子さん**。
写植でご協力いただいた、
WAVE DTPラボ、PROP、TMプランニングの方々。
本のカヴァー作りの際に、アイディアのサンプルを提供してくださった、
UPUの安藤哲也氏、パルコの中野圭子さん。
作品掲載について、快く相談に応じてくださった、
クリエイターやプロダクションの方々。
　最後になりましたが、登場したデザイナーたちと共に、いろいろとお世話をしてくださった各デザイン・オフィスの方々にも、感謝します。

ピエ・ブックス

Designers' Address

London Designers

MALCOLM GARRETT マルコム ギャレット
(AMX digital)
Victoria House, 64 Paul Street, London EC2A 4NA Tel: 0171 613 5300

THE DESIGNERS REPUBLIC デザイナーズ リパブリック
The Workstation, Unit 415, 15 Paternoster Row, Sheffield S1 2BX Tel: 0114 275 4982

RUSSELL MILLS ラッセル ミルズ
Loughrigg Holme, Under Loughrigg, Ambleside, Cumbria LA22 9LN Tel: 01534 31278

PETER SAVILLE ピーター サヴィル
Apartment 10, Audley court 32-34 Hill street, London W1X 7FT Tel: 0171 491 4350

DAVID CROW デヴィッド クロウ
48 Saxby Street Salford M6 7RG Tel: 0161 737 8960

DAVID JAMES デヴィッド ジェイムズ
(David James Associates)
23-25 Great Sutton Street, Clerkenwell, London EC1V 0DN Tel: 0171 608 1966

TWO トゥー

IAN SWIFT イアン スウィフト
(CCC)
P.O.BOX 10, London N.1 3RJ Tel: 0171 241 2183

TERRY JONES テリー ジョーンズ
71 Sheriff Road, West Hampstead, London NW6 Tel: 0171 624 4333

Tokyo Designers

CONTEMPORARY PRODUCTION コンテムポラリー プロダクション
Brill Building, 7-5 Daikanyama, Shibuya-ku, Tokyo 150 Tel: 03 5459 8221
〒150 東京都渋谷区代官山 7-5 ブリルビル 電話: 03 5459 8221

TADANORI YOKOO 横尾忠則
(Yokoo Tadanori Atelier, 横尾忠則アトリエ)
4-19-7 Seijo, Setagaya-ku, Tokyo 157 Tel: 03 3482 2826
〒157 東京都世田谷区成城 4-19-7 電話: 03 3482 2826

KENJI ISHIKAWA 石川絢士
(the GARDEN)
1-22-13 Minami-Aoyama, Minato-ku, Tokyo 107 Tel: 03 5410 3315
〒107 東京都港区南青山 1-22-13 電話: 03 5410 3315

HAJIME TACHIBANA 立花ハジメ
(Tachibana Hajime Design, 立花ハジメデザイン)
1-35-28 Higashigaoka, Meguro-ku, Tokyo 152 Tel: 03 3487 9711
〒152 東京都目黒区東が丘 1-35-28 電話: 03 3487 9711

NOBUAKI TAKAHASHI 高橋伸明
(bahaty)
#701 Nishiazabu-heights, 2-12-1 Nishiazabu, Minato-ku, Tokyo 106 Tel: 03 3409 1408
〒106 東京都港区西麻布 2-12-1 西麻布ハイツ701 電話: 03 3409 1408

KEN SAKAGUCHI 坂口 賢
(Sakaguchi Ken Factory, サカグチケン ファクトリー)
Avenue Ikejiri 204, 2-10-12 Ikejiri, Setagaya-ku, Tokyo 154 Tel: 03 3424 2304
〒154 東京都世田谷区池尻 2-10-12 アヴェニュー池尻204 電話: 03 3424 2304

Editorial Credits

GRAPHIC BEAT: THE SOFT MIX
LONDON / TOKYO, VOLUME 1

グラフィックビート: ソフトミックス 1
ロンドン／トウキョウ

JACKET DESIGN
Contemporary Production
ART DIRECTOR
Mitsuo Shindo
DESIGNER
Ryoji Ohya

JACKET DESIGN
コンテムポラリー プロダクション
ART DIRECTOR
信藤三雄
DESIGNER
大箭亮二

ART DIRECTOR
Patrick Glover

ART DIRECTOR
パトリック グローヴァー

DESIGNERS
Patrick Glover
Shinji Ikenoue
Kimiko Ishiwatari
Yutaka Ichimura

DESIGNERS
パトリック グローヴァー
池之上 信二
石渡君子
市村 裕

EDITORS
Ayako Aoyama
Shinichi Kadota
Tsutomu Hirata
Junko Wong
Kaoru Yamashita

EDITORS
青山文子
門多伸市
平田 義
ジュンコ ウォング
山下かおる

PHOTOGRAPHER (DESIGNERS WORK)
Shoichi Sato (Photo Studio Techne)

PHOTOGRAPHER (DESIGNERS WORK)
佐藤尚一（フォトスタジオ テクネ）

PHOTOGRAPHER (COVER / FRONT SECTION)
Patrick Glover

PHOTOGRAPHER (COVER / FRONT SECTION)
パトリック グローヴァー

BOOK PRODUCTION & COORDINATION
Cross World Connections

BOOK PRODUCTION & COORDINATION
クロスワールドコネクションズ

LONDON ARTISTS COORDINATOR
Sarah Philips

LONDON ARTISTS COORDINATOR
サラ フィリップス

PUBLISHER
Shingo Miyoshi

PUBLISHER
三芳伸吾

この本の売上の一部は、出品者の方々のご厚意によりユニセフに寄付されます。
Part of the sales of this book will be donated to UNICEF by courtesy of the submittors.

1997年12月18日初版第1刷発行

発行所　ピエ・ブックス
〒170　東京都豊島区駒込4-14-6 #301
編集: TEL 03-3949-5010　FAX 03-3949-5650
営業: TEL 03-3940-8302　FAX 03-3576-7361

製版 弘陽印刷
印刷・製本　（株）サンニチ印刷

©1997 P・I・E BOOKS
本書の収録内容の無断転載、複写、引用等を禁じます。
落丁・乱丁はお取り替え致します。

ISBN4-89444-071-7 C3070　　Printed in Japan

SOFT COVER COLLECTION SERIES

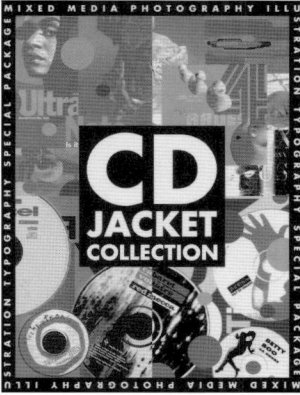

世界のCDジャケット・コレクション
CD JACKET COLLECTION

世界中のレコードCD・LPジャケットの中からデザイン的に優れた作品約700点を一挙掲載。
A collection features 700 of the world's most imaginative CD and LP covers from all musical genres.

ポストカード・コレクション vol.1
POSTCARD COLLECTION 1

年賀状、X'masカード、セール案内・招待状など小さなスペースにエッセンスが詰まったコレクション!!
The collection packed with graphics created for cards, announcements and invitations for personal and corporate use.

ポストカード・コレクション vol.2
POSTCARD COLLECTION 2

好評第2弾!トップクリエイター、企業、ファッションメーカーなどのポストカード1500作品紹介。
The collection of 1500 corporate and personal-use postcard from Japan and around the world.

カタログ&パンフレット・コレクション
CATALOG AND PAMPHLET COLLECTION

国内を中心にファッション/家電/車/流通等、様々な業種のカタログを約250点紹介。
A collection of the world's most outstanding brochures, catalogues and leaflets classified by industry such as fashion, restaurants, and so on.

世界のラベル&タグ・コレクション
LABELS AND TAGS COLLECTION

ファッションや雑貨など450ブランドのラベル&タグを選りすぐり1600点紹介。
Here is a collection of 1600 labels and tags from Japan's 450 top fashion names.

ワッペン・コレクション
FASHION INSIGNIA COLLECTION

120のファッション・ブランドの、お洒落でかわいいワッペン・エンブレムを約1000点紹介。
Over 3000 designs were scrutinized for this collection of 1000 outstanding emblems and embroidered motifs.

T-シャツ・コレクション vol.2
T-SHIRT COLLECTION 2

アパレルメーカーの市販品から企業PR用まで様々な世界のTシャツプリント約700点を紹介。
The 700 t-shirts introduced here were designed for a variety of purposes, from fashion brand products to corporate promotional items.

世界のスポーツグッズ・コレクション
SPORTS GOODS COLLECTION

スポーツ用品の斬新なグラフィックス、約1000点を一挙掲載。様々なグッズを幅広く紹介。
A collection of 1000 bold sporting-goods graphic works from all over the world. A wide variety of goods are shown.

世界の名刺・コレクション vol.2
BUSINESS CARD COLLECTION 2

個性あふれるビジネスカード、そしてアイデアたっぷりのショップカードなど約1000点紹介。
Unique personal business cards, creative shop cards, and more! Here are 1,000 of the best.

ダイアグラム・コレクション
DIAGRAM COLLECTION

グラフ/チャート/マップなど世界から寄せられたダイアグラム約400作品を厳選して紹介。
Nearly 400 graphs, charts, maps, and other diagrams, selected from the submissions of top designers worldwide.

ART CENTER COLLEGE OF DESIGN

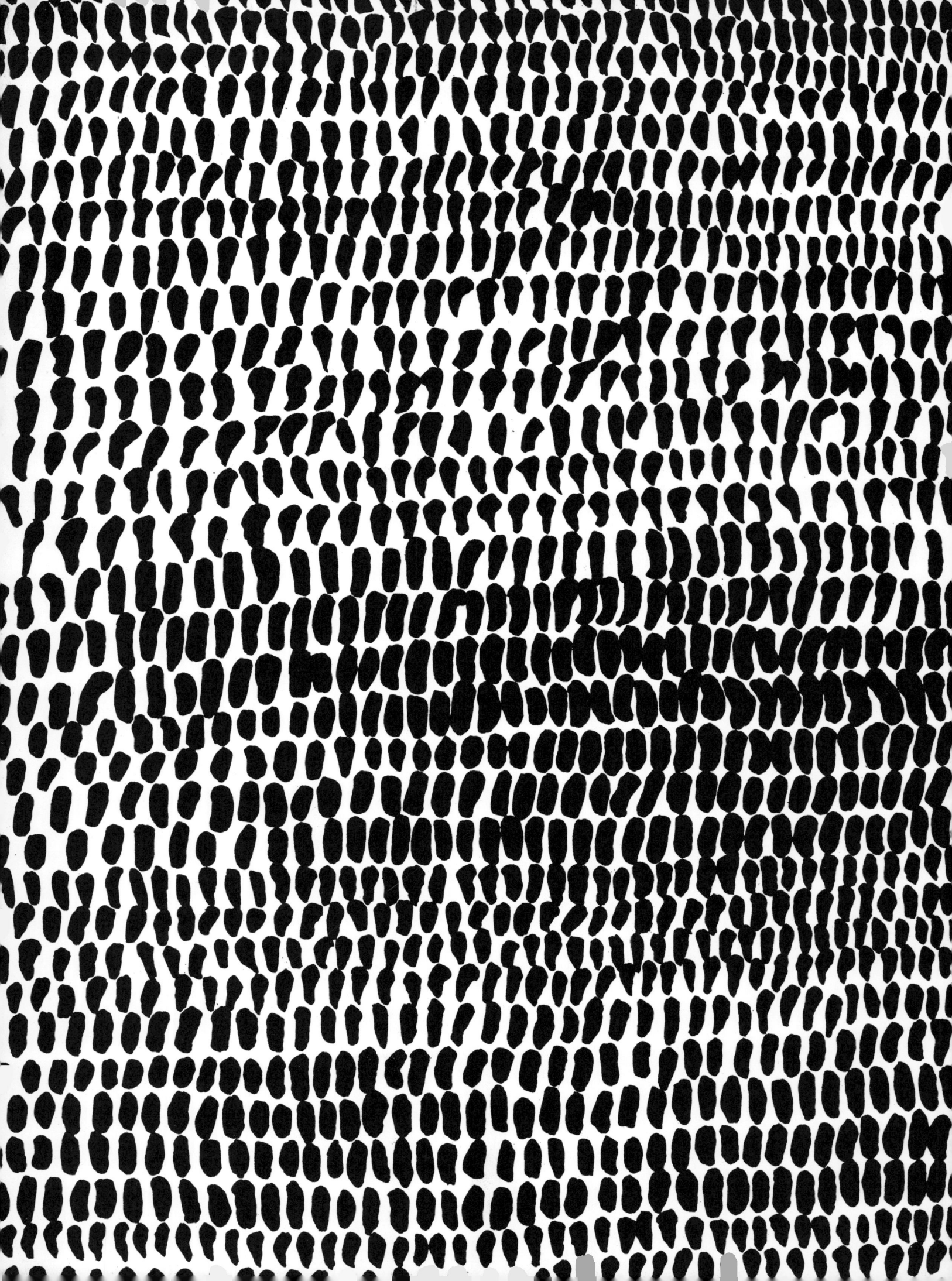